The Future of Memory

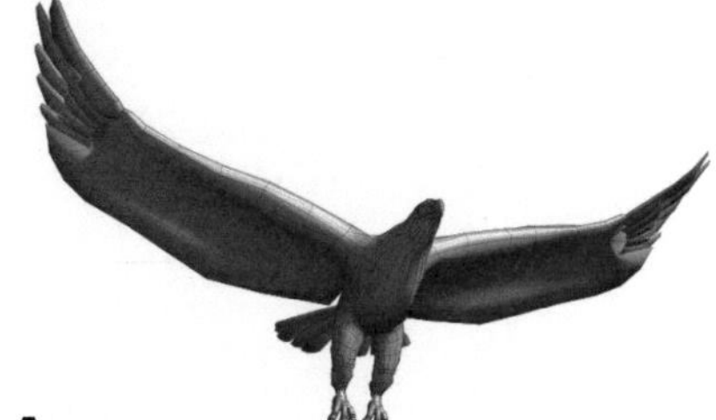

An Exhibition on the Infinity of the Present Time

04/02 – 29/03 2015

Kunsthalle Wien

The Future of Memory
An Exhibition on the
Infinity of the Present Time
(04/02 – 29/03)
Kunsthalle Wien

Digital communication and virtual
interlacing shape our world today
and influence our collective
memory. Remembering the past,
experiencing the present and
imagining the future all meld
to become part of a seemingly
equivalent imagery in digital space.
Held at Kunsthalle Wien from
February 4 until March 29, 2015, the
exhibition *The Future of Memory*
critically challenged constructions
of reality and investigated the
conditions under which individual
and collective memory evolve.

The Future of Memory
Eine Ausstellung über die
Unendlichkeit der Gegenwart
(04/02 – 29/03)
Kunsthalle Wien

Digitale Kommunikation und
virtuelle Vernetzung prägen nicht
nur unsere Gegenwart, sondern
beeinflussen auch unser kulturelles
Gedächtnis. Die Erinnerung an die
Vergangenheit, das Erleben der
Gegenwart und die Vorstellung
von der Zukunft vereinen sich im
digitalen Raum zu für uns scheinbar
gleichen Bildern. Die Ausstellung
The Future of Memory wurde vom
4. Februar bis 29. März 2015 in
der Kunsthalle Wien gezeigt. Die
ausgewählten Arbeiten untersuchten
Konstrukte von Realität und die
Bedingungen, zu denen individuelle
Erinnerung und ein kollektives
Gedächtnis entstehen.

Inhaltsverzeichnis / Table of Contents

The Future of Memory – Some Thoughts Developed in Advance of the Exhibition
<u>Nicolaus Schafhausen</u>

With the rapid increase of virtual memory space, the very nature of human memory is in the process of changing fundamentally. It is a circumstance that raises many urgent questions.

1. Whereas before our experiences were made up of what might be called "real" memories, i.e. memories of events and spaces we experienced personally, now we are being confronted more and more with the recall of experiences we have gained from virtual sources. Virtual memories are the memories and experiences, now available to us within the expanded realm of the digital. One need search no further than the screen you are looking at to see how readily this state of affairs has been adapted to by the culture as a whole. How it is to be understood is another question. The author of a new epistemology for the Digital Age will face an exceedingly complex task.

2. "Real" memory is understood as the classic model for truth: that which we have experienced personally and for the veracity of which we can vouch: we saw it with our own eyes... Virtual memory is, on the other hand, representative of the world of manufactured images. As Dessislava Dimova says, writing about the artist Pierre Bismuth: "An image in contemporary visual culture pertains less and less to reality and claims less and less truthfulness to any kind of nature — natural, artificial, naturally flavored, or artificially enhanced. Images are perfected and proliferated to the point of abstraction. Yet they refer neither to a transcendental reality, nor are a thing in themselves. Rather they create their parallel reality — the reality of magazine covers, of selfies, of billboards, of inhumanly perfect humans, of lives edited in pictures on social networks."[1]

3. The images we are inundated with today do not correlate with our actual experience, but as a facet of our contemporary existence images are a real part of everyday experience nonetheless. This would seem to expand the definition of what we understand to be "real."[2] Indeed, three recent cultural tendencies point to how "reality" has become a contested ground of contemporary experience, one that the culture as a whole is investigating: 1) over the past fifteen years "reality" has become a global TV genre[3], suggesting loosening standards for the term's definition; 2) on the other hand (to give just one of many possible examples) author James Frey[4] was exposed for fabrications in his addiction recovery memoir by no less a public figure than Oprah Winfrey[5] on global TV broadcasted from the US, suggesting a demand for more exacting standards of truth-telling than writers were previously held to; 3) by contrast, current discussion of the literary trend known as Autofiction[6], exemplified in books like Sheila Heti's *How Should a Person Be* (2012) and Karl Ove Knausgaard's *My Struggle* (2014) points to a coming acceptance of a truthful/fictive amalgam in the production of the self.

4. Beyond an increase in virtual memories, what we experience in the actual is arguably now remembered differently. The virtual alters human memory.

Three ways memory is changed by the digital:

I. Google makes you stupid
- "the capacity of electronics has exploded our ability to not remember things." (author emphasis).[7]
- "Search engines, we are told, remember for us and, as a consequence, we are forgetting to remember for ourselves. Of course, things are rarely as simple as a headline. The research behind these stories, published in the journal Science[8], found that when people knew information would be stored on a computer, they were less likely to remember it (although they were better at remembering where this information was stored)."[9]

II. The brain becomes more computer-like
"the digital age is changing what we use our brains for. Rather than store important facts, today we are more likely to store information about how to find those facts."[10]

III. Memory becomes more social
"more and more ephemera seems to be kept online – accidentally or otherwise…[therefore] memories are becoming increasingly public – social, even."[11]

5. Therefore, the alteration to memory is collective and "transactive"

I. As noted in *The Guardian*[12] "humans have long drawn on the power of "transactive memory". Memory has long been stored outside of our own individual bodies, but today we are storing it behind small screens rather than on shelves. Before the silicon chip was invented, pen and paper, the printing press and the camera all helped store information for us."

II. "For many people, this shared experience raises questions about the nature of memory. Remembering is often a deeply personal event – do we want to experience it collectively?"[13]

6. Connected to this change in the way we store and experience memories is how the image deluge effects a delocalization and alienation in relation to our physical location. While ever present in our minds and, so to speak, crowding out the real memories, virtual memories are mere images that connect us to no one and to nowhere. They are not connected to us. Because of the way digital technology provides access to it, cultural memory becomes experienced as an omnipresent totality in a manner it hasn't before[14]. However, this idea is as much figurative as it is literal. No one actually spends their time accessing all of it, and the idea of doing so isn't desirable or even meaningful. Awareness of this circumstance is, however, felt strongly by most people. Due to a professional – or temperamental – orientation, this contemporary condition seems to be experienced as a kind of pressure by those individuals who are receptive to it; hence the many instances in the visual art discipline that show signs of its influence.

Two examples:
I. MoMA's *The Forever Now*[15] exhibition posits atemporality in contemporary painting practice as an effect of this condition. Ecumenical painting style is understood as an expression of the contemporary memories-deluge that presumably is digitally induced. It is also possible to understand that painting today expresses an anachronism of human touch/marks — but expresses this negatively. Painting appears an anachronism when confronted with the human-neutral quality of digital marks.

II. Another way to explain the atemporal condition of contemporary painting…"In fact, it has been clear for quite some time now that meme[16] culture is setting the tone for what theorist Raymond Williams[17] would call today's "structure of feeling," the specific expressive texture that distinguishes the present from the past. This probably represents the most significant development of grassroots visual culture since the explosion of the graffiti scene in the 1970s: #YesAllWomen[18] or the "Ice Bucket Challenge"[19] (or, hell, the Harlem Shake[20]) are obviously powerful vehicles of collective experience."[21]

7. That meme culture is…today's most significant development of grassroots visual culture[22] is obvious. However, this reality is hard to grasp, for so many interesting reasons. Contemporary art is a professional discipline of visual culture. Meme culture falls within art's realm of competence, and yet even though vernacular digital culture (e.g. animated Gifs and their brethren) is clearly influencing contemporary art practice, at the same time it also presents a number of problems that make it all but elude the art establishment's cognizance. Reasons for this include: the human-neutral quality of digital image making, its lack of apparent gravitas, and its uncommodifiability, among other points. Further, MoMA's *The Forever Now* show appears to be about how painting flounders within today's image phantasmagory. This is not its stated intention, but the exhibition seems to demonstrate that painting struggles to even make contact with the surface of this reality. Painting represents a tradition of *individual visual expression* in a contemporary world where *collective modes of visual expression* are ubiquitous, easily accessible and arguably more relevant, for the reasons already suggested. Interestingly, however, understood in this way, painting negatively demonstrates its relevance. Painting as practiced today seems to be an outmoded form of engagement with the world – and yet it endures. Data may continue to increase exponentially, but there is still a limit on the ability of humans to meaningfully process it. Analogy is: painting>surface>touch = location>locatedness>individual experience.

8. In spite of all this, "real" memory is inevitably linked to our actual physical existence. Grounding in the physical, in the body, provides a good starting point for thinking about the problem, to be reminded what is real. Faithfulness to this idea that truth can be found in your bodily experience can help when negotiating an excessively demanding media environment. Daily life in the West proves, however, that adherence to this nostrum could never be that simple. Indeed, it's easy to imagine our image deluge culture could produce in reaction a kind of "image abstention" millennial cult — *back-to-nature* 21st century style. It would be another form of extremism, another type of fundamentalism, not unlike that which drove the recent massacre of the French cartoonists associated with *Charlie Hebdo*[23] for making provocative drawings about the Prophet Muhammed and Islamic culture. Such responses (one fictive, one all too real) are symptomatic of perhaps an inevitable, probably perennial strain of anti-modern reactionary feeling. In the wake of this horrible event, however, those who have suggested there might be some culpability on the part of the cartoonists indulge in, maybe unwittingly, a similar type of iconoclasm. It is a response that suggests a certain lack of self-awareness, especially when promoted via Facebook, a preeminently modern communication format. Discussions on social media by the digital generation seem to take civil rights traditions for granted at the same time as they question the right of the *Charlie Hebdo* cartoonists' to make provocations that this legacy makes possible. After all this is the tradition we are acting within when we make art and when we make exhibitions. Provocations are a vital component of this territory, which also includes the principal of art for art's sake.

A desire to simplify helps explain the anti-modern tendency — in whatever weak or extreme form it gets expressed. But like the proscription to believe in the truth of only what you experience in your own body, giving in to the impulse to resist the modern world is a false solution. Instead of disavowing the expanded reality of the image deluge and the wealth of complication it creates, the future will probably see our culture's wholesale recalibration according to some version of the Singularity, as popularized by the futurist Ray Kurzweil[24], but that's a topic for another exhibition.

Nicolaus Schafhausen is director of Kunsthalle Wien.

[1] Dessislava Dimova, "Life is probably round," Pierre Bismuth: Things I Remember I Have Done, but Don't Remember Why I Did Them, eds. Luca Lo Pinto and Nicolaus Schafhausen (Vienna: Kunsthalle Wien, 2015)
[2] It should be mentioned that this discussion completely side-steps perhaps the most useful definition of The Real, which comes from Lacan. To borrow a formulation from Wikipedia: "that which is outside language and that resists symbolization absolutely." http://en.wikipedia.org/wiki/The_Real
[3] "Reality television is premised on the idea of "providing viewers with an unmediated, voyeuristic, yet often playful look into what might into what might be called the ‚entertaining' real". (Murray and Ouellette, 2004: 4)" Global Television Formats: Understanding Television Across Borders , eds. Tasha Oren, Sharon Shahaf (Google eBook [London: Routledge, 2013]) 347.
[4] A contemporaneous thought piece in The New York Times gives a succinct account of the scandal: "James Frey's admission last week that he made up details of his life in his best-selling book „A Million Little Pieces" - after the Smoking Gun Web site stated that he „wholly fabricated or wildly embellished details of his purported criminal career, jail terms and status as an outlaw ‚wanted in three states' „ - created a furor about the decision by the
[5] "The Oprah Winfrey Show, was the highest-rated program of its kind in history and was nationally syndicated from 1986 to 2011. Dubbed the "Queen of All Media", Winfrey has been ranked the richest African-American of the 20th century, the greatest black philanthropist in American history, and is currently North America's only black billionaire. She is also, according to some assessments, the most influential woman in the world.", http://en.wikipedia.org/wiki/Oprah_Winfrey
[6] Autofiction: "novels [that] point to a new future wherein the self is considered a living thing composed of fictions," "2014: The Death of the Postmodern Novel and the Rise of Autofiction," Jonathon Sturgeon, Flavorwire, December 31, 2014., www.flavorwire.com/496570/2014-the-death-of-the-postmodern-novel-and-the-rise-of-autofiction
[7] "How the Digital Age Has Changed Memory," Big Think, http://bigthink.com/ideafeed/how-the-

digital-age-has-changed-memory

[8] *Science* is the academic journal of the American Association for the Advancement of Science, an organization based in Washington DC. First published in 1880, the peer-reviewed journal's focus is the publication of important original scientific research., http://www.sciencemag.org/

[9] Alice Bell, "Memory in the digital age," *The Guardian*, 14 January 2012, www.theguardian.com/lifeandstyle/2012/jan/14/memories-in-the-digital-age

[10] "How the Digital Age Has Changed Memory", http://bigthink.com/ideafeed/how-the-digital-age-has-changed-memory

[11] "Memory in the digital age", www.theguardian.com/lifeandstyle/2012/jan/14/memories-in-the-digital-age

[12] Ibid.

[13] Ibid.

[14] "For the first time, [curator] Laura Hoptman claims in her audacious catalogue essay, culture no longer "define[s] the time in which we live", but rather reflects "a new and strange state of the world in which, courtesy of the internet, all eras seem to exist at once." Jason Farago, "The Forever Now review: calling time on the avant garde," *The Guardian*, 12 December 2014., www.theguardian.com/artanddesign/2014/dec/12/the-forever-now-review-calling-time-avant-garde

[15] "The Forever Now: Contemporary Painting in an Atemporal World," Museum of Modern Art, New York, December 14, 2014–April 5, 2015, http://www.moma.org/visit/calendar/exhibitions/1498

[16] Coined by the evolutionary biologist Richard Dawkins, a "meme" is any idea (a catchphrase, behaviour, image or graphic, etc.) that ripples across a cultural field, its popularity explained because of the way it helps inflect and resonates within its moment in time. "We need a name for the new replicator, a noun that conveys the idea of a unit of cultural transmission, or a unit of imitation. ‚Mimeme' comes from a suitable Greek root, but I want a monosyllable that sounds a bit like ‚gene'. I hope my classicist friends will forgive me if I abbreviate mimeme to meme. If it is any consolation, it could alternatively be thought of as being related to ‚memory', or to the French word même. It should be pronounced to rhyme with ‚cream'. Richard Dawkins, The Selfish Gene, (Oxford: Oxford University Press, 1982), 192.

[17] "Raymond Williams (1921-1988) was one of the most original and prolific cultural writers and thinkers in English in the 20th century, opening up new areas of enquiry in literary and cultural studies, communications and social and political theory. His cultural work was rooted in his concept of a long revolution - the democratic transformation of society in order that inequality and oppression would cease to exist.", http://www.raymondwilliamsfoundation.org.uk/RW1.html

[18] "The suspect in Friday's killings in Santa Barbara, Calif. wrote a manifesto promising revenge on all the women who had rejected him. But Twitter users responded with their own thoughts on and experiences of misogyny, centered around the hashtag #YesAllWomen," "The Most Powerful #YesAllWomen Tweets," Nolan Feeney, TIME, May 27, 2014, www.time.com/114043/yesallwomen-hashtag-santa-barbara-shooting

[19] An initiative of the ALS Association, in the Ice Bucket Challenge films are posted on the Internet of participants getting a bucket of ice water pored over their head as a way to promote awareness about and raise funds for Amyotrophic lateral sclerosis (ALS), a progressive neurodegenerative disease that affects nerve cells in the brain and spinal cord. "When doing the challenge, please use the hashtags #icebucketchallenge, #alsicebucketchallenge, and #strikeoutals. The Ice Bucket Challenge may not be suitable for small children, the elderly, anyone in poor health or animals of any kind, so please use good judgment. Please be thoughtful about water usage. If you're in an area of the country or world affected by drought, please consider making a donation instead, or repurpose the water for later use.", http://www.alsa.org/fight-als/ice-bucket-challenge.html

[20] The Harlem Shake [BEST ONES!], https://www.youtube.com/watch?v=8f7wj_RcqYk

[21] Ben Davis, "After Ferguson, A New Protest Culture's Challenge to Art," ArtNet, 16 December 2014, www.news.artnet.com/art-world/after-ferguson-a-new-protest-cultures-challenge-to-art-194601

[22] Davis, "After Ferguson, A New Protest Culture's Challenge to Art."

[23] 42% of French Opposed to *Charlie Hebdo*'s Cartoons of the Prophet Muhammad, Poll Finds," Jack Linshi, TIME, January 18, 2015, www.time.com/3672921/charlie-hebdo-prophet-muhammad-muslim-cartoon-poll/

[24] "The Singularity is an era in which our intelligence will become increasingly nonbiological and trillions of times more powerful than it is today—the dawning of a new civilization that will enable us to transcend our biological limitations and amplify our creativity." Ray Kurzweil, THE SINGULARITY IS NEAR: When Humans Transcend Biology (New York: Viking Press, 2005), www.singularity.com

The Future of Memory – Some Thoughts Developed in Advance of the Exhibition
<u>Nicolaus Schafhausen</u>

Die permanenten Veränderungen in der Kommunikationskultur und die damit einhergehende Expansion der Internetarchive werden sich fundamental auf das kollektive Gedächtnis auswirken. Dieser gegenwärtige Wandel wirft mehrere relevante Fragen auf.

1. Vor der digitalen Revolution wurden Bilder und Spuren der Vergangenheit als Erinnerungen bezeichnet. Sie spiegelten Momente wider, die wir tatsächlich erlebten und bezogen sich auf Erfahrungen, die wir in der Realität machten.[1] Heute wird unsere Erinnerung vor allem von Bildern geprägt, die über elektronische Kommunikationsmedien geteilt und verbreitet werden. Virtuelle Erinnerungen setzen sich aus den Erfahrungen zusammen, die erst seit den technologischen Innovationen in der digitalen Welt möglich sind. Gleichzeitig führt uns die permanente Interaktion mit den neuen Kommunikationsgeräten vor Augen, dass diese Veränderungen alle Bereiche unseres Denkens und Handelns berühren und beeinflussen. Mit welchen Konsequenzen dieser Wandel einhergeht, bleibt allerdings eine offene Frage. Es wäre zu komplex, eine umfassende Epistemologie zum digitalen Zeitalter zu schreiben.

2. „Reale" Erinnerungen stehen in einem ambivalenten Bezug zum Wahrhaftigen. Sie können gewissermaßen als eine Rekonstruktion eines subjektives Erlebnisses verstanden werden, als eine Begebenheit, der man beiwohnte und die man unter dem Vorsatz bezeugen würde: „Ich habe es mit meinen eigenen Augen gesehen." Ganz anders verhält es sich mit virtuellen Erinnerungsbildern, sie sind die Repräsentation einer Welt aus konstruierten Inhalten. So schreibt die Autorin Dessislava Dimova über den Künstler Pierre Bismuth: „In der zeitgenössischen visuellen Kultur steht ein Bild immer weniger in Bezug zur Realität und hat immer weniger den Anspruch, irgendwie naturgetreu zu sein – natürlich, künstlich, natürlich aromatisiert oder künstlich verbessert. Bilder werden bis zur Abstraktion perfektioniert und verbreitet. Dennoch beziehen sie sich weder auf eine transzendentale Realität, noch sind sie ein Ding an sich. Vielmehr schaffen sie eine eigene parallele Realität – die Realität von Zeitschriftencovers, Selfies, Plakatwänden, unmenschlich perfekten Menschen und einem Leben, das in sozialen Netzwerken in Bildern aufbereitet wird."[2]

3. Die mediale Daten- und Bilderflut ist zu einem Zeichen des digitalen Zeitalters geworden. Obwohl die Medien von individuellen und kollektiven Erfahrungen vermittelt berichten, ist das Betrachten, Teilen und Kommunizieren von Daten und Bildern zu einer alltäglichen Erlebniswelt geworden. Daher bedarf die Definition des Begriffes „Realität" einer Aktualisierung und eventuell sogar einer zeitgemäßen Erweiterung. Anhand von drei aktuelleren Debatten lässt sich nachvollziehen, wie „die Realität" oder „das Reale" zu einem heiß diskutieren Begriff geworden ist. Genauer betrachtet weisen die Diskussionen auch darauf hin, dass der digitale Wandel den generellen Status der Gegenwartskultur angreift. 1.) „Reality TV[3]" wurde im Zuge der letzten 15 Jahre zu einem globalen Genre. Bereits daran ist ablesbar, dass sich die Begriffsdefinition schon früh gelockert hat. 2.) Im Jahr 2006 wurde der Romanautor James Frey[4] im US-amerikanischen Fernsehen von Oprah Winfrey[5] für die Fiktionen in seiner als real verkauften Geschichte *A Million Little Lies* öffentlich angeklagt. Aus seiner Autobiografie wurde schlagartig ein autobiografischer Roman. Im deutschen Kontext rankte sich um das Buch *Axolotl Roadkill* (2010) von Helene Hegemann eine ähnlich heftige Diskussion. Kurz nach der Veröffentlichung des Debütromans wurde Hegemann als besonders authentische Schriftstellerin hoch gelobt. Wenige Monate später wurde ihr Sampling und Plagiatismus vorgeworfen[6]. Es gibt weitere solcher Fälle. Debatten wie diese führten jedenfalls dazu, dass Schriftsteller/innen weltweit aufgefordert waren, anspruchsvollere Standards für die Begriffe Autorschaft und Authentizität zu formulieren. 3.) Die aktuellen Diskussionen um den Literaturtrend der Autofiktion[7] zeigen wiederum, dass im Moment eine literarische Mischung aus Wahrhaftigkeit und Fiktion auf weitverbreitete Akzeptanz stößt. Das lässt sich z.B. am Buch *Wie sollten wir sein* (2014) der Kanadischen Autorin Sheila Heti oder an Karl Ove Knausgårds autobiografisch angelegten Romanprojekt *Min Kamp* (2009) nachskizzieren.

Alle diese Beispiele verdeutlichen jedenfalls, dass das Digitale zwischen unsere Idee des Realen und Fiktiven getreten ist. Die Grenzen sind mittlerweile nicht nur aufgeweicht, sie richten sich je nach Diskussion stärker an der einen oder anderen Begriffsidee aus. Verwirrung ist Alltag.

4. Die willkürliche Verbreitung virtueller Bilder ohne Nennung der Urheberrechte nimmt immer weiter zu. Diese Entwicklung scheint sich auch auf unsere Erinnerungsprozesse an „reale" Erlebnisse auszuwirken. Das Virtuelle tastet sich also langsam vor und beginnt unser Denken zu beeinflussen.

Erinnerungsprozesse werden vom Digitalen in drei Punkten angegriffen:

I. Google macht doof.
- „Die Leistungsstärke elektronischer Geräte hat unsere Fähigkeit, sich nicht mehr an die Dinge erinnern zu können, auf ein Höchstmaß getrieben."[8] Diese Idee wird von wissenschaftlichen Erkenntnissen belegt.
- „Suchmaschinen, so sagt man, erinnern sich für uns und die Folge ist, dass wir vergessen, uns selbst zu erinnern. Natürlich sind die Dinge selten so simpel, wie es eine Überschrift vorzugeben scheint. Die Forschungsergebnisse, die hinter diesen Annahmen stehen, wurden im Journal *Science*[9] veröffentlicht und belegen, dass Menschen, die

wussten, dass bestimmte Informationen auf einem Computer gespeichert sind, auch weniger fähig waren sich an diese Informationen zu erinnern (gleichzeitig wussten sie aber bestens darüber Bescheid, wo diese Informationen abgespeichert waren.)"[10]

II. Unsere Denkmuster haben sich den computergesteuerten Technologien angepasst.
„Das digitale Zeitalter verändert, wie wir denken. Heute erinnern wir uns viel häufiger daran, wie man bestimmte Informationen finden kann, und viel weniger daran, was diese Informationen eigentlich alles umfassen."[11]

III. Erinnerungen werden immer öffentlicher.
„(...) immer mehr Ephemeres scheint online Preis gegeben zu werden – zufälligerweise oder gerade deswegen … werden die Erinnerungen immer öffentlicher – und (dadurch) immer sozialer."[12]

5. Der Wandel der Erinnerungsprozesse ist kollektiv und „transaktiv" zugleich.
I. Die Autorin Alice Bell hat im *The Guardian* angemerkt, dass „sich die Menschheit schon seit Ewigkeiten auf die Leistungsfähigkeit des „transaktiven Gedächtnisses" verlassen hat. Erinnerungen werden seit jeher außerhalb des menschlichen Körpers aufbewahrt, heute aber speichern wir sie viel schneller in unseren Devices als wir sie früher in den Regalen verstauen konnten. Bevor der Silikonchip erfunden wurde, haben der Stift und das Papier, der Buchdruck und die Kamera dabei geholfen Informationen zu archivieren."[13]
II. „Viele Menschen sind durch diese kollektiven Erfahrungen dazu angeregt worden, das Wesen der Erinnerung zu hinterfragen. Erinnern ist meist ein zutiefst subjektives Moment – wollen wir das wirklich kollektiv erleben?"[14]

6. Der Wandel kollektiver Erinnerungsprozesse scheint auch – bedingt durch die Bilderflut – mit einer Delokalisierung und Entfremdung von der fühlbaren Umwelt einherzugehen. Obwohl „reale" Erinnerungen sozusagen stetig vor unseren Augen präsent sind, leiden sie trotzdem unter einer zunehmenden Verdrängung durch das Digitale. Virtuelle Daten liefern im Vergleich zu echten Erfahrungen aber nur Bilder, die uns mit niemandem und nichts verbinden. Sie stehen nicht in direktem Zusammenhang mit unseren Gefühlen und Erlebnissen. Gerade weil die digitale Technologie ständig und überall verfügbar ist, werden die vermittelten Inhalte heute viel stärker als eine unzertrennbare Einheit wahrgenommen.[15] Diese Idee ist genauso bildlich wie wörtlich gemeint. Niemand verbringt seine ganze Zeit damit, Wissen aus dem gesamten Internet zu akkumulieren – und das wäre weder wünschenswert noch besonders sinnvoll. Jedoch ist das Bewusstsein, dass diese Möglichkeit bestünde, bei einigen Menschen sehr stark ausgeprägt. Dieser Möglichkeitszustand scheint von manchen Menschen sogar als eine Form des Zwanges oder Drucks empfunden zu werden. Aus dieser Gefühlslage heraus scheinen auch die zahlreichen Beispiele in der Kunst und dem Kunstdiskurs zu argumentieren, die versuchen eine Erklärung für diese emotionale Abhängigkeit und gleichzeitige Ohnmacht zu finden.

Zwei Beispiele:
I. Die Ausstellung *The Forever Now: Contemporary Painting in an Atemporal World* (2014) im New Yorker MoMA postuliert Zeitlosigkeit als

eine starke Tendenz in der Gegenwartsmalerei.[16] Das Internet habe eine Epoche der Gleichzeitigkeit eingeleitet, in der sich Vergangenheit, Gegenwart und Zukunft nicht mehr voneinander unterscheiden lassen. Als Reaktion auf den Daten- und Bilderstrom habe sich ein globaler Malstil herausgebildet, der alle Zeiten, Herkünfte, Bezüge und Interessen in einer Promiskuität der Stile unkenntlich macht. Warum aber wird diese Ausstellung heute so stark rezipiert? Sie kommuniziert Malerei nach einer ganz traditionellen Idee, nämlich als ein Kommentar zur menschlichen Geste und als Impuls für das Empathische. Verfolgt man diese Idee weiter, dann wäre die Form der Gegenwartsmalerei, die ohne jede Spur einer menschlichen Geste auskommt und nur durch einen digitalen Gestus gesteuert wird, ein reiner Anachronismus.

II. Einen anderen Argumentationsstrang, die Tendenz zur Zeitlosigkeit in der Gegenwartsmalerei zu erklären, verfolgt der New Yorker Kunstkritiker Ben Davis in einem Online-Artikel: „Es ist schon seit geraumer Zeit bekannt, dass der Internet-Hype der digitalen Meme[17] die gegenwärtigen „Gefühlsstrukturen" bestimmt, wie der Theoretiker Raymond Williams[18] die spezifischen Ausdrucksmittel, die Gegenwart und Vergangenheit voneinander unterscheiden lassen, bezeichnete. Diese Entwicklung ist wahrscheinlich die bedeutendste basisdemokratische und kulturelle Bewegung seit dem Ausbruch der Graffiti-Szene in den 1970er Jahren. Jedenfalls scheinen #YesAllWomen[19], die „Ice Bucket Challenge[20]" (oder hell, der Harlem Shake[21]) produktive Mittel für das Teilen von kollektiven Erlebnissen zu sein.[22]

7. Es liegt auf der Hand, dass die Reichweite der *„digitalen Meme heute die wohl bedeutendste basisdemokratische und kulturelle Bewegung ist."*[23] Trotzdem fällt es schwer, diese Entwicklung nachzuvollziehen und das hat sehr viele verschiedene Gründe. Die zeitgenössische Kunst reagiert mit ihrem eigenen Repertoire auf das Visuelle. Die digitalen Meme (z.B. Animationen, Gifs und ähnliche elektronische Tools) fallen in ihren Kompetenzbereich und dennoch hält der Slang der digitalen Kultur eine ganze Reihe an Hürden bereit, die ein Problem für die zeitgenössische Kunst darstellen. Beispiele sind u. a. die digitalisierte Bildproduktion ohne menschliche Züge, das Fehlen von sichtbaren Bedeutungsebenen und die Nicht-Kommodizifierbarkeit des Produzierten. Die Ausstellung *The Forever Now* in MoMA macht u. a. auch sichtbar, wie Abbildungen von aktuellen und historischen Malereien heute durch die gesamte digitale Bilderwelt geistern. Sie werden von Künstler/innen aufgegriffen, bearbeitet und dann wieder verworfen. Das ist sicher nicht ihre dezidierte Aussage, aber die Ausstellung scheint aufzuzeigen, dass es der Malerei schwer fällt, Kontakt zu ihrem eigenen Medium herzustellen. Vielmehr scheint sie die Tradition des *individuellen visuellen Ausdrucks* einer gegenwärtigen Welt zu repräsentieren, in der *kollektive Formen des visuellen Ausdrucks* onmipräsent, leicht zugänglich und – aus den bereits genannten Gründen – scheinbar relevanter sind als alle anderen künstlerischen Ausdrucksformen. Interessanterweise zeigt die Malerei ihre Relevanz damit in einem Umkehrschluss. Malerei, so wie sie heute praktiziert wird, repräsentiert eine veraltete Form der Auseinandersetzung mit der Welt und lebt trotzdem als Referenz der Referenz weiter fort. Außerdem werden wir nur bis zu einem gewissen Limit sinnvoll mit den Sammlungen der Internetarchive arbeiten können, auch wenn diese weiterhin exponentiell ansteigen. Die Analogie sieht also wie folgt aus: Malerei>Oberfläche>Geste = Ort>Verortung>individuelle Erfahrung.

8. Trotz allem sind „reale" Erinnerungen unweigerlich an unsere körperlichen und emotionalen Erlebnisse gebunden. Die Verankerung im Physischen oder Körperlichen ist ein guter Ausgangspunkt um darüber nachzudenken, was Erinnerungen sind und was im Gegensatz dazu das „Reale" sein kann. Der Idee treu zu bleiben, dass Wahrheiten auf körperlichen Erfahrungen beruhen, kann hilfreich sein, um mit den permanenten Überforderungen der Medienwelt umzugehen. Der Alltag in der westlichen Welt zeigt allerdings auch, dass das nicht immer einfach ist. Man kann sich gut vorstellen, dass unsere bildüberflutete Gesellschaft als Reaktion auf die gegenwärtigen Tendenzen eine ewig während „Bildabstinenz" heraufbeschwören könnte – Zurück-zur-Natur im Stil des 21. Jahrhunderts. Dies wäre eine andere Form des Bilderstreits, eine andere Form von Ikonoklasmus, die in ihrem Ursprung dem jüngsten Terroranschlag gegen die französische Satirezeitschrift *Charlie Hebdo*, die provokante Zeichnungen des Propheten Mohammed und der islamischen Kultur veröffentlichte ähnelt.[24] Solche Reaktionen (die eine fiktiv, die andere nur zu real) sind symptomatisch für eine unvermeidbare und wahrscheinlich länger andauernde Genese einer anti-modernen reaktionären Haltung. Eine ähnliche Form von Bilderverbot praktizieren aber auch diejenigen, die den Karikaturist/innen selbst einen Teil der Schuld an den erschütternden Ereignissen zusprechen. Reaktionen dieser Art sind zweifelhaft, vor allem wenn die Gedanken öffentlich über Facebook oder anderen Foren verteilt werden. In sozialen Netzwerksdiskussionen scheint die digitale Generation die Tradition der Bürgerrechte per se als gegeben hinzunehmen und stellt dann aber das Recht der *Charlie Hebdo* Satirist/innen Provokationen zu äußern in Frage. Provokationen sind ein wesentlicher Bestandteil der Legitimierung von Bürgerrechten. Sie gehören zur Tradition unseres Handelns, egal ob wir Kunstwerke oder Ausstellungen produzieren.

Unabhängig davon wie schwach oder extrem anti-moderne Tendenzen ausgedrückt werden, sie spiegeln den allgemeinen Wunsch danach wieder, die Dinge zu vereinfachen. Es ist weder eine zukunftsträchtige Lösung sich zu verbieten, an Wahrheiten zu glauben, die man am eigenen Körper erlebt hat, noch scheint es angemessen dem Impuls zu folgen, sich der modernen Welt einfach nur hinzugeben. Anstatt zu leugnen, dass die Bilderflut eine erweiterte Form der Realität geschaffen hat und eine Vielfalt an Komplikationen mit sich bringt, sollten wir überlegen, wie die Gegenwart aus der Zukunft betrachtet aussehen könnte. Von dort aus wird die kapitalistische Kalibrierung unserer Kultur wahrscheinlich wie eine Version von *Menschheit 2.0. Die Singularität naht*[25] wirken, die der Futurist Ray Kurzweil in seinem gleichnamigen Buch beschrieben hat. Aber das wäre ein Thema für eine weitere Ausstellung.

Nicolaus Schafhausen ist Direktor der Kunsthalle Wien.

[1] Anm.: Realität ist ein komplexer Begriff, der hier im Gegensatz zum Virtuellen verwendet wird. Es ist anzumerken, dass jede Form der Erinnerung nur subjektiv und fragmentarisch sein kann. Erinnerungen setzen sich aus Bildern, Momenten und Spuren zusammen. Sie bilden einen Gegenspieler zum dem, was wir als Wirklichkeit bezeichnen. Vgl. Jacques Derrida: „Mémoires", hrsg. Peter Engelmann, Wien 2012.
[2] Dessislava Dimova: „Das Leben ist wahrscheinlich rund.", in: Pierre Bismuth: Things I Remember I Have Done, but Don't Remember Why I Did Them, Luca Lo Pinto, Nicolaus Schafhausen (Hg.), Kunsthalle Wien, Wien 2015., in Engl. "An image in contemporary visual culture pertains less and less to reality and claims less and less truthfulness to any kind of nature — natural,

artificial, naturally flavored, or artificially enhanced. Images are perfected and proliferated to the point of abstraction. Yet they refer neither to a transcendental reality, nor are a thing in themselves. Rather they create their parallel reality — the reality of magazine covers, of selfies, of billboards, of inhumanly perfect humans, of lives edited in pictures on social networks.",
Übersetzung: Georg Bauer
[3] „Reality TV basiert auf der Idee, „den Zuschauern einen unmittelbaren, voyeuristischen, oft auch spielerischen Blick in die sogenannte „unterhaltsame" Realität zu bieten." (Murray und Ouellette, 2004)", in: Global Television Formats: „Understanding Television Across Borders", Hrsg. Tasha Oren und Sharon Shahaf, Google eBook, London 2013, S. 347.
[4] Iris Alanyali: „US-Präsidenten verzeiht man Lügen eher als mir", Die Welt, 20. November 2014., http://www.welt.de/kultur/literarischewelt/article133475644/US-Praesidenten-verzeiht-man-Luegen-eher-als-mir.html
[5] Oprah Gail Winfrey (*1954 in Kosciusko, Mississippi, USA) ist eine US-amerikanische Talkshow-Moderatorin, Schauspielerin und Unternehmerin. Sie ist bekannt für *The Oprah Winfrey Show*, die bei weitem erfolgreichste Talkshow des amerikanischen Fernsehens. 2006 hatte die wöchentliche Show 21 Millionen Zuschauer in 105 Ländern.", http://de.wikipedia.org/wiki/Oprah_Winfrey
[6] David Hugendick: „Total egoistisch und gedankenlos", Die Zeit, 8. Februar 2010, http://www.zeit.de/2010/08/Helene-Hegemann-Plagiat
Josef Joffe: „Über das Plagiat", Die Zeit, 18. Februar 2010, http://www.zeit.de/2010/08/Helene-Hegemann-Plagiat
[7] Als Autofiktion werden Selbstdarstellungen in Romanen bezeichnet, die ein fiktives Leben des Protagonisten in der Zukunft schildern. Vgl.: Jonathon Sturgeon: „2014: The Death of the Postmodern Novel and the Rise of Autofiction", Flavorwire, 31. Dezember 2014.
www.flavorwire.com/496570/2014-the-death-of-the-postmodern-novel-and-the-rise-of-autofiction
[8] Big Think Editors: „How the Digital Age Has Changed Memory", o. D.
http://bigthink.com/ideafeed/how-the-digital-age-has-changed-memory
[9] *Science* ist eine Fachzeitschrift des Instituts American Association for the Advancement of Science mit Sitz in Washington DC. Science wurde erstmalig im Jahr 1880 publiziert, arbeitet nach dem Peer-Review-Verfahren und fördert die Veröffentlichung einflussreicher naturwissenschaftlicher Forschungsberichte., http://www.sciencemag.org/
[10] Alice Bell: „Memory in the digital age", *The Guardian*, 13. Januar 2012.,
www.theguardian.com/lifeandstyle/2012/jan/14/memories-in-the-digital-age
[11] Big Think Editors: „How the Digital Age Has Changed Memory", o. D.,
http://bigthink.com/ideafeed/how-the-digital-age-has-changed-memory
12 Alice Bell: „Memory in the digital age", *The Guardian*, 13. Januar 2012. www.theguardian.com/lifeandstyle/2012/jan/14/memories-in-the-digital-age
[13] ebd
[14] ebd
[15] „Erstmalig stellt Laura Hoptman (Kuratorin) in ihrem radikalen Katalogbeitrag die These auf, dass „Kultur nicht mehr die Zeit definiert, in der wir leben", sondern vielmehr zum Ausdruck für „einen neuen und seltsamen Zustand der Welt geworden ist. Dank des Internets scheinen nun alle Epochen gleichzeitig zu existieren." in: Jason Farago: „The Forever Now review: calling time on the avant garde", *The Guardian*, 12. Dezember 2014., www.theguardian.com/artanddesign/2014/dec/12/the-forever-now-review-calling-time-avant-garde
Vgl.: Claudia Steinberg: „Die Zombies zieht es ins Museum", Die Zeit, 25. Januar 2015.
http://www.zeit.de/2015/02/moma-new-york-malerei-zeitlos
Susanne von Falkenhausen: „Too Much Too Fast", Frieze d/e, Ausgabe 17, Dezember 2014., http://frieze-magazin.de/archiv/features/too-much-too-fast/
[16] *The Forever Now: Contemporary Painting in an Atemporal World*, Museum of Modern Art, New York, 14. Dezember 2014 – 5. April 2015., http://www.moma.org/visit/calendar/exhibitions/1498
[17] Der Evolutionsbiologe Richard Dawkins bezeichnet Meme als jede mögliche Idee (ein Schlagwort, Verhalten, Bild oder Grafik etc.), die über einen bestimmten Interessensbereich hinaus Wellen schlägt. Ihre Popularität erklärt sich ihrer schnellen Veränderbarkeit und der stetigen Anpassung an die Zeit. Vgl.: Richard Dawkins: *Das egoistische Gen*, Berlin und Heidelberg 2014.
[18] „Raymond Williams (1921–1988) war einer der bedeutendsten und einflussreichsten Denker und Dichter im England des 20. Jahrhundert. Er eröffnete den Zugang zu neuen Forschungsbereichen in Literatur- und Kulturwissenschaft, der Kommunikation, sowie der sozialen und politischen Theorie. Seine Kulturarbeit basierte auf dem Konzept der langen Revolution, derzufolge der demokratische Wandel der Gesellschaft schließlich auch zu einem Ende von Ungleichheit und Unterdrückung führen würde.", http://www.raymondwilliamsfoundation.org.uk/RW1.html
[19] „Der Amokläufer im Kalifornischen Santa Barbara schrieb vor seiner Tat ein Manifest, in dem er verspricht, Rache an all den Frauen zu üben, die ihn zurückgewiesen hätten. Darauf reagierten Twitter-Nutzer mit ihren eigenen Gedanken zum Thema Frauenfeindlichkeit, alles unter dem Hashtag #YesAllWomen." in: Nolan Feeney: „The Most Powerful #YesAllWomen Tweets", TIME, 27. Mai 2014., www.time.com/114043/yesallwomen-hashtag-santa-barbara-shooting
[20] http://www.alsa.org/fight-als/ice-bucket-challenge.html
[21] The Harlem Shake. https://www.youtube.com/watch?v=8f7wj_RcqYk
[22] Ben Davis: „After Ferguson, A New Protest Culture's Challenge to Art", ArtNet, 16. Dezember 2014., www.news.artnet.com/art-world/after-ferguson-a-new-protest-cultures-challenge-to-art-194601
[23] ebd
[24] Anm.: Laut einer Umfrage sind 42% der Franzosen gegen die Charlie Hebdo Karikaturen des Propheten Mohammed, in: Jack Linshi: „42% of French Opposed to Charlie Hebdo's Cartoons of the Prophet Muhammad, Poll Finds", TIME, 18. Januar 2015., www.time.com/3672921/charlie-hebdo-prophet-muhammad-muslim-cartoon-poll/
[25] Ray Kurzweil: Menschheit 2.0. Die Singularität naht, 2., durchgesehene Auflage, Berlin 2014.

Always Futurize!
<u>Clint Burnham</u>

In his latest novel, *The Peripheral* (2014), science fiction writer William Gibson describes a future with various pasts. In that future, the rich can interfere with recent history, changing events that lead to a "stub", a timeline that stops (and so does not interfere with the contemporary). The action of the novel takes place in one of these stubs, a near-present of animated tattoos, ubiquitous drones, government marijuana and 3D printers at your local shopping mall. History as a stub suggests the Wikipedia stub, or short article that requires more information. And this question of history, the present, the future, and what our memories can do to process this information, is very much relevant to the artworks in "The Future of Memory," which are deeply metahistorical even as they think about the future. Here we learn to be disgusted by past, by our politics, by our everyday cruelty. But we also learn that this cruelty and violence have historical precedents.

Consider, first of all, two of the artists whose video works deal with Balkan history: Igor Bošnjak and Aleksandra Domanović. In *Balkan Hotel* (2013), Bošnjak takes us into one of Marshall Tito's bunkers in Yugoslavia. As a gritty, postindustrial soundtrack gloomily drones on, the camera shows us a mix of the fantastic and the utilitarian: mid-century modern chairs lined up at teletype machines, a key in a doorknob, banks of fluorescent lights, or a mural of swimmers at a beachside resort. Given that the bunker was designed for the Yugoslav apparatchiks in the event of a nuclear war, who did they think would be on the other end of the communication devices? At least the operators had chic, Danish-looking chairs to sit on. And the generals and cabinet ministers would be able to remember better days, in the sun and at the seaside, as they cowered, eating canned food and waiting for the radiation to dissipate.

Domanović's *Turbo Sculptures* (2005-2013) capture a more recent twisting of history. Sculptures of Bruce Lee, Bob Marley, and (proposed but abandoned) Samantha Fox, mark some attempts, after the Balkan Wars of the 1990s, to provide public sculptures that circumvent the recent past. And they suggest a popular attempt at memory-making that is at least more refreshing than the crude forms of nationalism to be found in Macedonia, such as, Suzana Milevska recently wrote in *e-flux*, monuments in Skopje "of unrecognized and incomplete identities, marginal heroes, and exaggerated victories from the past were used as strategies for inducing collective enjoyment, and ultimately self-delusion."[1] But Domanović's turbo monuments are more properly sublime, especially the Bruce Lee sculpture unveiled in Mostar, Bosnia and Herzegovina, in 2005. A shiny, chromed figure, Bruce Lee represents an attempt to suture over the recent past of the Balkans, the fractious war, claims and counter-claims of atrocity, victim-hood, shame and blame. In Domanović's video, pop culture icons (Batman, Fox, Bob Marley…) are layered over standard images of war (a tank facing the audience). The form of that video — its corporatized and clunky format, over-identifying with the format of cheesy TV news — then attempts to match the very "turbo" quality of what we might call low postmodernism (or lo pomo). But

Bošnjak's video is more stylish and cool. The bunkers, its modern furniture and grey-steel teletype machines would not be out of place in a hipster boutique in Brooklyn or Kreuzberg.

So too, the retro-kitsch concept of folk sculptures are very much in keeping with our present-day fascination with recent pop culture. Since the 1990s, that is, global pop culture has successively mined the recent past (first the 1970s, then the 1980s, now the 1990s, as the 20th anniversary of Nirvana's *Nevermind* album reminded us). What those pop culture moments do, especially Domanović and Bošnjak's art, is to bring to the fore the troubled way in which we, as social subjects, deal with our history, our memory.

First of all, the sculptures are fetishes, which allow the Balkan subjects to disavow their (our) history. For Lacan, the fetish is what allows the subject to misrecognize its lack (or surplus), to forget about it. Domanović's images (the freeze frames that circulate as metonyms of the work) offer viewers the unwrapping of a Bruce Lee sculpture, for instance, next to a peeled back slide curled on a stack of pictures. That is, the images are simultaneously photograph, video or moving image, and object. Such an accelerated wrapping/unwrapping (like the veritable money shot that is the YouTube genre of unboxing devices) is all the more necessary to distract us from our violent past and present. That is, the form of the video functions all the more hurriedly, hysterically, perhaps: #Accelerationism, is after all, a hysterical philosophy *par excellence*.

This operation of fetishistic disavowal, Slavoj Žižek reminds us, is one of four ways in which we negate, repress, or deny the past. In his book *Less than Nothing* (2013), Žižek distinguishes between Freud's four "main forms" of Ver- : "*Verwerfung* (foreclosure/rejection); *Verdrängung* (repression); *Verneinung* (denial); *Verleugnung* (disavowal)." Žižek continues: "In *Verwerfung*, the content is thrown out of the symbolic, de-symbolized, so that it can only return in the Real (in the guise of hallucinations). In *Verdrängung*, the content remains within the symbolic but is inaccessible to consciousness, relegated to the Other Scene, returning in the guise of symptoms. In *Verneinung*, the content is admitted into consciousness, but marked by a denial. In *Verleugnung*, it is admitted a positive form, but … it is not really integrated into the subject's symbolic universe."[2]

Domanović's *Turbo Sculptures* suggest disavowal, or *Verleugnung*, in that the horrors of the Balkan wars are "admitted into consciousness": "Nobody from the wars of the 1990s or from the former Yugoslavia deserves a monument, because all our leaders did was to prevent us from progressing," declares Bojan Marceta, who helped organize a statue of Rocky/Sylvester Stallone in the Serbian town of Zitiste. But the horrors are disavowed, isolated, by being transformed into the fetish of the Turbo sculpture, the celebrity monument, a kind of fan art writ large. Domanović's naming of Turbo Sculpture owes much to an indigenous postmodern kitsch found in the Balkans during and after the wars. From gaudy architecture to nationalist politics, Turbo denotes a frenetic striation of affect, ornament, and aesthetics. This effect is in turn mimicked, perhaps, in Domanović's video's curvy layers of images which, placed one on another, build an argument through sheer excess.

For all its elegance, Bošnjak's *Hotel Balkan*, meanwhile, is more horror movie-like in its use of tracking shots down long, cramped corridors, and its forensics' focus pulling that will remorselessly move from one telephone or object to another. With no narration, the role of sound is important, while with the imagery Bošnjak provides us with a way to think historically about technology and what Egyptian artist Basim Magdy calls "our futuristic past." That is, the sound has an ambient feel, with static, buzzing, and hums that suggest the feedback caused by deteriorating electronic machinery. The machinery depicted in the video: old turntables and microphones and bulky plastic desk phones, a switchboard with dozens of openings waiting for input jacks — the sounds, and technology, of the 1970s and 80s. Now and then the soundtrack is a bit more modern: is that the buzzing and screech of a dial-up modem? The beeping of 8-bit video games?

The connection made between analogue tech to Balkan history suggests that Tito's bunker may be re-figured as a symptom of our past. That is, the "future" of that Communist past is surely what is now repressed (the operation of *Verdrängung*) in our neoliberal present, as repressed as the bulky communications technology, computers, and switchboards have been relegated to the scrapheap of history. In both cases, a metahistorical sensibility is at work, one with a self-conscious awareness of the visual and narrative elements of history. So too with Jon Rafman's video, *Mainsqueeze* (2014), but with the addition of the affective (thus making it psychoanalytic) via registers of disgust, anxiety, and paranoia, if not anger.

Writers such as Sara Ahmed and Sianne Ngai have helped us to think about emotions, or affect, in queer and feminist and postcolonial ways that exceed those ideas' origins in Lacan, Deleuze, or Kristeva. To which we can add questions of a historical attitude towards digital networks evident in Rafman's work. And so what of the history of that technology, or digital or computer memories that are internal to those systems? It is easier, perhaps, to wipe the history of one's browsing than to wipe bodily fluids off the keyboard — and it is such an "ugh factor" that we encounter with *Mainsqueeze*. With Rafman, instead of Ngai''s "ugly feelings," then, we have "ugh feelings."

In *Mainsqueeze*, we see a discontinuous series of images, often scenes of destruction: a washing machine running until it self-destructs, photos of passed-out drunks with their faces covered in black marker; a watermelon crushed between a muscleman's thighs, an office worker smashing his laptop, a young woman stepping on a crayfish, violent historical paintings such as Caravaggio's *Judith Beheading Holofernes* (1598-1599). Someone in a turtle costume tries to escape from rope, while a dog barks and a cellphone buzzes.

The graffiti'd drunks walk that fine line between college hazing pranks and Abu Ghraib "soft torture," reminding us of how both practices also tend to be relentlessly documented by the perpetrators: no one is so ashamed of their actions that they also won't upload it to Facebook. This is a different kind of memory, perhaps: acknowledged, not even disavowed. Rafman's work suggests we may need a fifth category for Žižekian or Freudian repression: here, everything is disgusting, anxiety-inducing, and even while nothing is hidden (the Internet, and Rafman, will show us almost anything), we cannot help but feel paranoid about what we aren't watching, what is hidden in the society of total transparency and uploading.

Mainsqueeze is thus difficult to watch, and it is no wonder that, in the U.S., a country where torture and drone warfare is disavowed but carried on furtively, Rafman's work should itself be censored (as when the video was cut from his recent St. Louis Museum exhibition). But this is as it should be, and in a post *Charlie Hebdo* political sphere, where art critics and iconophobia are vilified, a little old-fashioned censorship is to be welcomed as bracingly honest. For really, there is no rational (or realist) criticism possible with Rafman: no point in breaking down the origins of a given image, its progress from event or its simulacra to digital dissemination and (mock) outrage. That social media cycle is all too well known, as predictable and banal as a philistines and the gutter press in a former age. What I mean here, is that no matter how much information one reads about the etiology of a given *Mainsqueeze* image or sequence, one is still disgusted. You could learn, for instance, that the shellfish that a woman steps on while a voice-over discusses caring for an infirm relative was in fact a robotic shellfish or that the image was CGI'd. No matter: the look is amateur internet video, the crack and squish have done their work, and we can never deny our disgust retroactively.

The title of this essay, Always Futurize! is a reference to Fredric Jameson's well-known call, in The Political Unconscious (1981), to "always historicize!", to always contextualize cultural objects in history. Today we face a different task, as suggested by these artworks. What future do we have in front of us? The apocalyptic end times suggested by so many Hollywood films? The "peak oil" moment of wind turbines and hippies? The shiny, unproblematic connectivity promised by cellphone ads? The sped-up contradictions philosophized by #Accelerationism? We do not know, of course, but to think about the future, and to inquire into its relation with our past, our history, our emotions and our memory, may be the most important question today.

Clint Burnham is an associate professor in the English department at Simon Fraser University in Vancouver, Canada. He has published in Flash Art, Canadian Art, Artforum, Momus.ca, and Camera Austria, and for galleries and museums in Europe and America. He is currently writing books on Slavoj Žižek and digital culture, and on Fredric Jameson and The Wolf of Wall Street.

---

[1] Suzana Milevska, "Ágalma: The 'Objet Petit a,' Alexander the Great, and Other Excesses of Skopje 2014," e-flux 57 (Sept. 2014).
[2] Slavoj Žižek, Less Than Nothing. (London: Verso, 2012), 859.

Always Futurize!
<u>Clint Burnham</u>

In seinem neuesten Roman *The Peripheral* (2014) beschreibt der Science-Fiction-Autor William Gibson eine Zukunft mit verschiedenen Vergangenheiten. In dieser Zukunft können die Reichen in die jüngste Geschichte eingreifen und Ereignisse so verändern, dass sie zu einem Platzhalter führen, zu einer Zeitleiste, die endet (und auf diese Weise die Gegenwart nicht behindert). Die Handlung des Romans spielt in einem dieser Platzhalter – einer nahen Zukunft mit animierten Tattoos, allgegenwärtigen Drohnen, Marijuana von der Regierung und 3D-Druckern in der örtlichen Shopping Mall. Geschichte als Platzhalter – das erinnert an den Platzhalter bei Wikipedia: ein kurzer Artikel, der nach mehr Informationen verlangt. Und diese Frage nach der Geschichte, der Gegenwart, der Zukunft und danach, was unser Gedächtnis tun kann, um diese Informationen zu verarbeiten, ist von großer Bedeutung für die Kunstwerke in dieser Ausstellung. Denn sie sind zutiefst metahistorisch, selbst wenn sie sich mit der Zukunft befassen. Hier lernen wir die Abscheu vor der Vergangenheit, vor unserer Politik, vor unserer alltäglichen Grausamkeit. Aber wir erfahren auch, dass es für diese Grausamkeit und Gewalt historische Vorbilder gibt.

Richten wir unser Augenmerk zunächst auf zwei Künstler, in deren Videoarbeiten es um die Geschichte der Balkanregion geht: Igor Bošnjak und Aleksandra Domanović. Bošnjak nimmt uns mit in einen von Marschall Titos Bunkern in Jugoslawien. Zu einem düsteren, post-industriellen und bedrückenden Soundtrack zeigt uns die Kamera moderne, an Fernschreibern aufgereihte Stühle aus der Mitte des letzten Jahrhunderts oder ein Wandbild von Schwimmern in einem Urlaubsort am Meer. Ein Schlüssel an einem Türknauf, Reihen von Neonleuchten. Eine Mischung aus dem Abstrusen und Nützlichen also. Angesichts der Tatsache, dass der Bunker für die jugoslawischen Funktionäre im Fall eines Atomkriegs entworfen wurde – wer, dachten sie, würde am anderen Ende der Leitungen sitzen? Zumindest hatten die Telefonisten schicke, dänisch aussehende Stühle. Und die Generäle und Minister konnten sich an bessere Tage in der Sonne und am Meer erinnern, während sie sich duckten, Dosennahrung aßen und darauf warteten, dass sich die Strahlung abbaute.

Domanovićs *Turbo Sculptures* greifen aktuellere historische Ereignisse auf. Die Skulpturen von Bruce Lee, Bob Marley und – vorgeschlagen, aber wieder aufgegeben – Samantha Fox stellen den Versuch dar, nach den Balkankriegen der Neunzigerjahre für den öffentlichen Raum Kunstdenkmäler zu entwickeln, die sich nicht auf die jüngste Vergangenheit beziehen. Und sie propagieren eine geläufige Art der Erinnerungskonstruktion, die wohltuender ist als die plumpen Formen des Nationalismus, die sich in Mazedonien finden lassen. Hiermit gemeint sind, wie Suzana Milevska kürzlich auf *e-flux* schrieb, die in Skopje zu findenden „Monumente verkannter und unvollendeter Persönlichkeiten, marginaler Helden und übertriebener Siege aus der Vergangenheit, die dazu benutzt wurden, kollektive Freude und damit letztlich Selbsttäuschung zu erzeugen."[1] Domanovićs Turbo-Skulpturen sind erhabener, vor allem die Statue von Bruce Lee, die 2005 in Mostar (Bosnien und Herzegowina) enthüllt wurde. Die chromglänzende Figur des Bruce Lee verkörpert den Versuch, eine Wunde zu schließen – die Wunde der jüngsten Vergangenheit der Balkanregion, des schrecklichen Krieges, der Behauptungen und Gegenbehauptungen von Gräueltaten und Opferstatus, von Schande und Schuld. In Domanovićs Video überlagern Ikonen der Popkultur (Batman, Fox, Bob Marley) übliche Bilder des Krieges (z.B. einen dem Publikum zugewandter Panzer). Auf eine kommerziell wirkende, schwerfällige, sich stark auf billige Nachrichtenformate im Fernsehen beziehende Weise versucht das Video, den „Turbo"-Qualitäten von etwas zu entsprechen, das man als „Postmoderne auf niedrigem Niveau" bezeichnen könnte. Bošnjaks Video ist stylisher und cooler. Die Bunkerarchitektur, das moderne Mobiliar und die Fernschreiber aus grauem Stahl würden sich auch in einer Hipster-Boutique in Brooklyn oder Kreuzberg gut machen.

Das Retrokitsch-Konzept volkstümlicher Denkmäler entspricht von daher in großem Maße unserer heutigen Faszination für die neuere Popkultur. Denn seit den Neunzigerjahren hat die weltweite Popkultur nach und nach die jüngere Vergangenheit ausgegraben – zuerst die Siebziger, dann die Achtziger und jetzt die Neunziger, woran uns der zwanzigste Jahrestag des Nirvana-Albums *Nevermind* erinnert. Was diese popkulturellen Momente, vor allem aber die Kunstwerke von Domanović und Bošnjak bewirken, ist die Sichtbarmachung der gestörten Art und Weise, in der wir als soziale Wesen mit unserer Geschichte und unserem Gedächtnis umgehen.

In erster Linie sind die Skulpturen Fetische, die es den Bürgern des Balkans ermöglichen, ihre (unsere) Geschichte zu leugnen. Für Lacan ist der Fetisch das, was dem Subjekt erlaubt, seinen Mangel (oder seinen Überschuss) zu ignorieren, ihn zu vergessen. Die Bilder von Domanović, d.h. die Stills, die als Metonymien ihrer Arbeit zirkulieren, zeigen uns z.B. das Auspacken einer Statue von Bruce Lee während die Bilder im Video wie ein Stapel durchgeblättert werden. Auf diese Weise sind die Bilder zugleich Foto, Video oder Film – und Objekt. Ein solch beschleunigtes Verpacken und Auspacken (vergleichbar mit einem *money shot*, d.h. mit der YouTube-Version des Auspackens) ist umso nötiger, um uns von unserer brutalen Vergangenheit und Gegenwart abzulenken. Also wird das Video immer eiliger und hysterischer, und vielleicht ist #Accelerationism am Ende die hysterische Philosophie *par excellence*.

Dieser Vorgang der fetischistischen Verleugnung ist, wie Slavoj Žižek uns erinnert, eine der vier Arten, auf die wir unsere Vergangenheit negieren, verdrängen und abstreiten. In seinem Buch *Weniger als nichts* unterscheidet Žižek Freuds vier „Hauptformen" des Ver-: Verwerfung, Verdrängung, Verneinung und Verleugnung. Žižek fährt fort: „Bei der Verwerfung wird der Inhalt aus dem Symbolischen hinausgeworfen, ent-symbolisiert, sodass er nur im Realen in Form von Halluzinationen wiederkehren kann. Bei der Verdrängung bleibt der Inhalt im Symbolischen, ist aber unzugänglich für das Bewusstsein, wird der Anderen Szene zugeschrieben und kehrt in Form von Symptomen wieder. Bei der Verneinung wird der Inhalt ins Bewusstsein gelassen, aber mit Ablehnung gekoppelt. Bei der Verleugnung wird er als positive Form zugelassen, aber […] nicht wirklich in das symbolische Universum des Subjekts integriert."[2]

Domanovićs *Turbo Sculptures* deuten eine Verleugnung an, da die Schrecken der Balkankriege „ins Bewusstsein gelassen" werden: „Niemand aus den Kriegen der Neunzigerjahre oder aus dem ehemaligen Jugoslawien verdient ein Denkmal, denn alles was unsere Anführer taten, war, uns vom Fortschritt abzuhalten", erklärt Bojan Marceta, der bei der Aufstellung einer Statue von Rocky/Sylvester Stallone in der serbischen Stadt Zitiste planend mitgeholfen hat. Doch die Gräuel werden verleugnet und isoliert, indem sie in den Fetisch einer Turbo Sculpture verwandelt werden, in ein Denkmal für eine Berühmtheit, in Fan-Kunst wie sie im Buche steht. Domanovićs Bezeichnung *Turbo Sculpture* ist dem postmodernen Kitsch geschuldet, der während und nach den Kriegen auf dem Balkan zu finden war. Für pompöse Architektur und nationalistische Politik gleichermaßen gültig, steht Turbo für das hemmungslose Übereinanderlagern von Emotion, Ornament und Ästhetik. Vielleicht wird dieser Effekt in den miteinander verknüpften Bildebenen in Domanovićs Video seinerseits imitiert. Eine über die andere gelegt, stellen sie durch ihre bloße Menge eine Behauptung in den Raum.

Trotz seiner Eleganz ähnelt Bošnjaks *Hotel Balkan* dagegen eher einem Horrorfilm – vor allem in den Kamerafahrten durch lange, enge Korridore und in der geradezu forensischen Einstellung einer Bildschärfe, die sich erbarmungslos einem Telefon oder Objekt nach dem anderen anpasst. Wenn es keine Erzählung gibt, spielt der Ton eine wichtige Rolle, doch hier bietet uns Bošnjak allein durch seine Bildsprache die Möglichkeit, unter historischen Vorzeichen über Technik nachzudenken und über das, was der ägyptische Künstler Basim Magdy „unsere futuristische Vergangenheit" nennt. Der Sound liefert die passende Atmosphäre hierzu – sein Rauschen, Brummen und Summen erinnert an die Rückkopplungen einer defekten Elektronik. Die Gerätschaften im Video sind alte Mischpulte und Mikrofone sowie sperrige Telefone aus Plastik. Eine Schaltzentrale mit Dutzenden von Öffnungen, die auf Stecker warten. Die Klänge und die Technik der Siebziger und Achtziger. Ab und zu wird der Soundtrack etwas moderner: Ist dies das Schnarren und Krächzen eines Modems? Das Piepsen von 8-Bit-Videospielen?

Diese Verbindung zwischen analoger Technik und der Geschichte des Balkans suggeriert, dass Titos Bunker als ein Symptom unserer Vergangenheit neu begriffen werden kann. Die „Zukunft" dieser kommunistischen Vergangenheit ist von daher mit Sicherheit das, was heute dem Vorgang der Verdrängung unterworfen ist – genauso wie die sperrigen Kommunikationsgeräte, die Computer und die Schaltwände auf den Müllhaufen der Geschichte entsorgt wurden. In beiden Fällen ist eine metahistorische Sensibilität am Werk, die sich der visuellen und narrativen Elemente von Geschichte auf eine reflektierte Art und Weise bewusst ist. So ähnlich ist es auch in Jon Rafmans Video *Mainsqueeze* von 2014, doch tritt hier durch Regungen des Ekels, der Angst und Paranoia, wenn nicht sogar des Zorns, ein affektives Element hinzu und verleiht der Arbeit eine psychoanalytische Komponente.

Autorinnen wie Sara Ahmed und Sianne Ngai haben dazu beigetragen, dass über Emotionen und Affekte aus einer queeren, feministischen und postkolonialen Perspektive nachgedacht wird, die den Ursprung dieser Ideen bei Lacan, Deleuze oder Kristeva hinter sich lässt. Hier lassen sich die Fragen nach einer historischen Einstellung zu digitalen

Netzwerken hinzufügen, die in Rafmans Schaffen sichtbar werden. Was hat es also mit der Geschichte dieser Technologien oder besser: der digitalen Datenspeicher, die sich in diesen Systemen befinden, auf sich? Es ist vielleicht einfacher, die eigene Browsing-Historie zu löschen, als ganz real Flüssigkeiten von der Tastatur zu entfernen. Und es ist genau dieser „Igitt-Faktor", auf den wir in *Mainsqueeze* stoßen. Statt der „hässlichen Gefühle" bei Ngai haben wir bei Rafman „Igitt-Gefühle".

In *Mainsqueeze* sehen wir eine unzusammenhängende Bildfolge, oftmals Szenen der Zerstörung: Eine Waschmaschine, die schleudert, bis sie sich von selbst zerlegt. Fotos von ohnmächtigen Trinkern, die Gesichter mit schwarzem Filzstift übermalt. Eine Wassermelone, die zwischen den Schenkeln eines Muskelmannes zerdrückt wird, ein Büroangestellter, der seinen Laptop zertrümmert, eine junge Frau, die einen Krebs zertritt – brutale Historienbilder im Stil von Artemisia Gentileschis „Judith enthauptet Holofernes". Jemand in einem Schildkrötenkostüm versucht, seinen Fesseln zu entkommen, während ein Hund bellt und ein Handy klingelt.

Die Trinker mit den geschwärzten Gesichtern bewegen sich auf dem schmalen Grat zwischen erniedrigenden College-Ritualen und der „sanften Folter" von Abu Graib. Sie erinnern daran, dass beide Praktiken immer öfter von den Tätern schonungslos dokumentiert werden: Niemand schämt sich seiner Taten genug, um sie nicht doch auf Facebook hochzuladen. Vielleicht ist dies eine andere Art der Erinnerung – eine anerkannte, eine noch nicht einmal verleugnete. Rafmans Arbeit suggeriert, dass wir womöglich eine fünfte Kategorie der Verdrängung im Sinne Freuds und Žižeks bräuchten: Hier ist alles abstoßend und angsteinflößend, doch obwohl nichts versteckt bleibt (das Internet und Rafman zeigen und fast alles), können wir doch nicht anders als paranoid werden angesichts dessen, was wir uns nicht ansehen, was unsichtbar bleibt in einer Gesellschaft totaler Transparenz und Hochladewut.

Mainsqueeze ist schwer anzuschauen, und es ist nicht verwunderlich, dass Rafmans Arbeit in den USA – einem Land, in dem Folter und Drohneneinsätze zwar geleugnet, aber heimlich weiterhin praktiziert werden – zensiert werden sollte: In der Rafman-Ausstellung im Contemporary Art Museum in St. Louis im Sommer 2014 war das Video jedenfalls nicht zu sehen. Aber so sollte es auch sein. In einer politischen Sphäre nach *Charlie Hebdo*, in der Kritik an der Kunst und Angst vor Bildern verunglimpft werden, ist ein bisschen altmodische Zensur als Ausdruck erfrischender Ehrlichkeit begrüßenswert. Denn bei Rafman ist wirklich keine rationale (oder realistische) Kritik möglich: Es hat keinen Sinn, die Herkunft eines bestimmten Bildes zu entschlüsseln, seine Entwicklung seit dem ursprünglichen Ereignis nachzuzeichnen oder Motive zu finden, zu denen es hinsichtlich ihrer digitalen Verbreitung und der durch sie ausgelösten (Pseudo-)Empörung Parallelen gibt. Diese Bilderfolge aus den sozialen Medien ist zu altbekannt, zu vorhersehbar und so trivial wie ein Spießbürger in früherer Zeit. Was ich meine, ist Folgendes: Egal wieviel man liest über die Ätiologie eines bestimmten Bildes oder einer bestimmten Szene aus *Mainsqueeze* – man ist immer noch angeekelt. Man konnte z.B. erfahren, dass das Schalentier, das die Frau zertritt, während eine Stimme aus dem Off von der Pflege einer kranken Angehörigen erzählt, in Wirklichkeit ein Roboter war oder dass es sich um ein computergeneriertes Bild handelte. Gleichviel – der Look entspricht dem eines Amateurvideos aus dem Internet, die Knack- und

Quetschlaute haben ihre Schuldigkeit getan, und wir können niemals rückwirkend unseren Ekel leugnen.

Der Titel diese Essays – Always Futurize! – bezieht sich auf Fredric Jamesons bekannten Aufruf „Always historicize!" in *Das politische Unbewusste*, d.h. auf seine Forderung, kulturelle Phänomene immer in ihrem historischen Kontext zu betrachten. Heute haben wir eventuell eine andere Aufgabe, darauf weisen die hiesigen Kunstwerke hin. Was für eine Zukunft liegt vor uns? Die apokalyptische Endzeit, die so viele Hollywoodfilme suggerieren? Der *Peak* Oil-Moment mit Windrädern und Hippies? Die wunderbaren, unkomplizierten Vernetzungsmöglichkeiten, die die Mobilfunkwerbung verspricht? Die beschleunigten Widersprüche, über die auf #Accelerationism philosophiert wird? Wir wissen es natürlich nicht, aber das Nachdenken über die Zukunft und das Erforschen ihrer Beziehung zu unserer Vergangenheit, unserer Geschichte, unseren Emotionen und unserem Gedächtnis könnte die wichtigste Aufgabe von heute sein.

Clint Burnham ist Associate Professor am Institut für Anglistik der Simon Fraser University in Vancouver. Er hat in Flash Art, Canadian Art und Artforum, auf Momus.ca und in Camera Austria publiziert, außerdem für Galerien und Museen in Europa und Amerika. Augenblicklich arbeitet er an Büchern über Slavoj Žižek und die digitale Kultur sowie über Fredric Jameson und den Film The Wolf of Wall Street.

[1] Suzana Milevska: "Ágalma: The 'Objet Petit a', Alexander the Great and Other Excesses of Skopje 2014', e-flux 57 (Sept. 2014).
[2] Slavoj Žižek, zit. nach der engl. Ausg.: Less Than Nothing. London: Verso 2012, S. 859.

Documentation/
Dokumentation

32

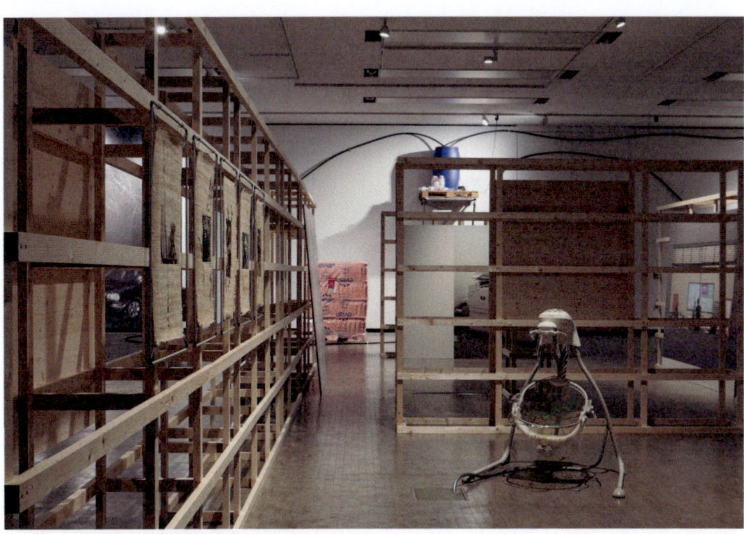

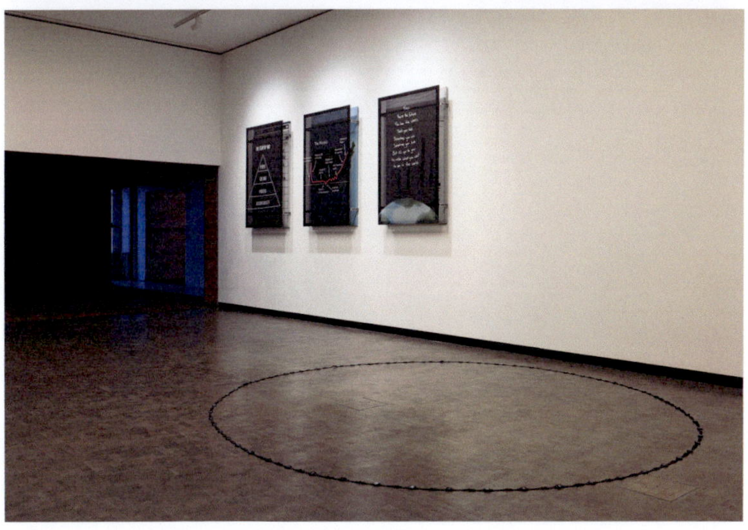

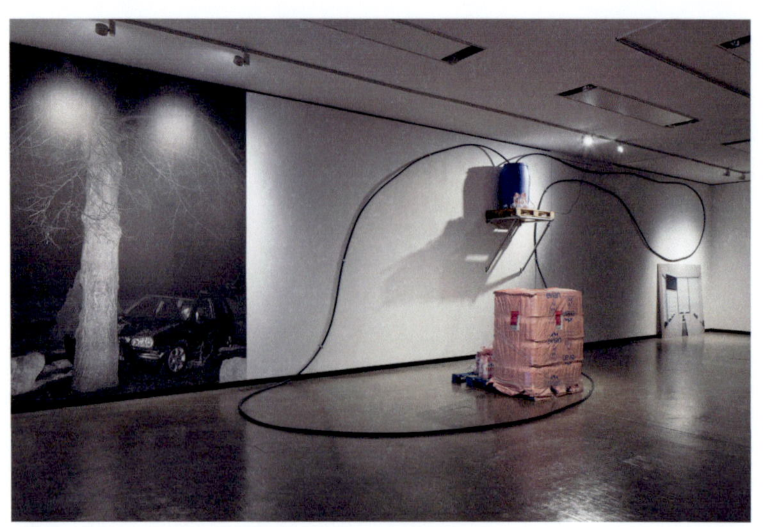

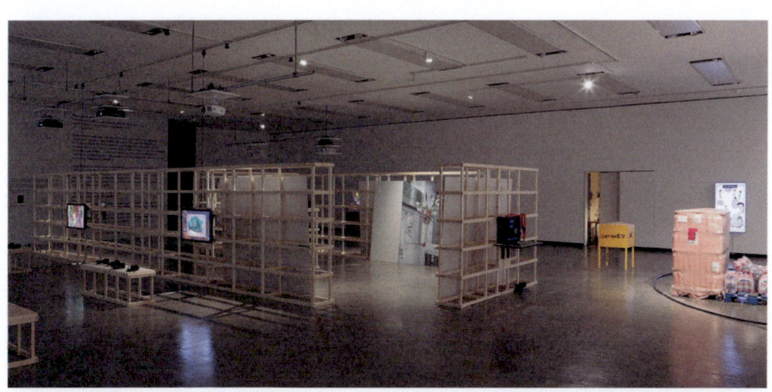

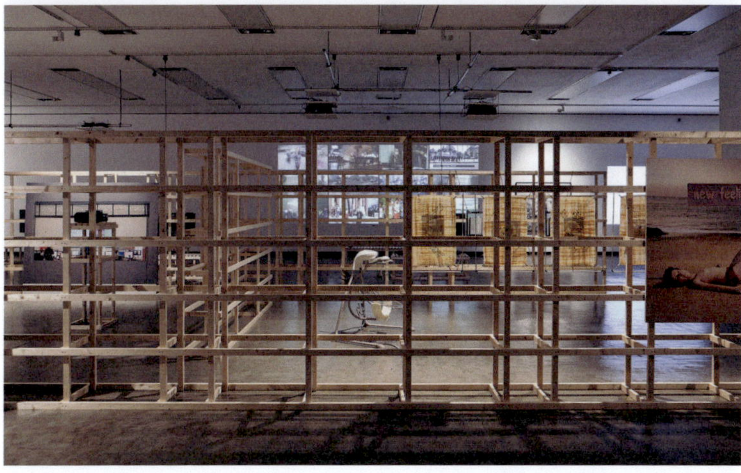

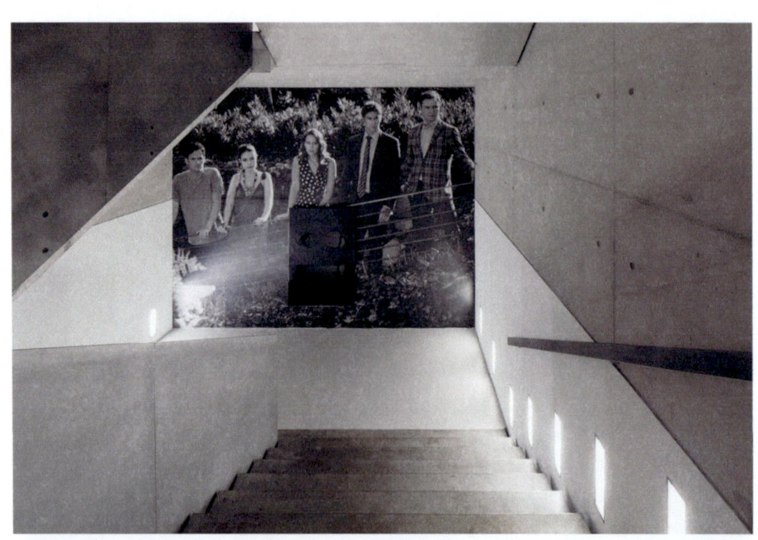

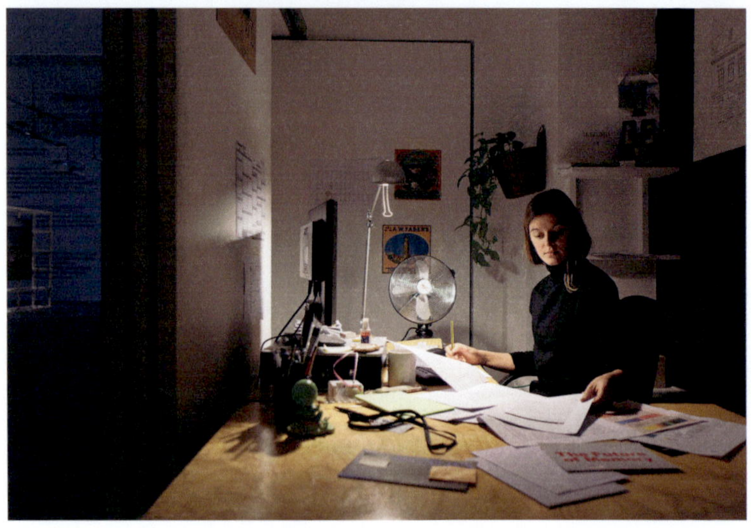

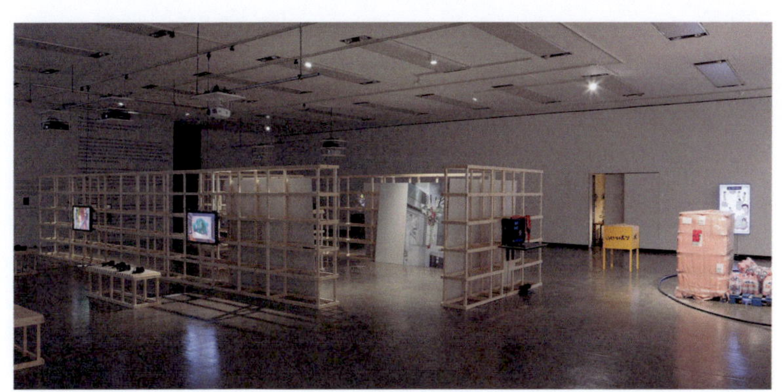

Algorithmic Cruelty and the Promise of Deceit
Michael Connor

Maybe it's a conversation best had while stoned, and in fact a conversation I have had in that state, most notably with my ex-roommate C, a devoted futurist. Among many other technological developments that terrified me, C eagerly anticipated external brain storage becoming a reality; she wanted to be able to learn, rewrite, and store memory freely and fluidly, unbounded by the one-to-one relationship between lived experience and memory. When will we be able to inscribe our memories directly into computational media, as in the movie *Johnny Mnemonic* (1995)? When will be able to have memories directly inscribed into our brains, as in *Total Recall* (1990)?

This was ten years ago; now we live in the age of the cloud, and I wonder if C's vision of the external brain has shifted at all. It's hard to think of digital media today as anything but semi-public. Everything written to disk in 2015 seems destined to become part of a shared archive someday, if only in a forgotten corner of the NSA's enormous vaults or an accidentally uploaded folder on a cloud server. Does the ability to write our memories directly to disk erode the boundary between social memory — how and what we collectively remember — and individual memory?

And to what extent is this line already beginning to shift?

In the last days of 2014, Facebook invited me to create a "Year in Review" for 2014. A post appeared at the top of my timeline; "Here's what your year looked like!" it announced, displaying against a background of clip art paintbrush strokes a photo from 2004 of a late night curry in Liverpool. "See Your Year," it suggested. When I clicked, a bot automatically collated my most popular content of the year into a decidedly underwhelming composition: seven images, two of them duplicates of the same curry house image, accompanied by one work-related fundraising plea. I was invited to share this content with other users, along with the suggested caption, "It's been a great year! Thanks for being a part of it!" I changed the caption, but not with any particular wit.

A week later, I posted a link to a widely circulated news article with the headline, "Facebook apologizes for 'algorithmic cruelty' in its Year in Review."[1] It told the story of Eric Meyer, for whom the prompt to create a "Year In Review" was automatically populated with an image of his recently deceased daughter. Still early in his grieving process, he was repeatedly, horribly confronted with an image that seemed to maliciously celebrate her passing.

**

As the data accumulation of the typical computer user increases apace, it no longer becomes realistic to expect them to manually create a representation of their data. We assiduously make an effort to drag and drop our files into folders, and then nest those within subfolders. But I mean, come on, are we going to keep that up forever? At some point it becomes too much. Already, there are tools that organize our content automatically (photo albums arranged by date, for example). The Facebook Year in Review bot is kind of a worst case scenario of what this might look like — a bot-generated interface to our data that seems to impose an emotional mandate on our lived experience.

**

In 1982, the anthropologist Eric Michaels moved from Texas to Australia to take up the task of assessing the "impact" of satellite television's introduction on remote Indigenous Australian communities. He focused his research on Yuendumu, a small town which, if you get bored, is a mere 350 km from the nearest settlement of even a modest size, Alice Springs (population 20,000)[2]; there, he wrote a series of ethnographic studies beginning with a text called "The Aboriginal Invention of Television in Central Australia."[3] The title seemed to destabilize the underlying assumptions behind his assignment: television, it suggested, could be re-invented through the practices of its users, and not merely be an invader from without.[4]

Cinema had never really taken off in Yuendumu, in part because of the small size of the community and perhaps also because its kinship structures prohibited certain members of the community from being in the same room at the same time, making auditorium gatherings difficult. Television and the VCR, suitable for more intimate viewing environments, did not present the same problems. At that time, maintaining a VCR in the bush required no small investment, and community members found that they could share a single machine among a number of scattered households by setting up pirate TV antennas, broadcasting a tape to the surrounding areas according to a pre-announced schedule.

For Michaels, part of the reinvention of television by the Warlpiri in Yuendumu lay in the re-interpretation of imported films according to local custom. He wrote, for example:

"Narrative [in Warlpiri stories] will provide detailed kinship relationships between all characters, as well as establishing a kinship domain for each. When Hollywood videos fail to say where Rocky's grandmother is, or who's taking care of his sister-in-law, Warlpiri viewers discuss the matter and fill in the missing content."[5]

It was not only a matter of re-reading existing works, though. As part of this ad hoc broadcast network, the people of Yuendumu began to make and broadcast their own programs, both live and pre-recorded. In particular, Michaels focuses on:

"Warlpiri videotape is at first disappointing to the European observer. It seems unbearably slow, involving long landscape pans and still takes that seem empty… Yet Warlpiri audiences view these tapes with great attention and emotion, often repeatedly … The camera in fact traces tracks and locations where ancestors, spirits or historical characters travelled. The apparently empty shot is full of life and history to the Aboriginal [viewer]."[6]

In both of these scenarios, the video itself is incomplete; information about the characters or landscapes depicted therein is supplied by the viewers and becomes part of a collectively held memory, stored in fragments across the videotape and the social network. For the Warlpiri people, Michaels argued that culture was:

"itself information, and [that] kinship structures are communication systems which bring certain people together, but exclude others protecting communications pathways and the value of the information they carry."[7]

Here, Michaels tells a story of a culture that involves humans and media objects participating together in a process of elaborating social memory that is structured by communications networks.

Under the ascendant regime of Big Data and mostly in places far from Yuendumu, the roles fulfilled by humans and media objects have shifted. The communication systems that "bring certain people together, but exclude others" are being hard-coded into privacy settings, and the media object is now often treated as canonical social memory. These are tendencies we can further extrapolate into a future in which our memory sits on an external drive.

**

Despite my initial antipathy to the Year in Review, I found myself clicking on and liking other users' entries in that format, even when fellow users failed to change the default status update. The content of any Year in Review was less interesting than the question of how different users' Facebook practices were reflected in varying ways by the algorithm. The Year in Review bot created a representation of 2014 that amplified certain kinds of behaviors while omitting others.

Even if the bot often seemed to misunderstand us, Facebook's Year in Review can be thought of as a form of training. It's like the equivalent of a blog editor rounding up their reporters at the end of the year to celebrate the stories that generated the most traffic, in hopes of generating more such stories in the year to come. Facebook wants us to maximize our social lift. In 2015, we will remember the lessons of our 2014 Years in Review each time we post. We will remember that we are adding to our end-of-year archive with each new post. When I recognize that my feed is too sparse, and Eric Meyer recognizes that his feed is too sad, this isn't accidental; this is the Year in Review's intended purpose.

These are the kind of "demands" that Rob Horning had in mind when he recently asked, in a conversation with Amalia Ulman:

"Is there a presumption of Facebook innocence — a benefit of the doubt given to any particular user that they are using Facebook in good faith and aren't trying to somehow trick audiences, or sell them something? Or does the fact that Facebook demands that one perform oneself so explicitly make such presumption of innocence impossible? What could guileless Facebook use look like, given that it's understood that the "normal" way to use it is to promote oneself…?"[8]

41

But innocence is overrated. We have never been innocent. We do not want to be innocent. We do not want innocent, guileless art. Horning agrees; later in the same interview, he writes:

"Perhaps this will orient people toward seeing the "real" or the "true" in the effort one puts toward faking something, and that "something" will not even need to be assessed in terms of its genuine-ness. But instead we seem to be moving toward more elaborate efforts to hide effort (the "#nofilter," "I woke up like this" wave), to represent the fake as true instead of as a true fake."[9]

On the one hand, the obvious effort required to craft a Facebook profile might be a way for us to understand the provisional nature of identity, the porousness of selfhood. On the other, Facebook might be merely fostering ever more sophisticated forms of deceit.

It seems to me that creating deceitful data on Facebook may actually be quite productive, though, in maintaining a healthy interplay between humans and digital objects in the creation of social memory. The images and utterances we make in the context of Facebook are elaborated through complex social interactions that may continue across other platforms. A single "like" may acquire levels of meaning that a bot would be hard-pressed to parse, from sarcasm to mourning — and the codes only get more complex from there.

**

One of the most perceptive criticisms I read of Michaels' work in Yuendumu focused on his excessive attempts to frame his story of Warlpiri television as a narrative of community self-determination — "the Aboriginal invention of television." As evidence, Melinda Hinkson cited the very first television broadcasts that were made at Yuendumu in August 1985. Her description:

"In viewing these tapes, one observes a group of Warlpiri men in what was then the broadcasting room, with a non-Warlpiri voice audible in the background, recognisably that of Adult Educator, Peter Toyne, who was also integrally involved in the inception of WMA [Warlpiri Media Association], discussing technical problems with the planned transmission. Conversation between the young men is in Warlpiri, with much joking and playing around. When Toyne advises the men that the transmission link has been established and they are 'on air', two Warlpiri men seated side-by-side in front of the camera compose themselves and start talking to each other in English. Their discussion takes a question-answer format, one asks the other, 'What's your name?', 'Where do you live?', 'What do you work?'"

The anecdote suggests that the young men were perhaps more savvy users of media than Michaels gave them credit for —already altering their performances in preparation for its inscription in media objects, and seemingly more aware of the cultural politics surrounding these videos than Michaels' account suggests.

What I especially like about this analysis is that the media object itself offers the evidence of this "deceit," and becomes part of the elaboration of its meaning after the fact. It gives me a sense of optimism about the potential for media objects to illustrate their own lack of authenticity, undercutting canonical interpretations and continuing to confound the bots.

**

Eric Michaels passed away in 1988, and kept a diary in the last year of his life, Unbecoming. In its opening pages, he pondered the decision to tell friends of his status, or to inscribe the information only in his diary.

I rather like the choice to tell my computer, to engage in the curious restrictive circuit which makes electronic inscription seem such a narcissistic jerk-off. I don't much want to publicize my disease any further — but, of course, I will have to.

For whom do I write? And worse yet, from what position? I could hedge and claim that I write for myself, in the hope that I can preserve for myself some clarity in a process which is likely to become very clouded very soon. And for myself, in the sense of a nearly biological drive to self-inscription which we recognize (but do not always forgive) at such moments.

It's time to forgive. The process of self-inscription always involves these moments of self-doubt, and the realization that one is writing for an audience, and the modulation of one's appearance in negotiation with this imagined interlocutor. This process of negotiation doesn't make us less "authentic," it is part of what makes us anything at all.

Michael Connor is Artistic Director of the art and technology organization Rhizome, which has been on-line since 1996 and in residence at the New Museum since 2003. He is an adjunct faculty member at NYU and Parsons the New School for Design.

[1] "Facebook apologizes for 'algorithmic cruelty' in its Year In Review," RT, December 27, 2014, www.rt.com/news/218071-facebook-apologize-year-review.

[2] "A brief history of Alice Springs," www.toddys.com.au/toddys-about-alice-springs

[3] Eric Michaels, "The Aboriginal Invention of Television in Central Australia," (Canberra: Australian Institute of Aboriginal Studies, 1986); Michaels' work in Yuendumu was the basis for several other notable papers, most of which were collected in the book Bad Aboriginal Art (University of Minnesota Press, 1993).

[4] See in particular R. Hodge, "Aboriginal truth and white media: Eric Michaels meets the spirit of Aboriginalism." Continuum 3(2) (1990): 201–25.

[5] Ibid, 119.

[6] Ibid, 1998: 120-1.

[7] Ibid, 153.

[8] Rob Horning and Amalia Ulman, "Perpetual Provisional Selves," Rhizome, Accessed 14 January 2015., http://rhizome.org/editorial/2014/dec/11/rob-horning-and-amalia-ulman/

[9] Ibid.

Algorithmische Grausamkeit und das Versprechen der Täuschung
<u>Michael Connor</u>

Vielleicht war es eine Unterhaltung, die man am besten auf Drogen führte, und tatsächlich habe ich sie in diesem Zustand geführt – interessanterweise mit meiner ehemaligen Mitbewohnerin C, einer eifrigen Futuristin. Neben vielen anderen technischen Entwicklungen, die mir Angst machten, ersehnte C die Möglichkeit der externen Speicherung von Wissen. Sie wollte sich frei und unabhängig Daten merken, sie neu formulieren und sie speichern können, ungehindert von der Eins-zu-Eins-Beziehung zwischen gelebter Erfahrung und Gedächtnis.
Wann werden wir in der Lage sein, unsere Erinnerungen direkt in den Computer einzugeben wie in dem Film *Vernetzt – Johnny Mnemonic* (1995)? Wann wird es uns möglich sein, uns Erinnerungen direkt in unsere Gehirne einpflanzen zu lassen wie in *Total Recall* (1990)?

Das war vor zehn Jahren. Heute leben wir im Zeitalter der Cloud, und ich frage mich, ob die Vision meiner Mitbewohnerin vom externen Gehirn sich überhaupt verändert hat. Es ist schwer, sich digitale Medien heutzutage anders als halböffentlich vorzustellen. Alles, was 2015 auf eine Festplatte geschrieben wird, scheint dafür bestimmt zu sein, eines Tages Teil eines großen gemeinschaftlichen Archivs zu werden – und sei es nur in einem vergessenen Winkel in den riesigen Kellern der NSA oder in einem versehentlich hochgeladenen Verzeichnis auf einem Cloud Server. Verwischt die Möglichkeit, unsere Erinnerungen direkt auf eine Festplatte zu schreiben, die Grenze zwischen sozialem Gedächtnis – also wie und woran wir uns gemeinsam erinnern – und individuellem Gedächtnis?
Und in welchem Maße beginnt sich diese Grenze jetzt schon zu verschieben?

**

Ende 2014 lud mich Facebook ein, einen persönlichen "Jahresrückblick" zu erstellen. Ganz oben in meiner Chronik erschien ein Posting: "So sah Ihr Jahr aus!", verkündete es. Zu sehen war ein Schnappschuss von einem abendlichen Curry-Essen in Liverpool nach einer Filmvorführung. Den Hintergrund bildeten Pinselstriche im Stil der Clip Art. "Erleben Sie Ihr Jahr!", empfahl mir das Posting. Als ich es anklickte, stellte ein Web-Agent meinen beliebtesten Content des Jahres automatisch zu einer ausgesprochen enttäuschenden Komposition zusammen: sieben Bilder, zwei davon Duplikate des Bildes aus dem indischen Restaurant, dazu ein beruflicher Fundraising-Aufruf. Ich wurde eingeladen, diesen Content mit anderen Usern zu teilen – zusammen mit der vorgeschlagenen Bildunterschrift „Es war ein tolles Jahr! Danke dass du ein Teil davon warst!" Ich änderte den Text, allerdings nicht besonders geistreich.

Eine Woche später postete ich den Link zu einem weit verbreiteten Artikel mit der Überschrift „Facebook entschuldigt sich für ‚algorithmische Grausamkeit' in seinem Jahresrückblick".[1] In dem Bericht war von Eric Meyer die Rede, dessen Computerbefehl, einen „Jahresrückblick" zu erstellen, automatisch ein Bild seiner kürzlich verstorbenen Tochter generierte. In einem frühen Stadium seines Trauerprozesses wurde er auf grausame Weise immer wieder mit einem Bild konfrontiert, das ihren Tod bösartig zu feiern schien.

**

Da die Datenmenge eines typischen Avid-Computers sich schnell vergrößert, ist es nicht länger realistisch zu erwarten, dass ein User manuell eine Darstellung seiner Daten kreieren kann. Zwar sind wir emsig dabei, unsere Dateien via *drag and drop* in Ordnern abzulegen und diese dann in Unterordner zu gliedern. Aber wollen wir damit ewig weitermachen? Irgendwann wird es überwaltigend. Schon jetzt gibt es Tools, die unseren Content automatisch verwalten, die z.B. Fotoalben nach Datum ordnen. Die Jahresrückblick-Funktion auf Facebook ist so etwas wie das *worst case scenario* – eine maschinell gesteuerte Verknüpfung mit Daten, die die emotionale Vollmacht über unsere gelebte Erfahrung beansprucht.

**

1982 zog der Anthropologe Eric Michaels von Texas nach Australien, um die „Auswirkungen" zu studieren, die die Einführung des Satellitenfernsehens auf zurückgezogen lebende indigene Gemeinschaften hatte. Er konzentrierte seine Forschungen auf die Kleinstadt Yuendumu, die – falls man sich langweilt – nur 350 Kilometer von Alice Springs mit seinen 20000 Einwohnern entfernt liegt.[2] Hier schrieb er eine Reihe ethnografischer Aufsätze, von denen der erste den Titel „Die Erfindung des Fernsehens durch die Aborigines in Zentralaustralien" trägt.[3] Dieser Titel scheint die grundlegenden Thesen seines Vorhabens zu destabilisieren: Das Fernsehen, so suggeriert er, könnte durch die Gewohnheiten der Nutzer neu erfunden werden und nicht nur wie ein Eindringling von außen agieren.[4]

Das Kino hatte sich nie wirklich durchgesetzt in Yuendumu, zum Teil aufgrund der geringen Größe der Gemeinde, vielleicht aber auch weil die Verwandtschaftsverhältnisse es einigen Bürgern verboten, zur selben Zeit im selben Raum zu sein. Das machte größere Zusammenkünfte schwierig. Fernsehen und Videorekorder passten besser zu Filmabenden im kleinen Kreis und brachten weniger Probleme mit sich. Zu der Zeit war ein Videorekorder im Busch eine größere Investition, und die Gemeindemitglieder waren der Ansicht, dass mehrere Haushalte sich einen Rekorder teilen könnten. Also montierten sie illegale Fernsehantennen und sendeten Videofilme nach einem zuvor verkündeten Zeitplan.

Doch für Michaels lag die Neuerfindung des Fernsehens durch die Warlpiri in Yuendumu auch in einer Neuinterpretation importierter Filme entsprechend den lokalen Gebräuchen. Er schreibt:

„Eine Erzählung [bei den Warlpiri] enthält detaillierte Informationen zu den Verwandtschaftsbeziehungen aller Figuren und legt für jede Figur eine Aufgabe im Kreis der Verwandten fest. Wenn Hollywoodfilme nichts darüber sagen, wo Rockys Großmutter ist oder wer sich um seine Schwägerin kümmert, dann diskutieren die Warlpiri darüber und fügen den fehlenden Inhalt hinzu."[5]

Aber es blieb nicht nur bei einer neuen Sicht auf bereits existierende Filme. Im Rahmen ihres improvisierten Fernsehsenders begannen die Einwohner von Yuendumu damit, eigene Programme zu entwickeln und auszustrahlen – sowohl live als auch als Aufzeichnung. Hierzu hebt Michaels hervor:

„Die Videoaufnahmen der Warlpiri sind zunächst einmal enttäuschend für den europäischen Betrachter. Sie erscheinen unerträglich langsam mit ihren langen Schwenks über die Landschaft und mit ihren Still Takes, die wie inhaltslos wirken [...] Doch die Warlpiri schauen sich diese Aufnahmen aufmerksam und mit großer emotionaler Beteiligung an, oft mehrmals hintereinander. [...] Denn tatsächlich folgt die Kamera den Spuren und Aufenthaltsorten von Vorfahren, Geistern und historischen Gestalten. Die anscheinend inhaltslosen Aufnahmen sind für die Aborigines voller Leben und Geschichte."[6]

In beiden geschilderten Fällen ist der Film an sich unvollständig – die zusätzlichen Informationen zu den dargestellten Figuren oder Landschaften liefern die Zuschauer: Sie lassen sie dadurch zu einem Teil ihres kollektiven Gedächtnisses werden. Eine bestimmte Erinnerung wird in den miteinander in Zusammenhang stehenden Gedächtnissen des sozialen Netzwerks abgespeichert. Für die Warlpiri, so argumentiert Michaels, bedeutet Kultur Information, und verwandtschaftliche Strukturen sind Kommunikationssysteme, die manche Menschen zusammenbringen, andere aber ausschließen. Dadurch schützen sie die Kommunikationswege und den Wert der Informationen, die sie verbreiten.[7]

Wenn er über die Warlpiri schreibt, erzählt Michaels die Geschichte einer Kultur, in der Menschen und Medien gemeinsam ein soziales Gedächtnis erschaffen, das auf Kommunikationsgeflechten beruht.

Unter der Vorherrschaft von Big Data und hauptsächlich an Orten weit weg von Yuendumu haben sich die Rollen von Menschen und Medien verändert. Die Kommunikationssysteme, die „manche Menschen zusammenbringen, andere aber ausschließen", werden zum festen Bestandteil der privaten Umgebung, und die Medien werden als das anerkannte soziale Gedächtnis betrachtet. Dies ist der Trend, von dem wir auf eine Zukunft schließen können, in der unser Gedächtnis seinen Platz auf einem externen Laufwerk finden wird.

**

Trotz meiner ursprünglichen Abneigung gegen den Jahresrückblick auf Facebook ertappte ich mich dabei, wie ich die Inhalte anderer User in dieser Rubrik aufrief und bewertete, auch wenn einige User es nicht schafften, ihre Standardeinstellungen zu aktualisieren. Die Inhalte der Jahresrückblicke waren weniger interessant als die Frage, wie sich die Facebook-Gewohnheiten diverser User auf verschiedenste Art und Weise im Algorithmus widerspiegelten. Der Jahresrückblick-Roboter schien eine doppelte Funktion zu haben – nämlich nicht nur eine Darstellung von 2014 zu erstellen, sondern auch unser Verhalten im kommenden Jahr zu strukturieren.

Man kann den Jahresrückblick auf Facebook als eine Art Trainingsmaßnahme begreifen. Es ist wie bei einem Blog, wenn der Herausgeber am Ende des Jahres seine Reporter um sich versammelt, um die Storys zu feiern, die in dem Jahr den meisten Traffic generiert haben – in der Hoffnung, dass auf diese Weise noch mehr solcher Storys entstehen. Facebook möchte, dass wir unsere soziale Performance optimieren. 2015 werden wir uns bei jedem Posting an den Jahresrückblick von 2014 erinnern. Uns wird klar sein, dass wir mit jedem Posting zu unserem Jahresarchiv beitragen. Wenn ich erkenne, dass meine Beiträge zu spärlich sind, und Eric Meyer erkennt, dass seine zu traurig sind, dann ist das kein Zufall, sondern die beabsichtigte Wirkung des Jahresrückblicks.

Diese und ähnliche "Interessen" hatte Rob Horning im Sinn, als er kürzlich im Gespräch mit Amalia Ulman die Frage stellte:

„Kann man sich einen unschuldigen Umgang mit Facebook vorzustellen? Einen Vertrauensvorschuss für alle User, der die Vermutung beinhaltet, dass sie Facebook in guter Absicht nutzen und nicht versuchen, andere zu betrügen oder ihnen etwas zu verkaufen? Oder macht die Tatsache, dass Facebook einen so explizit zur Selbstdarstellung auffordert, eine solche Vorstellung von Unschuld unmöglich? Wie könnte eine unschuldige Facebook-Nutzung aussehen, wenn man voraussetzt, dass eine ‚normale' Nutzung darin besteht, sich selbst zu vermarkten?"[8]

Doch die Unschuld wird überschätzt. Wir waren niemals unschuldig. Wir wollen nicht unschuldig sein. Wir wollen keine unschuldige, harmlose Kunst. Horning stimmt dem zu. Später schreibt er in demselben Interview:

„Vielleicht wird dies die Menschen dazu bringen, die ‚Realität' oder die ‚Wahrheit' in dem Bemühen zu sehen, etwas vorzutäuschen. Und noch nicht einmal dieses ‚Etwas' muss auf seine Echtheit überprüft werden. Stattdessen neigen wir scheinbar immer mehr zu aufwendigen Versuchen, unser Bemühen zu verschleiern (vgl. die ‚So-bin-ich-aufgewacht'-Welle auf #nofilter) und die Täuschung als Wahrheit und nicht als eine wahre Täuschung darzustellen."[9]

Einerseits könnte die offensichtliche Mühe, die es kostet, um ein Facebook-Profil zu gestalten, für uns ein Weg sein, das Provisorische im Wesen der Identität und die Durchlässigkeit des eigenen Selbst zu begreifen. Andererseits ist es möglich, dass Facebook lediglich immer raffinierte Arten der Täuschung begünstigt.

Ich glaube allerdings, dass falsche Angaben auf Facebook auch ganz ergiebig sein können: Im Zuge der Gestaltung eines sozialen Gedächtnisses wird auf so nämlich ein gesunder Diskurs zwischen den

Menschen und der digitalen Welt aufrechterhalten. Unsere Bilder und Äußerungen auf Facebook verfeinern sich durch komplexe soziale Interaktionen, die sich auch auf anderen Plattformen fortsetzen. Ein einziges „Like" kann Bedeutungen annehmen, die ein Bot kaum erfassen könnte – von Sarkasmus bis hin zu Trauer, und darüber hinaus werden die Codes noch komplexer.

**

Eine der scharfsinnigsten Rezensionen, die ich zu Michaels' Arbeit in Yuendumu gelesen habe, beschäftigt sich mit seinem Versuch, den Bericht über das Fernsehen der Warlpiri als eine Erzählung über kommunale Selbstbestimmung zu formulieren – als „die Erfindung des Fernsehens durch die Aborigines". Als Beweis führt Melinda Hinkson die allerersten Sendungen an, die im August 1985 in Yuendumu entstanden sind. Ihre Beschreibung:

„Wenn man sich diese Bänder ansieht, erkennt man eine Gruppe Warlpiri-Männer im damaligen Senderaum. Im Hintergrund ist die Stimme eines Nicht-Warlpiri zu hören. Es ist erkennbar die Stimme von Peter Toyne, einem Lehrer für Erwachsenenbildung, der auch wesentlich an der Gründung der WMA [Warlpiri Media Association] beteiligt war. Er spricht über Probleme bei der geplanten Übertragung. Die Unterhaltung zwischen den jungen Männern findet auf Warlpiri statt, begleitet von vielen Scherzen und Spielereien. Als Toyne die Männer darüber informiert, dass die Übertragung jetzt funktioniert und sie on air sind, nehmen sich zwei der Warlpiri-Männer, die nebeneinander vor der Kamera sitzen, zusammen und beginnen, sich auf Englisch zu unterhalten. Ihr Gespräch ist ein Frage-Antwort-Spiel. Einer fragt den anderen 'Wie heißt du?', 'Wo wohnst du?', 'Was arbeitest du?'"

Diese Anekdote suggeriert, dass die jungen Männer als Mediennutzer womöglich cleverer waren, als Michaels ihnen zugestanden hatte. Sie änderten ihr Verhalten bereits vor dessen medialer Fixierung und waren sich der kulturellen Bedingungen, unter denen diese Videos entstanden, in stärkerem Maße bewusst als Michaels' Bericht glauben macht. Besonders gefällt mir an dieser Analyse, dass das Medium selbst das Beweismaterial für den "Betrug" liefert und an der nachträglichen Ausschmückung seiner Bedeutung Anteil hat. Sie macht mich optimistisch hinsichtlich der Möglichkeit der Medien, ihren eigenen Mangel an Authentizität zu veranschaulichen, dabei anerkannte Interpretationen zu unterlaufen und Bots zu verwirren.

**

Eric Michaels starb 1988. In seinem letzten Lebensjahr führte er unter dem Titel Ungebührlich ein Tagebuch. Auf den ersten Seiten denkt er darüber nach, ob er Freunden von seinem Zustand erzählen soll oder ob er die Angaben nur in sein Tagebuch schreiben soll:

„Ich ziehe es vor, meinem Computer alles zu erzählen, mich in diesen merkwürdigen und beschränkten Kreislauf zu begeben, der elektronische Bekenntnisse wie ein einziges narzisstisches Gewichse aussehen lässt. Ich möchte meine Krankheit eigentlich nicht noch öffentlicher machen – aber ich werde es natürlich tun müssen. […] Für wen schreibe ich? Und schlimmer noch: von welchem Standpunkt aus? Ich könnte ausweichen

49

und behaupten, dass ich für mich selbst schreibe – in der Hoffnung, dass ich mir ein wenig Klarheit bewahren kann innerhalb eines Vorgangs, der wahrscheinlich alles sehr bald sehr stark verdüstern wird. Und auch für mich selbst im Sinne eines beinah biologischen Triebs zur Selbstdarstellung, den wir in solchen Momenten erkennen – aber den wir uns nicht immer vergeben."

Es ist Zeit zu vergeben. Der Vorgang der Selbstbeschreibung beinhaltet immer auch diese Momente des Selbstzweifels, daneben die Erkenntnis, dass man für ein Publikum schreibt, und die Anpassung des eigenen Auftretens an die Auseinandersetzung mit dem imaginären Gesprächspartner. Dieser Prozess der Auseinandersetzung macht uns nicht weniger „authentisch". Er ist ein Teil dessen, was uns überhaupt zu etwas macht.

Michael Connor ist Artistic Director der Kunst- und Technologie-Organisation Rhizome, die seit 1996 online und seit 2003 am New Museum ansässig ist. Er ist Lehrbeauftragter der New York University und der Parsons The New School of Design.

1 "Facebook apologizes for 'algorithmic cruelty'in its Year In Review", RT, December 27, 2014, www.rt.com/news/218071-facebook-apologize-year-review/
2 "A brief history of Alice Springs", www.toddys.com.au/toddys-about-alice-springs
3 Eric Michaels, "The Aboriginal Invention of Television in Central Australia," (Canberra: Australian Institute of Aboriginal Studies, 1986); Michaels Arbeit in Yuendumu war die Grundlage für mehrere andere bemerkenswerte Papiere, von denen die meisten in dem Buch gesammelt Bad Aboriginal Art (University of Minnesota Press, 1993)
4 Vgl. vor allem Hodge, R.: „Aboriginal truth and white media: Eric Michaels meets the spirit of Aboriginalism", Continuum 3, 2 (1990), 201–225.
5 Ebd,119
6 Ebd, 1998; 120-1
7 Ebd, 153.
8 Rob Horning and Amalia Ulman, "Perpetual Provisional Selves," Rhizome, http://rhizome.org/editorial/2014/dec/11/rob-horning-and-amalia-ulman
9 Ebd

Artists / Künstler

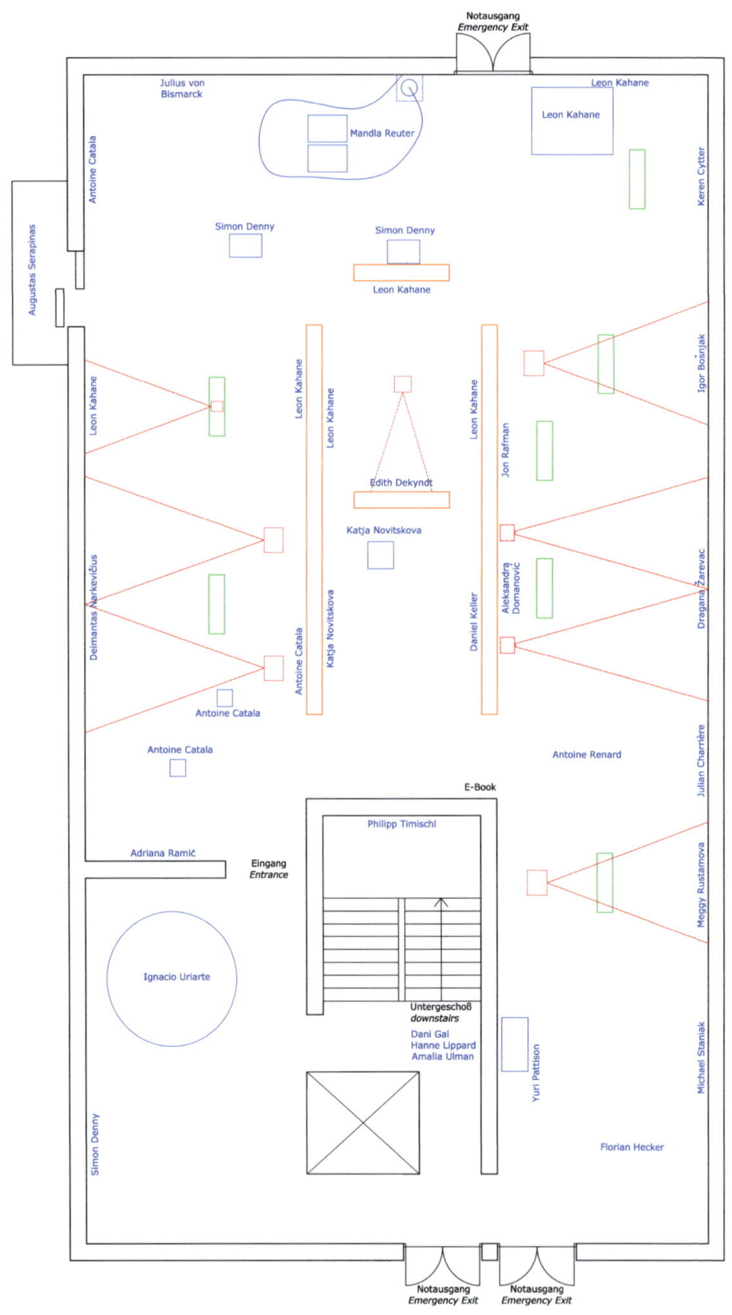

Julius von Bismarck
Igor Bošnjak
Antoine Catala
Julian Charrière
Keren Cytter
Edith Dekyndt
Simon Denny
Aleksandra Domanović
Dani Gal
Florian Hecker
Leon Kahane
Daniel Keller
Hanne Lippard
Deimantas Narkevičius
Katja Novitskova
Yuri Pattison
Jon Rafman
Adriana Ramić
Antoine Renard
Mandla Reuter
Meggy Rustamova
Augustas Serapinas
Michael Staniak
Philipp Timischl
Amalia Ulman
Ignacio Uriarte
Dragana Žarevac

Julius von Bismarck

Unfall am Mittelpunkt Deutschlands

Following the reunification of Germany on 26 February 1991, a *Kaiserlinde* or "commemorative lime tree" was planted in the village of Niederdorla in Thuringia, the geographical centre of Germany. On the morning of 15 April 2013, passers-by informed the police that a black VW Golf had crashed into this tree. The police recorded the incident, began to investigate and a few weeks later received a letter that claimed responsibility for it, revealing that the artist Julius von Bismarck had staged the incident. This accident occurring at the centre of Germany was not actually an accident at all, but instead exists in police and press reports as documentation of an ultimately fictive story.
The photographic record of the supposed accident resembles evidence photography for police files, insurance documents or media reports. In visual terms, the photographs of *Unfall am Mittelpunkt Deutschlands* are reminiscent of those found in newspaper reports. As an information medium, the newspaper photo stands for factuality and gains validity on this basis. These photographic motifs form part of the collective visual memory: the photo document that refers to something that happened — although in this case the associations evoked cannot be attributed to any real event that the photos allegedly verify. *Unfall am Mittelpunkt Deutschlands* does not involve a manipulated photo but instead an accident that was itself only simulated, thus raising questions about the authenticity of the event itself. What really happened?
Unfall am Mittelpunkt Deutschlands carries a strong historical charge. In Germany, majestic lime trees and oak trees are planted for the commemoration of political events and historically significant persons, symbolizing a trans-generational cultural memory. When it was reunified after the end of the Cold War, this turning point in German history was commemorated with tree plantings in the village of Niederdorla. At the same time, the hedonistic youth of the 1980s was dubbed the "Generation Golf" — in reference to the car's popularity with this demographic. Julius von Bismarck lets these symbols quite literally collide in a scenario that is clearly staged. And so *Unfall am Mittelpunkt Deutschlands* expresses above all scepticism about identity-conferring metaphors in themselves.
(ME)

*1983 in Breisach am Rhein. Lives / lebt in Berlin.
www.juliusvonbismarck.com

Nach der Wiedervereinigung Deutschlands am 26. Februar 1991 wurde eine Kaiserlinde in Niederdorla in Thüringen, dem geografischen Mittelpunkt Deutschlands, gepflanzt. Am Morgen des 15. April 2013 benachrichtigten Passanten die Polizei, weil ein schwarzer VW Golf in diesen Baum gerast war. Die Beamten nahmen den Sachverhalt auf, begannen mit den Ermittlungen und wurden einige Wochen später in einem Bekennerschreiben darüber informiert, dass der Künstler Julius von Bismarck das Ereignis inszeniert hatte. Der *Unfall am Mittelpunkt Deutschlands* war in Wirklichkeit gar kein Unfall, sondern existiert in Polizei- und Presseberichten als Dokumentation einer letztlich fiktiven Geschichte.
Die fotografische Aufnahme der vermeintlichen Unfallsituation erinnert an Beweisfotografien für Polizeiakten, Versicherungsdokumente oder Medienberichte. Motive wie dieses sind Teil eines kollektiven Bildgedächtnisses. Sie evozieren Assoziationen, obschon sie in diesem Fall auf kein Ereignis zurückzuführen sind, das diese rechtfertigen würde. Visuell handelt es sich bei der Fotografie von *Unfall am Mittelpunkt Deutschlands* um ein Bild, das an Zeitungsfotos erinnert. Es entspricht einem bestimmten Standard und wird deshalb nicht weiter hinterfragt. Als Informationsmedium steht es für Faktizität und entwickelt daraus seine Beweiskraft. Da es sich bei *Unfall am Mittelpunkt Deutschlands* jedoch nicht um eine manipulierte Fotografie handelt, sondern der Unfall selbst simuliert wurde, legt sich über die medienkritische Ebene auch die Frage nach der Authentizität des Ereignisses an sich. Was ist wirklich passiert? Inwieweit ist die Geschichte manipuliert? Der *Unfall am Mittelpunkt Deutschlands* ist zudem stark historisch aufgeladen, da am neuen Zentrum der Bundesrepublik Deutschland ein VW mit einer Linde kollidiert, die anlässlich der Wiedervereinigung dort gepflanzt wurde. Die Kollision ist deshalb nicht nur eine von Kraftfahrzeug und Baum, sondern von Sinnbildern, die die deutsche Geschichte prägen. Stattliche Linden und Eichen wurden im Gedenken an politische Ereignisse und Persönlichkeiten gepflanzt, erinnern an historische Momente und symbolisieren ein Generationen übergreifendes kulturelles Gedächtnis. Mit der Wiedervereinigung Deutschlands nach dem Ende des Kalten Krieges würdigte man in Niederdorla eine Zäsur der Geschichte. Zugleich wurde für die hedonistische Jugend der 1980er Jahre der Begriff „Generation Golf" geprägt. Julius von Bismarck lässt diese Symbole in einem Szenario, das keine Zweifel an der Inszenierung zulässt, buchstäblich kollidieren. Der *Unfall am Mittelpunkt Deutschlands* bewirkt damit vor allem eine Skepsis gegenüber identitätsstiftenden Metaphern an sich. (ME)

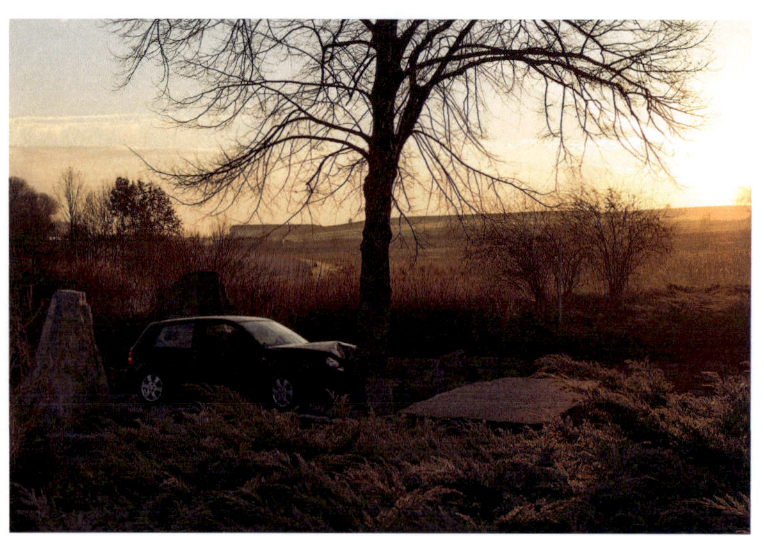

Julius von Bismarck
Unfall am Mittelpunkt Deutschlands, 2013
Fictive story / fiktive Geschichte
Courtesy the artist / der Künstler; Alexander Levy, Berlin

Igor Bošnjak

Hotel Balkan

Every present was once part of the future, but nonetheless the imagining of a tomorrow that is initially just a projection is irretrievably different from the causality that thinks in terms of temporal moments between the actual and the becoming. *Hotel Balkan* is a video that makes use of atmospheric images that can only partially be assigned to a concrete epoch to examine futuristic memories of the past and present imaginings of the future. The film was shot in the nuclear bunker of Tito, the former president of Yugoslavia, and centres on the question of why images from the past often appear more futuristic than plausible images of an imagined future. Even science fiction films often look like a journey not so much into the future but rather into an unknown past: it is not the unimaginable that finds expression in such cases, but rather those variants of the past that obviously failed to be realized. Igor Bošnjak's film *Hotel Balkan*, too, presents a future of the past that apparently never managed to become the present, although it actually exists. In line with this approach, the nuclear bunker in Konjic in the present-day Bosnia-Herzegovina is introduced as a sort of hotel: not a place for the protection of yesterday's ruling class, but somewhere for the people of today to relax. However, without guests, the deserted hotel resembles a spectral film set.

Jacques Derrida defined the spectre as that which both is and is not; it represents temporalities that cannot be adequately grasped by present-oriented thought, because they involve a past that has not passed as well as a future that breaks with the present. Both the past and the future, as temporal dimensions, are thus seen in an interrelationship: without memories of the past there will be no future. This vision of the past and the future as temporalities that do not merge fully with the present is central to Derrida's concept of the "spectral": the living present's asynchrony with itself. A temporal schism is expressed in the spectral, and thus also the element that eludes the linearity of sequential present moments.

Tito's Yugoslavia was the most progressive socialist country in terms of architecture, design and the thought given to living environments in general. In cities such as Neo Beograd and Skopje one can still see the architecture and urban design of a progressive socialist society. In retrospect, much from that time seems like a future of the past, with goals that ultimately remained just promises. The bunker in *Hotel Balkan*, with its furniture dating from somewhere between the outmoded and the timeless, has a similarly retro-futuristic effect: a place of power, encapsulated in an intermediate realm of time, with the paradoxical status of a spectre that pushes out of the past into a present that doesn't live in harmony with itself. (VJM)

*1981 in Sarajevo. Lives / lebt in Trebinje.
www.igorbosnjak.com

Jede Gegenwart war einmal die Zukunft der Vergangenheit, und doch scheint die Vorstellung eines Morgens, das vorerst nur Projektion ist, unwiederbringlich anders als jene Kausalität, die in zeitlichen Momenten zwischen Ist und Werden denkt. *Hotel Balkan* ist ein Video aus atmosphärischen, nur bedingt einer konkreten Epoche zuzuordnenden Bildern, das sich mit der futuristischen Erinnerung an das Vergangene und gegenwärtigen Zukunftsvorstellungen beschäftigt. Im Zentrum des im Atombunker des ehemaligen jugoslawischen Präsidenten Tito gedrehten Films steht die Frage, warum Bilder aus der Vergangenheit oft progressiver erscheinen als eingängige Bilder einer imaginierten Zukunft. Selbst Science Fiction Filme sehen nicht selten weniger wie Reisen in die Zukunft denn wie solche in eine unbekannte Vergangenheit aus: Nicht das Unvorstellbare kommt in ihnen zum Ausdruck, sondern jene Variation der Vergangenheit, die offenbar nicht realisiert worden ist. Auch Igor Bosniaks Film *Hotel Balkan* präsentiert eine Zukunft der Vergangenheit, die scheinbar niemals gegenwärtig geworden ist, obschon sie real existiert. Deshalb auch die Vorstellung des Atombunkers in Konjic im heutigen Bosnien-Herzogovina als eine Art Hotel: ein Ort der Erholung für die Menschen von heute statt eines Schutzortes für die Herrschenden von gestern. Ohne Gäste jedoch gleicht das menschenleere Hotel einer gespensterhaften Kulisse.

Als das, was zugleich ist und nicht ist, hat Jacques Derrida das Gespenst beschrieben. Es repräsentiert Zeitlichkeiten, die vom Denken der Gegenwart nicht angemessen begriffen werden können, denn sie umfassen eine Vergangenheit, die nicht vergangen ist, sowie eine Zukunft, die mit dem Gegenwärtigen bricht. Vergangenheit wie Zukunft stehen als zeitliche Dimensionen deshalb in einer Wechselbeziehung: ohne Erinnerung an das Vergangene wird es keine Zukunft geben. Dieses Verständnis von Vergangenheit und Zukunft als Zeitlichkeiten, die nicht vollständig in der Gegenwart aufgehen, ist für Derridas Konzept des Gespensterhaften, des *Spektralen*, zentral: als Ungleichzeitigkeit der lebendigen Gegenwart mit sich selbst. Im Spektralen drückt sich eine zeitliche Spaltung aus und damit das, was sich der Linearität einander abwechselnder Gegenwarten entzieht.

Das Jugoslawien unter Tito war das progressivste sozialistische Land in Bezug auf Architektur, Design und die Gestaltung des Lebensraums insgesamt. In Städten wie Neo Beograd und Skopje zeigt sich die gebaute Idee einer progressiven sozialistischen Gesellschaft bis heute. Retrospektiv wirkt vieles aus der damaligen Zeit wie eine Zukunft der Vergangenheit, deren Ziele letztlich Versprechen geblieben sind. Der Bunker mit seinem aus der Zeit gefallenen Mobiliar in *Hotel Balkan* wirkt auf ähnliche Weise retro-futuristisch: ein Ort der Macht, eingekapselt in einem Zwischenreich der Zeit, mit dem paradoxen Status eines Gespenstes, das aus der Vergangenheit in eine selbst mit sich nicht in Einklang lebende Gegenwart drängt. (VJM)

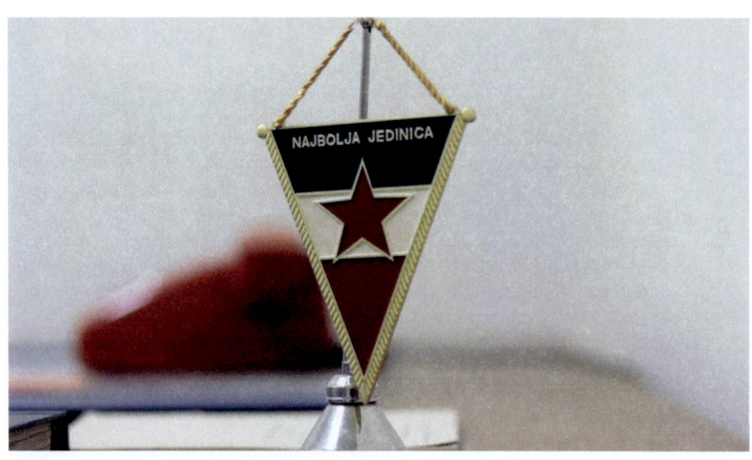

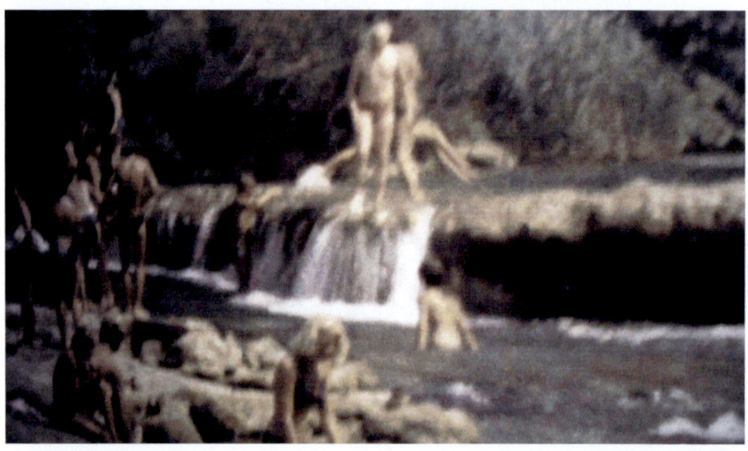

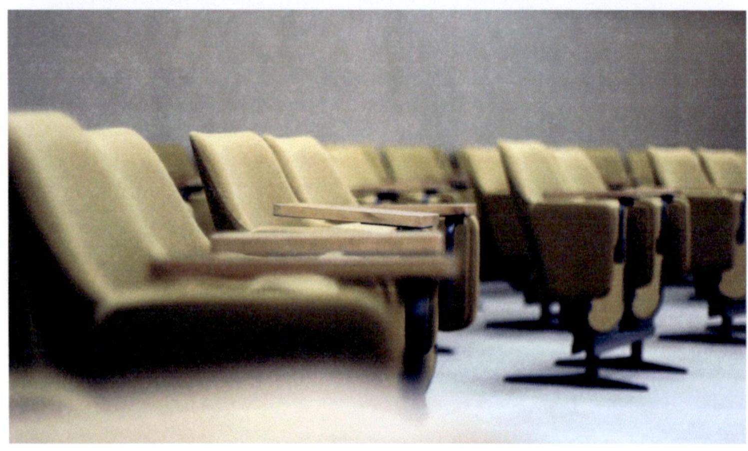

Igor Bošnjak
Hotel Balkan, 2013
HD video, 10 Min.
Courtesy the artist / der Künstler

Antoine Catala

Le Petit Antoine
New Feelings
Logo to Self-Consciousness
Collective Feelings Memory ()

Antoine Catala has developed his practice around our physical and psychological relationship to images and the machines that generate them. With a focus on spacialization and the tactile character of pictures — moving or still — the artist highlights the affective connection we have with them. As the machine turns into a relational tool between humans, it also becomes, for Catala, one of the vehicles for our mutation, developing into a new form of language. Catala insists as well on the importance of the mechanical repetition of the machine: "Their movement comes from my obsession with moving images, the logic being is that if a moving image is translated to a sculpture, the sculpture would have to be moving, too." Using 3D printing, fog displays, holograms, projections as well as more developed technology, Catala's performances and installations are often laced with humour, but without distracting from their primary intent to question the means of communication, language and emotions. Indeed, despite their machine veneer and plastic quality, a need for human warmth and understanding seem to somehow exude from Catala's work regardless.
For *The Future of Memory*, the artist exhibits four technology-based pieces tied together by a narrative that explores the memories and feelings they trigger. *New feelings* (2014) is a computer generated rendering of the artist with a young boy's body, lying on the beach, thinking. Directly associated to this piece is *Le Petit Antoine* (2014), a comic strip depicting again the artist as a kid, trying to approach and understand other people's behaviors. Underlying this piece is Catala's experience as a French expatriate living in New York, where relationships, often superficial, are difficult to comprehend for a foreigner. For the piece, Catala specifically chose words that belong to the American imaginary dictionary of France. As the artist points out, "Everybody here can understand those words: Le Petit Antoine", suggesting therefore a new, simple way for the artist to try and communicate. The title *Le Petit Antoine* might strike a deep chord of memory and some nostalgia for French people as it refers to the adventures of a young schoolboy, a cartoon character named *Le Petit Nicolas*. Drawn by Jean-Jacques Sempé, it is part of the cultural collective memory in France, and is so deeply entrenched that Catala himself had not noticed the correlation at first.
Emanating from the two other pieces is a desire for texture and sensory feeling. Created for the show, the installation *Collective Feelings Memory ()* (2015) ressembles a sandbox but is filled with multicolored balls of polystyrene foam. They retain their shape when touched by visitors, leaving a small fragment of physical memory for the next person. Looking like a flesh-colored balloon-brain, the installation *Logo to Self-Consciousness* (2014), inflates and deflates, rendering on the outside the shape it contains within. While the flesh color and the brain shape exacerbate the human dimension of this machine, the texture of the work seems to invite being touched, and therefore establishes an intimacy and a physical connection with the viewer. (EL)

*1975, Toulouse. Lives / lebt in New York.
www.aaaaaaa.org

In Antoine Catalas Kunst geht es um unsere körperliche und seelische Beziehung zu Bildern und zu den Apparaten, die diese Bilder erzeugen. Mit einem Schwerpunkt auf der Raumhaftigkeit und dem taktilen Charakter von bewegten oder unbewegten Bildern beleuchtet der Künstler die affektive Verbindung, die wir zu ihnen haben. Da die Maschine immer mehr zu einem Werkzeug der Beziehungen zwischen Menschen wird, wird sie für Catala auch zu einem der Instrumente unserer Veränderung und lässt eine neue Form der Sprache entstehen. Catala hebt auch die Bedeutung der mechanischen Wiederholung für die Maschine hervor: *„Ihre Bewegung ergibt sich aus meiner Sucht nach bewegten Bildern.* Die Logik dabei ist folgende: Wenn ein bewegtes Bild in eine Skulptur übertragen wird, müsste sich die Skulptur eigentlich auch bewegen." Catala nutzt 3D-Drucke, Fogscreens, Hologramme, Projektionen und noch weiter entwickelte Technologien. Seine Performances und Installationen enthalten oft einen Schuss Humor, verlieren aber nie ihre primäre Absicht aus den Augen – das Hinterfragen der Möglichkeiten von Kommunikation, Sprache und Gefühlen. Tatsächlich scheinen Catalas Arbeiten trotz ihres hauptsächlich maschinellen Aussehens und ihrer plastischen Qualitäten irgendwie immer auch ein Bedürfnis nach menschlicher Wärme und menschlichem Verständnis zu verströmen.
In *The Future of Memory* ist der Künstler mit vier Arbeiten vertreten, die durch eine Erzählung verbunden sind, in der Erinnerungen und die sie auslösenden Gefühle untersucht werden. *New Feelings* ist eine computergenerierte Darstellung des Künstlers mit dem Körper eines kleinen Jungen. Er liegt am Strand und denkt nach. Direkt damit verbunden ist *Le Petit Antoine* – ein Comicstrip, der nochmals den Künstler als ein Kind zeigt, das versucht, sich dem Benehmen anderer Leute anzunähern und es zu verstehen. Dieser Arbeit liegen Catalas Erfahrungen als Franzose in New York zugrunde, wo die oftmals oberflächlichen Beziehungen für einen Ausländer schwer nachzuvollziehen sind. Für dieses Werk hat Catala eigens Worte gewählt, die im imaginären Frankreich-Lexikon der Amerikaner zu finden sind. Wie der Künstler betont, kann jeder diese Worte verstehen: „Le Petit Antoine." Er schlägt damit eine neue, einfache Art und Weise vor, wie man als Künstler kommunizieren kann. Der Titel *Le Petit Antoine* könnte hierbei eine tief liegende Erinnerung und auch eine gewisse Sehnsucht nach den Franzosen auslösen, denn er bezieht sich auf einen kleinen Schuljungen, eine Comicfigur namens *Le Petit Nicolas*. Diese von Jean-Jacques Sempé gezeichnete Figur ist in Frankreich Teil des kollektiven kulturellen Gedächtnisses – eines Gedächtnisses, das so tief verwurzelt ist, dass Catala selbst den Zusammenhang zunächst nicht erkannt hat.
Die beiden anderen Werke strahlen ein Verlangen nach Textur und Sinneseindrücken aus. Die für die Ausstellung geschaffene Installation *Collective Feelings Memory ()* ähnelt einem Sandkasten, der jedoch mit bunten Blasen aus Polysterol-Schaum gefüllt ist. Wenn ein Besucher eine der Blasen berührt, behält sie die Form, die diese Person ihr gegeben hat, und hinterlässt auf diese Weise dem nächsten Besucher ein kleines Stück physikalisches Gedächtnis. Die Installation *Logo to Self-Consciousness* sieht wie ein fleischfarbenes „Ballon-Gehirn" aus, das sich aufbläst, wieder in sich zusammenfällt und an der Außenseite die Form wiedergibt, die sie in sich birgt. Während die Fleischfarbe und das hirnähnliche Aussehen die menschliche Dimension dieses Apparates verstärken, scheint die Textur danach zu verlangen, berührt und erfühlt zu werden und auf diese Weise eine Art Vertrautheit und körperliche Verbindung mit dem Betrachter zu entwickeln. (EL)

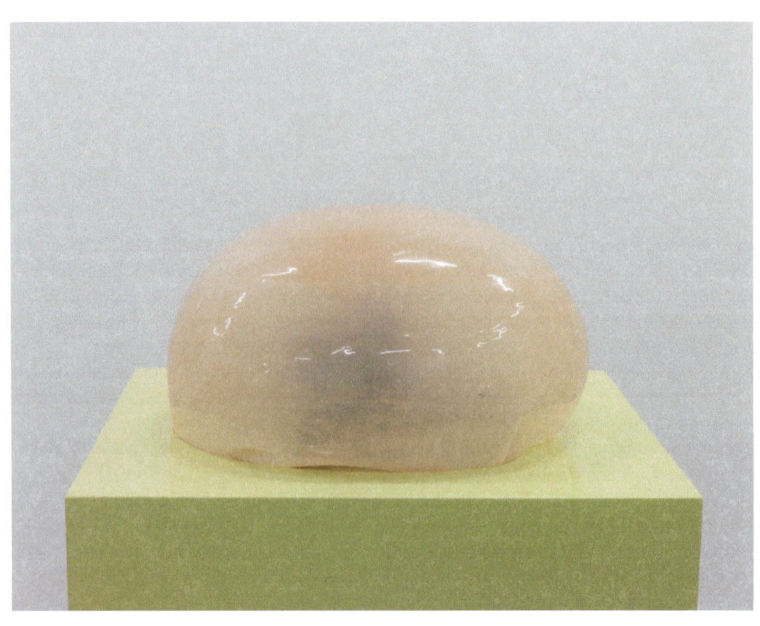

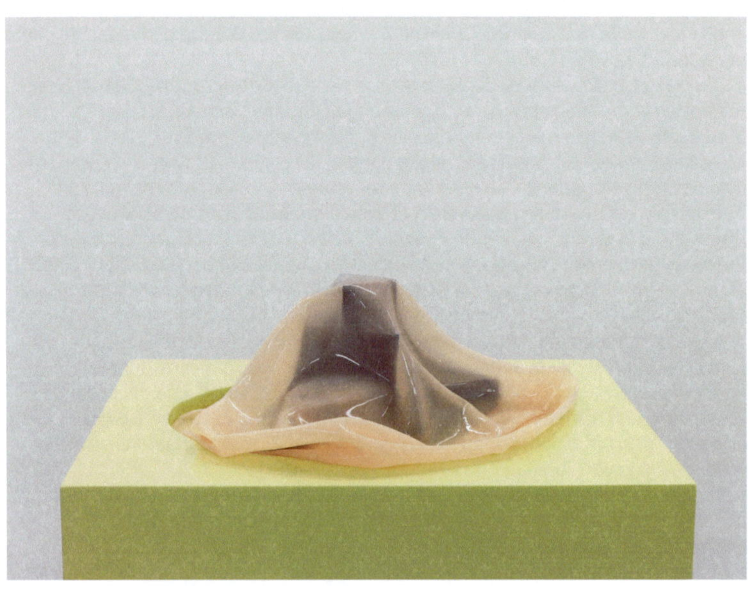

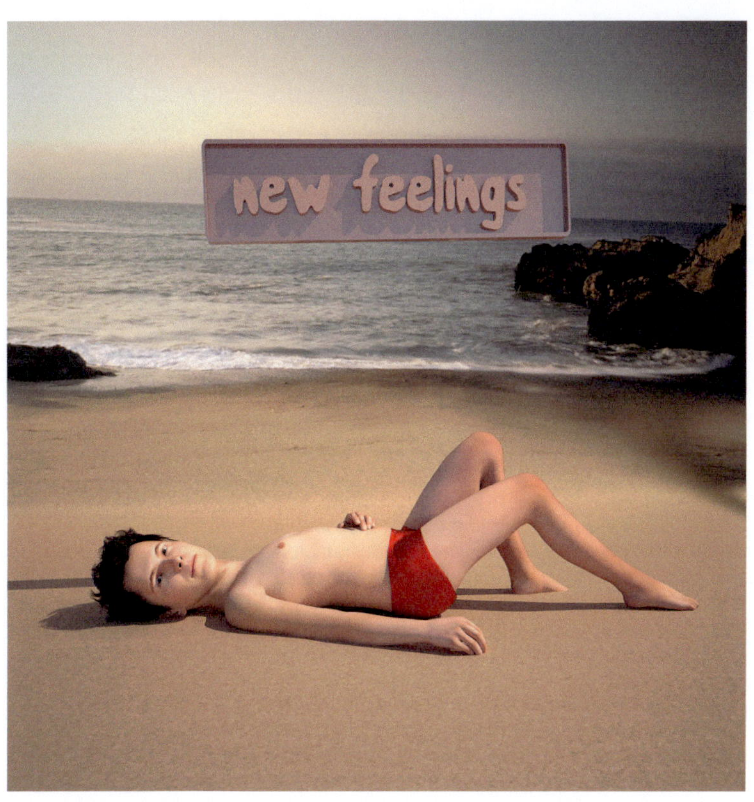

Antoine Catala
New Feelings, 2014
Courtesy the artist / der Künstler; 47 Canal, New York

<-   *Logo to Self-Consciousness*, 2014
Courtesy the artist / der Künstler; 47 Canal; Greene Naftali, New York

Various materials / Verschiedene Materialien
Images / Bilder: Joerg Lohse; the artist / der Künstler

Julian Charrière

Polygon XII

A hyperobject[1] is a large and spatially extensive entity that can only be perceived through complex auxiliary constructions. On the one hand it is very real and thus effective, but as a whole highly invisible. A hyperobject can resemble a simulacrum, but in contrast to the latter it actually exists. Julian Charrière succeeds in creating a visual representation of such an object in the *Polygon XII* series. These photographs show views of a former nuclear weapons testing site in the east of Kazakhstan, close to the towns of Semipalatinsk and Kurchatov.[2] The landscape still bears the recognizable traces of the explosion of nuclear weapons, measurement towers, bunkers and underground mines. In this region, 19,000 km^2 in size, some 460 tests were carried out between 1949 and 1989, many of them underground. The nuclear arms race between the USA and the Soviet Union was expressed in real terms here — the area became the de facto arena of a geopolitical public relations war. In historical terms, this location represents the age of the atom bomb and the East-West conflict. As Nadim Samman observes, Semipalatinsk also symbolizes the Anthropocene Era.[3] This is the designation given to the geological epoch characterized by the influence of human beings on their environment. The characteristics of the Anthropocene — climate change, species extinction, exploitation of resources and the release of radionuclides — highlight the empowerment of the human race with respect to the natural world and, in turn, can be viewed as hyperobjects.

Julian Charrière examines this phenomenon in *Polygon XII*, with a focus on the measurement towers of the polygon-shaped test site in eastern Kazakhstan. The photographs were taken on location with a medium format camera and document the landscape and the derelict buildings as relics of a bygone era. Since the area was closed only twenty-five years ago, it can only be entered with protective clothing. The radioactivity of plutonium disappears very slowly, with a half-life of 100,000 years, and thus still maintains the intensity of the active test period. Light and dark patches on the photographs are the result of the negatives coming into contact with radioactive excavation residues in the test area. After processing, the photos become objects that are simultaneously: documents of the historic ruins and of the phenomenon of continuing radioactive contamination, and at the same time represent a future archaeology of the nuclear age.

In these works by Charrière, it is not possible to draw a clear boundary between the past, the present and the future. A linear concept of temporality limits comprehension of their scale unless one interprets them, as the artist proposes, as future fossils. In 1964 J.G. Ballard described the dystopia of an atomically contaminated atoll in the Pacific, which inspired Julian Charrière to visit Semipalatinsk. A landscape that normally provides a key to the past for geologists sometimes needs an interpretation from the future. (ME)

*1987 in Morges. Lives/lebt in Berlin.
www.julian-charriere.net

Ein Hyperobjekt[1] ist ein großes und raumzeitlich weit verzweigtes Gebilde, das nur über komplexe Hilfskonstruktionen wahrnehmbar ist. Einerseits ist es sehr real und damit wirkungsvoll, als Ganzes jedoch extrem unsichtbar. Ein Hyperobjekt kann einem Simulakrum ähneln, ist im Gegensatz zu diesem jedoch tatsächlich existent.

Julian Charrière gelingt die visuelle Repräsentation eines solchen Objektes in *Polygon XII*. Die Fotografien dieser Serie zeigen Ansichten eines ehemaligen Atomwaffentestfeldes im Osten Kasachstans nahe der Städte Semipalatinsk und Kurtschatow.[2] In der Landschaft befinden sich noch heute erkennbare Markierungen für den Abwurf von Kernwaffen, Messtürme, Bunker und unterirdische Minen. In dem 19.000 km^2 großen Gebiet wurden zwischen 1949 und 1989 etwa 460 Tests durchgeführt, viele davon unterirdisch. Das atomare Wettrüsten zwischen den USA und der Sowjetunion erfuhr hier seine reale Manifestation – das Areal wurde zum faktischen Schauplatz eines fiktiven Krieges. Historisch repräsentiert der Ort das Zeitalter der Atombombe und des Ost-West-Konfliktes. Wie Nadim Samman konstatiert, symbolisiert Semipalatinsk ebenfalls das Zeitalter des Anthropozäns.[3] Damit wird jene geozeitliche Epoche bezeichnet, die von der Einflussnahme des Menschen auf seine Umwelt geprägt ist. Die Merkmale des Anthropozäns – Klimawandel, Artensterben, Ressourcenausbeute und Freisetzung von Radionukliden – veranschaulichen die Ermächtigung des Menschen gegenüber der Natur und könnten ihrerseits als Hyperobjekte verstanden werden.

Julian Charrière befasst sich mit diesen Phänomenen, fokussiert in *Polygon XII* jedoch die Messtürme des polygonal geformten Testgeländes in Ost-Kasachstan. Die Fotografien wurden vor Ort mit einer Mittelformatkamera aufgenommen und dokumentieren die Landschaft und die grotesken Gebäude als Hinterlassenschaften einer vergangenen Ära. Da die Stilllegung des Feldes erst 25 Jahre zurückliegt, kann das Areal nur mit Schutzkleidung betreten werden. Die radioaktive Strahlung von Plutonium schwindet mit einer Halbwertszeit von 100.000 Jahren und entspricht somit heute noch der einstigen Intensität. Die hellen und dunklen Flecken auf den Fotografien resultieren aus dem Kontakt der Negative mit radioaktiven Ausgrabungsresten des Testgebietes. Die Strahlung der Steine wirft helle und dunkle Schatten auf das Material und hinterlässt dadurch eine sichtbare Spur der unsichtbaren Kontaminierung. Wenngleich die Bilder nachträglich bearbeitet wurden, verschmelzen in ihnen Bestandsaufnahmen historischer Ruinen, bestehende radioaktive Verseuchung und eine zukünftige Archäologie des nuklearen Zeitalters.

Eine klare Abgrenzung zwischen Vergangenheit, Gegenwart und Zukunft ist nicht möglich. Ein lineares Konzept von Zeitlichkeit beschneidet den Maßstab des Gegenstandes, es sei denn man interpretiert ihn, wie der Künstler vorschlägt, als zukünftiges Fossil: James Graham Ballard beschreibt 1964 die Dystopie eines nuklear verstrahlten Atolls im Pazifik, die Julian Charrière zum Besuch Semipalatinsks inspirierte. Eine Landschaft, die für Geologen normalerweise den Schlüssel zur Vergangenheit liefert, bedarf manchmal einer Interpretation aus der Zukunft. (ME)

[1] Timothy Morton, Hyperobjects: Philosophy and Ecology after the End of the World, (Minneapolis: University of Minnesota Press, 2013); see also, Timothy Morton, Dawn of the Hyperobjects, A talk at the New Climes conference, Exeter University (UK), June 13, 2011 (www.youtube.com/playlist?list=PL70427836EA4E7F95) and "Ursula K. Heise reviews Timothy Morton," Critical Inquiry, June 04, 2014, www.criticalinquiry.uchicago.edu/ursula_k._heise_reviews_timothy_morton

[2] Igor Vasilyevich Kurchatov was the director of the Soviet atom bomb project. The town Kurchatov was named after him and is a closed city and the administrative centre of the test area.

[3] Nadim Samman, "The End of the World, Again," Charrière, Julian: Future Fossil Spaces, Catalogue Musée cantonal des Beaux-Arts de Lausanne (Milan: Mousse Publishing, 2014) 30-39.

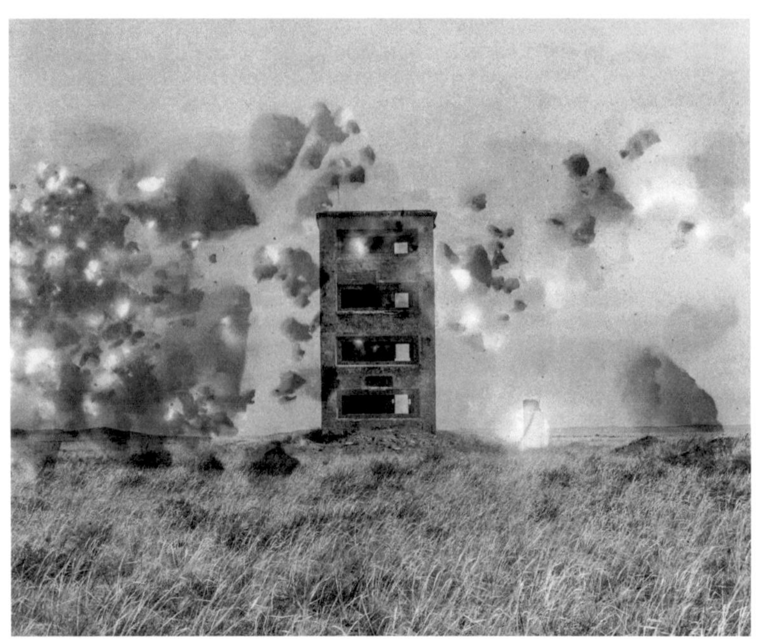

Julian Charrière
Polygon XII, 2014
B/W photography / S/W Fotografie, 150 x 180 cm
Courtesy the artist / der Künstler

Keren Cytter

Ocean

Ocean begins with instructions telling viewers to position their head at one point and their shoulders at another. Then a disembodied voice slowly induces a state of relaxation and meditative concentration: "If you don't want to drown, be an ocean. You are waking up to the sound of the waves. Your mind is an island. You are facing reality by yourself. Relax. Concentrate on the screen in front of you and face your own reflection." Keren Cytter's video work presents an elliptical narrative about a family, a lover, a beach house and a lonely boy. However, the fragmentarily recounted story is embedded in the language of hypnosis that superimposes mental images over reality. When in hypnosis the patient is transported to another place that, as an imaginary reality, he or she attempts to fill with life. In Cytter's work we encounter cinematographic images that generate an alternative reality and fill our consciousness with life. Similar scenes with different performers, atmospheric music and a non-linear form of narrative could put the viewer in a state of confusion, but the disembodied voice repeats its instructions, telling them what to do and feel when encountering the suggestive but ultimately distant worlds of images that they see. The immersive experience of this filmic construction is thus steered less by the dramatic composition or any identification with the performers, but instead by the gently insistent voice that directs viewer attention, promising positive feelings and a sense of oneness with the self.

Narrating from various perspectives, this voice guides us through the circular logic of the film, ending with instructions similar to those at the beginning: "Concentrate, look at your reflection. You are relieved. Your mind is empty… You recognize your reflection and smile with the embarrassment of a blind date. Relax. Your mind is now an ocean." In the last shot, a young man finds an iPhone buried in the sand. On the phone, we see a film that shows exactly the same scene as the one in front of him: the calm sea, the sun, the beach. The contemporary form of hypnosis that promotes mental self-optimization is no longer intended to shift the consciousness into a state of sleep and so reveal unassimilated elements, but now creates a paradoxical state of increased wakefulness. Cytter's filmic self-experience study takes up this promise, but between the stereotypically romantic scenes we glimpse the fractures of social conditioning, as well as the latent loneliness of every nonconformist who doesn't wish to become one with the ocean. Digital media sometimes create a hypnotic pull, asking for the user's concentrated attention in exchange for the promise of feeling better once embedded in its virtual world. But just as the sea gets filmed with an iPhone, instead of simply being an object of contemplation, so the flat glass surface of the screen gets insistently pushed in front of reality until this seems just as untactile, as unreal, as the data streams from our beloved gadgets. (VJM)

*1977 in Tel Aviv. Lives / lebt in New York.
www.kerencytter.com

Am Anfang steht die schriftliche Anweisung, den Kopf an der einen und die Schultern an der anderen Stelle zu positionieren. Dann versetzt uns eine Stimme aus dem Off langsam in einen Zustand der Entspannung und meditativen Konzentration: „If you don't want to drown, be an ocean. You are waking up to the sound of the waves. Your mind is an island. You are facing reality by yourself. Relax. Concentrate on the screen in front of you and face your own reflection." Keren Cytters Videoarbeit *Ocean* ist ein elliptisches Narrativ um ein Paar, eine Familie, eine Geliebte, ein Haus am Strand und einen einsamen Jungen. Die fragmentarisch erzählte Geschichte ist jedoch eingebettet in die Sprache der Hypnose, die die mentale Bilderzeugung wie eine Folie über die Realität blendet. Die Hypnose führt den Patienten an einen anderen Ort, den er als imaginäre Realität mit Leben zu füllen sucht. Hier sind es kinematografische Bilder, die eine alternative Wirklichkeit erzeugen und unser Bewusstsein mit Leben füllen. Ähnliche Szenen mit unterschiedlichen Darstellern, atmosphärische Musik und eine non-lineare Erzählweise könnten den Zuschauer verwirren, doch die Stimme aus dem Off wiederholt ihre Anweisungen, was wir tun und fühlen sollen angesichts der suggestiven und doch letztlich fernen Bildwelten, die wir betrachten. Das immersive Eintauchen in das filmische Konstrukt wird so weniger von der Dramaturgie oder der Identifikation mit den Darstellern gelenkt, sondern von der sanft insistierend unsere Aufmerksamkeit fordernden Stimme, die positive Gefühle und ein Einssein mit uns selbst verspricht.
Aus verschiedenen Blickwinkeln erzählt, leitet uns diese Stimme aus dem Off durch die zirkuläre Logik des Films, der mit ähnlichen Anweisungen endet wie er begonnen hat: „Concentrate, look at your reflection. You are relieved. Your mind is empty … You recognize your reflection and smile with the embarrassment of a blind date. Relax. Your mind is now an ocean." In der letzten Einstellung findet ein junger Mann ein im Sand vergrabenes iPhone. Auf dem Bildschirm ist ein Film zu sehen, der genau jene Szene zeigt, die vor ihm liegt: das ruhige Meer, die Sonne, der Strand. Die zeitgenössische, der mentalen Selbstoptimierung dienende Hypnose soll nicht mehr das Bewusstsein in einen Schlafzustand versetzen und Unverarbeitetes zum Vorschein bringen, sondern einen paradoxen Zustand gesteigerter Wachsamkeit erzeugen. Cytters filmische Selbsterfahrungsstudie greift dieses Versprechen auf, aber zwischen den nur Stereotype rekapitulierenden romantischen Szenen blitzen die Brüche gesellschaftlicher Konditionierung ebenso auf wie die latente Einsamkeit jedes Nonkonformisten, der nicht mit dem Ozean eins werden will. Digitale Medien erzeugen manchmal eine hypnotischen Sog, ihnen konzentrierte Aufmerksamkeit zu schenken im Austausch für das Versprechen, dass wir uns besser fühlen werden, wenn wir in ihre virtuellen Welten eingebettet sind. Doch so wie mit dem iPhone das Meer gefilmt wurde, statt es selbst zu betrachten, schieben sich
die flachen Glasscheiben der Bildschirme insistierend vor die Realität, bis diese genauso wenig taktil erscheint wie die Datenströme aus den geliebten Gadgets. (VJM)

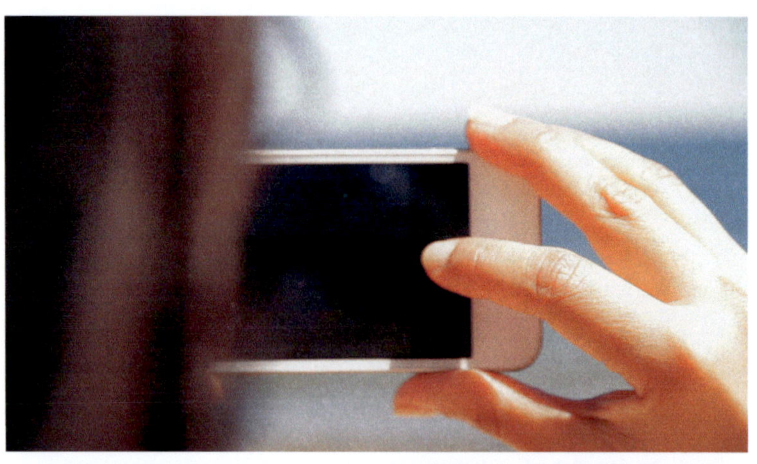

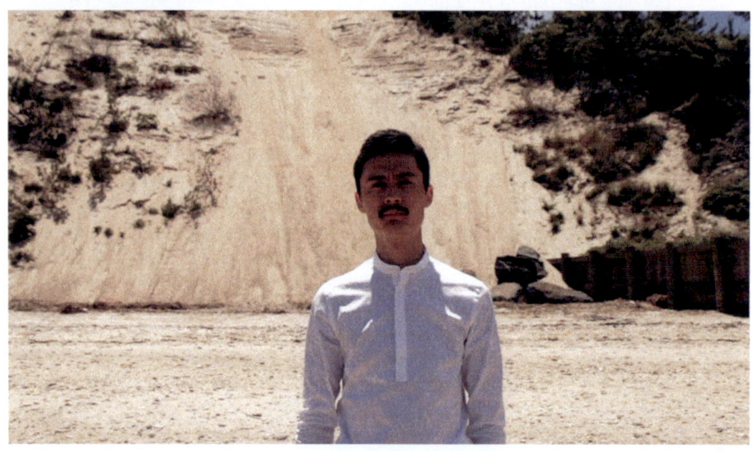

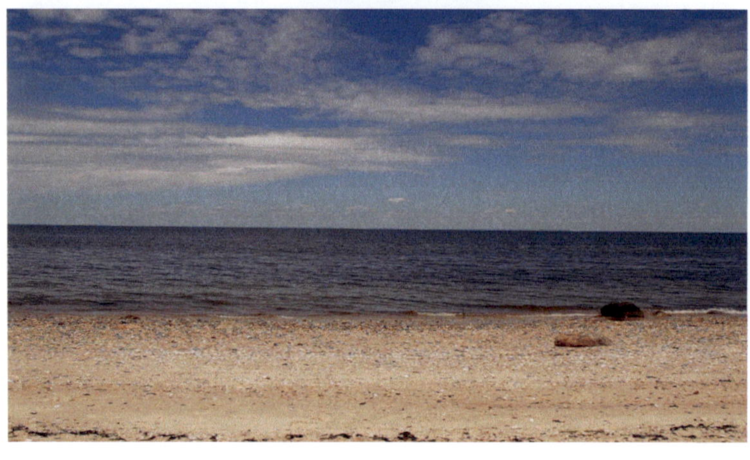

Keren Cytter
Ocean, 2014
Video, 15:40 Min.
Courtesy the artist / die Künstlerin; Galerie Nagel Draxler, Berlin; Galerie
Pilar Corrias; London

Edith Dekyndt

Carousel

In the television series *Mad Men*, set in the advertising industry in the 1960s, there is an iconic scene that portrays a slide projector as a nostalgia device. During the creation of an advertising campaign for Kodak, an almost magical quality is attributed to the projector. Images of an earlier time awake memories in us that reach far beyond what a slide actually depicts; seen in the light of a projector, the past seems to come to life and confront us directly. And it is a *carousel* that transports the slides. It makes the past rotate, carrying it at slightly dizzying speed into the present.
Edith Dekyndt's installation *Carousel* takes up this concept of the virtual journey into the past, but without showing concrete images. Instead of presenting personal memories, *Carousel* confronts the viewer with the evidence of what actually is: dust that has accreted in the empty slide frames; dust as microscopic particles of time that settle on everything; dust as physical traces of the past that betray nothing of this apart from the idea that it is very distant. The total of eighty slide frames that fill the carousel of a Kodak projector are over fifty years old and were acquired by the artist in their original packaging. Each slide frame has two thin glass plates between which a developed slide can be inserted. Some of the glass plates have been treated with an emulsion that has dried out over the years and developed cracks. Along with the dust, these cracks form a further level of the visible that appears when the image is magnified. As soon as the projector loads another empty slide frame in front of the lens, viewers see correspondingly minimal traces of "nothing" that points to the past. These are images created without intent and exposure, coincidental products of a storage process that presents itself as a perceptible sedimentation of time. The clicking noise of the projector emphasizes the mechanical quality of the presentation. And despite the sparse array, the minimalistic imagery and the conceptual nature of the installation, it is above all the poetic quality of the slides with their almost invisible dust compositions and their slight craquelure that unfolds as a mnemonic projection surface. Here, the supposed nothingness does not mean an absence of something but rather the absence of something specific. *Carousel* is rather like a perception machine that directs one's gaze to the existence of the bygone in the here and now: it is a projection that imbues dust with its magical presence.
Due to falling demand and high costs, Kodak ended production of the famous Kodachrome slide film in June 2009. Three years later the company filed for bankruptcy, followed by the end of production of all other analogue films. (VJM)

*1960 in Yper. Lives / lebt in Tournai.

In der amerikanischen, in der Werbebranche der 1960er Jahre spielenden Fernsehserie *Mad Men* gibt es eine ikonische Szene, die einen Diaprojektor als nostalgische Zeitmaschine inszeniert. Dem Gerät wird bei der Konzeption einer Werbekampagne für die Firma Kodak eine quasi magische Qualität zugeschrieben: Die Bilder der Vergangenheit wecken Erinnerungen in uns, die über das auf den Diapositiven Dargestellte weit hinausgehen, denn die Vergangenheit wird im Licht des Projektors quasi verlebendigt und konfrontiert uns unmittelbar mit ihr. Es ist deshalb ein Karussell, das die Dias transportiert. Es lässt die Vergangenheit rotieren und überführt sie mit einer Geschwindigkeit in die Gegenwart, die uns leicht schwindeln lässt.

Edith Dekyndts Installation *Carousel* greift dieses Konzept der virtuellen Reise in die Vergangenheit auf, ohne jedoch konkrete Bilder zu zeigen. Statt mit persönlichen Erinnerungen konfrontiert *Carousel* den Betrachter mit der Evidenz des Faktischen: Staub, der sich in leeren Diarahmen abgelagert hat; Staub als mikroskopisches Partikel Zeit, das sich auf alles legt; Staub als physische Spur der Vergangenheit, die nichts von dieser preisgibt außer der Tatsache, dass sie weit in der Ferne liegt. Die insgesamt achtzig Diarahmen, die das Karussell eines Kodak-Projektors füllen, sind über fünfzig Jahre alt und wurden von der Künstlerin originalverpackt erworben. Jeder der Diarahmen hat zwei dünne Glasplatten, zwischen die ein entwickeltes Diapositiv eingebettet werden kann. Einige der Glasplatten wurden offenbar mit einer Emulsion behandelt, die über die Jahre hinweg ausgetrocknet ist und Risse bekommen hat. Neben dem Staub bildet sie eine weitere Sichtbarkeitsebene, die in der Vergrößerung zur Erscheinung tritt. Sobald der Projektor mit einem Klacken einen weiteren leeren Diarahmen vor die Linse schiebt, sehen wir entsprechend minimale Spuren eines Nichts, das auf die Vergangenheit verweist. Es sind Bilder, die ohne Intention und Entwickler entstanden sind, Zufallsprodukte einer Lagerung, die sich als wahrnehmbare Sedimentierung von Zeit präsentiert. Das Klacken des Projektors wird von einem Lautsprecher verstärkt, was die mechanische Qualität der Vorführung unterstreicht. Und doch ist es trotz der nüchternen Anordnung, der minimalistischen Bildlichkeit und des konzeptuellen Charakters der Installation vor allem die poetische Qualität der Dias mit ihren fast unsichtbaren Staubkompositionen und ihrem leichten Krakelee, die sich als mnemotechnische Projektionsfläche präsentiert. Das vermeintliche Nichts bedeutet hier keine Abwesenheit von etwas, sondern die Abwesenheit von etwas Spezifischem. *Carousel* ist so etwas wie eine Wahrnehmungsmaschine, die den Blick auf das Dasein des Vergangenen im Jetzt lenkt: Es ist die Projektion, die dem Staub seine magische Präsenz verleiht.

Die Firma Kodak beendete aufgrund sinkender Nachfrage und hohen Kostenaufwandes im Juni 2009 die Produktion des berühmten Kodachrome-Diafilms. Drei Jahre später stellte die Firma einen Insolvenzantrag, gefolgt von der Einstellung der Produktion auch aller anderen analogen Filme. (VJM)

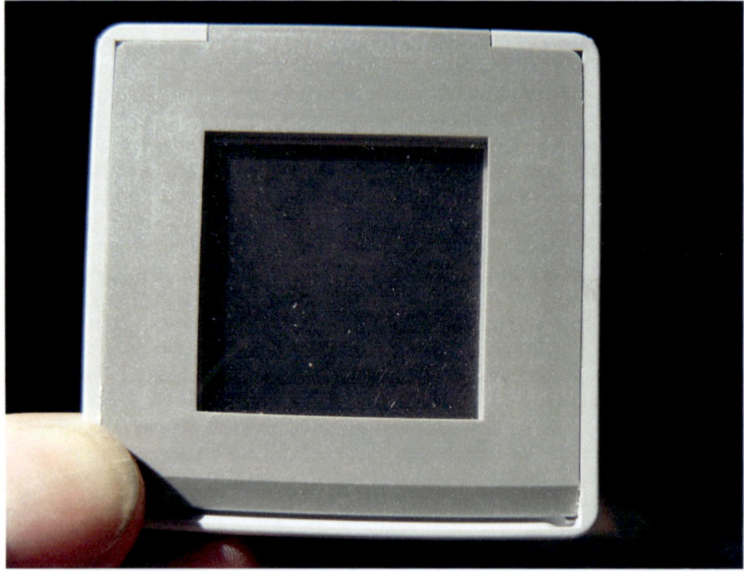

Edith Dekyndt
Carousel, 2010
Dia projection / Diaprojektion
Installation: Get out of my cloud, KIOSK, Gent
Courtesy the artist / die Künstlerin; Galerie Greta Meert

<u>Simon Denny</u>

The Startup Way Snapchat Legal Evidence
You Disruptive Technologies
The Process SeedCamp American Tour
Berlin Startup Case Mod: Sociomantic
Startup Case Mod: Snapchat

Snapchat is an instant messaging app for smartphones that allows one to send photos only visible to the message recipient for a fixed number of seconds before disappearing completely. This subverts the principle of the Internet that once information has been uploaded it is stored forever. However, the Snapchat developers recently had to admit that full deletion does not always work. In 2013, Snapchat became the victim of a hacker attack which published the supposedly deleted photos of several million users on an Internet website. The logo of the Los Angeles-based company – a little ghost – may be understood as a reference to the further existence of the images in the 'intermediate realm' of the Internet: digital ghosts from the past that reappear in the present, no longer alive but also not fully dead, "neither substance nor essence nor existence". In Simon Denny's installations, digital worlds such as these undergo a metaphorical materialization. The New Zealand-born artist brings the accelerated processes of the stock-exchange-listed Internet economy to a momentary standstill and thus creates an image of the status quo. *Startup Case Mod: Snapchat* presents the company's "ghost icon" as a three-dimensional laser engraving in a Plexiglas cube. The transparent being guards not only the emptiness but also a computer which, in turn, is encased in a Plexiglas shrine. The fetishization of the equipment collides in its materiality with the virtual worlds the hardware enables to explore, and, as well, with the promise evoked by a startup like Snapchat. Denny is interested in the interplay between venture capital and the spirit of invention, as well as the unbroken faith in the future and its infinite possibilities. In his installation-based works he portrays companies which, driven by the pioneering spirit, celebrate success in the Internet sector. By concentrating elements of a digital culture outside the mainstream he creates snapshots of a present that sees startup companies as tomorrow's heroes. The artist extracts readymade materials from their cultural niche and treats them as part of a globally interlinked community of nerdy inventors and venture capital investors. This creates a homage to technology, innovation and the unremitting search for the new, including its economic interrelations. *The Startup Way Snapchat Legal Evidence* introduces the concept behind Snapchat. Denny has illustrated the pyramid of its entrepreneurial success on a standard mesh fabric used for outdoor advertising. "Accountability" forms the base, followed by the units "process" and "culture", and ends with the heading "people", which stands at the summit. This is the "Startup Way" to success. The artist does not apply critical distance in his works. It is reality itself that may jeopardize or bring down the high-flying ambitions. (VJM)

*1982 in Auckland. Lives / lebt in Berlin.

Snapchat ist eine Instant-Messaging Anwendung für Smartphones, die das Versenden von Fotos ermöglicht, die für den Empfänger der Nachricht nur eine bestimmte Anzahl an Sekunden sichtbar sind und sich dann selbst zerstören. Das Prinzip des Internets, einmal hochgeladene Information für immer zu speichern, wird damit unterwandert. Auch die Snapchat-Entwickler mussten allerdings einräumen, dass das vollständige Löschen nicht immer funktioniert: 2013 wurde Snapchat Opfer eines Hackerangriffs, der die vermeintlich gelöschten Fotos von mehreren Millionen Usern auf einer Internetseite publik machte. Das Logo des Unternehmens aus Los Angeles, ein kleines Gespenst, verweist insofern auch auf das Fortleben der Bilder im Zwischenreich des World Wide Web: digitale Gespenster, die aus der Vergangenheit in die Gegenwart drängen, nicht mehr lebend, aber auch nicht vollständig tot, „weder Substanz, noch Essenz, noch Existenz".

In Simon Dennys Installationen finden digitale Welten wie diese eine metaphorische Materialisation. Die beschleunigten Prozesse der börsennotierten Netzökonomie versetzt der neuseeländische Künstler in einen Zustand des Stillstands und erzeugt damit ein Bild des Status quo. *Startup Case Mod: Snapchat* präsentiert das „ghost icon" der Firma als dreidimensionale Lasergravur in einem Plexiglaswürfel. Wie ein Computer ohne Hardware bewacht das transparente Wesen die Leere, aber auch einen seinerseits in einem Plexiglasschrein bewahrten Rechner. Die Fetischisierung des Equipments in seiner Materialität trifft auf die virtuellen Welten, die von diesem erkundet werden sowie die Versprechen, die ein Startup wie Snapchat evoziert. Denny interessiert das Zusammenspiel von Risikokapital und Erfindergeist sowie der ungebrochene Glauben an die Zukunft und deren unendliche Möglichkeiten. In seinen installativen Werken porträtiert er Unternehmen, die vom Pioniergeist getrieben in der Internetbranche Erfolg feiern. In der konzentrierten Kombination von Elementen einer Digitalkultur jenseits des Mainstream stellt er insofern Momentaufnahmen einer Gegenwart her, die in Startup-Unternehmen die Helden von Morgen findet. Er löst Readymade-Materialien aus ihrer kulturellen Nische heraus und behandelt sie als Teil einer global vernetzten Szene aus nerdigen Erfindern und Investoren von Risikokapital. So entsteht eine Hommage an Technologie, Innovation und die unaufhaltsame Suche nach dem Neuen inklusive ihrer ökonomischen Verflechtung. *The Startup Way Snapchat Legal Evidence* präsentiert das Konzept hinter Snapchat. Auf einem handelsüblichen Netzstoff für Außenplakate hat Denny die Pyramide von dessen unternehmerischen Erfolg abgebildet. „Accountability" bildet die Basis, gefolgt von den Einheiten „process" und „culture". Am Ende steht die Rubrik „people", die an der Spitze stehen: der „Startup Way" zum Erfolg. Kritische Distanz kennt Denny in seinen Werken nicht. Es ist die Realität, die im Zweifelsfall krisenhaft in die hochfliegenden Ambitionen interveniert. (VJM)

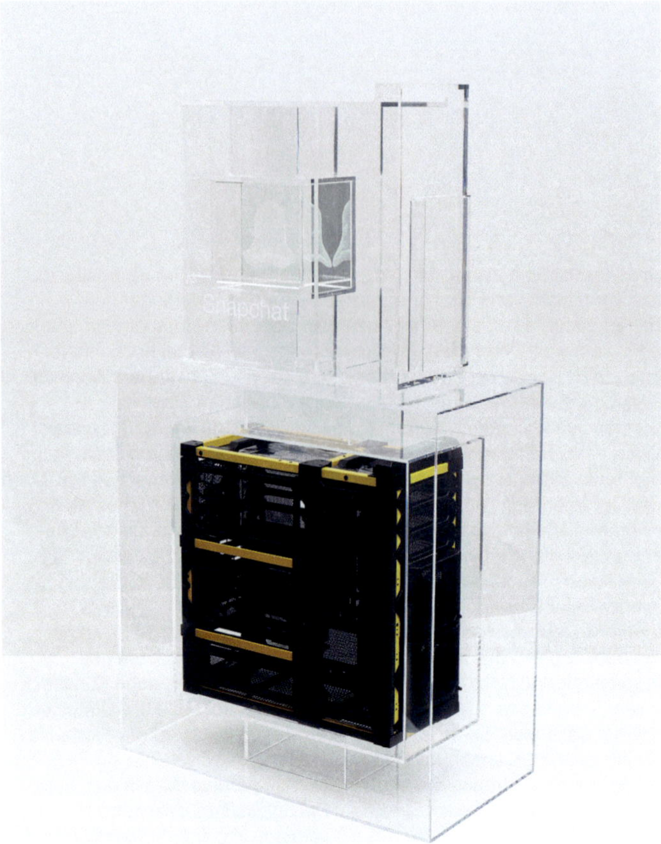

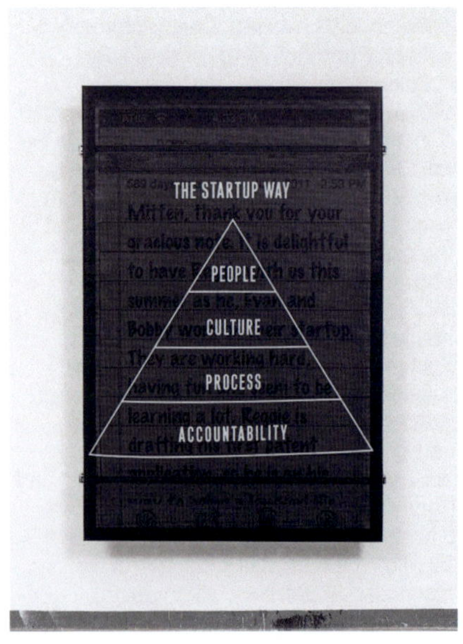
THE STARTUP WAY
PEOPLE
CULTURE
PROCESS
ACCOUNTABILITY

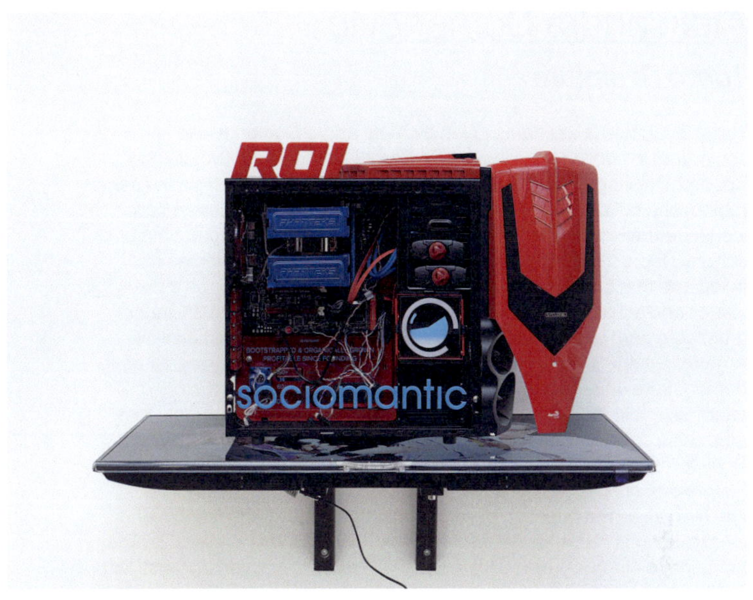

Simon Denny
Berlin Startup Case Mod : Sociomantic, 2014
Custom computer case, heavy-duty computer hardware, Metal fittings,
custom plexiglas components, digital prints on plexiglas, Samsung
UE40F6500 SS, Video on USB stick
79,5 x 91 x 54 cm
Courtesy Alastair Cookson

<--   *Startup Case Mod: Snapchat*, 2014
Antec Lan Boy Air Midi-Tower PC case, engraved custom plexiglas boxes,
3d laser photo in glass
126 x 72,2 x 38 cm

The Startup Way Snapchat Legal Evidence, 2014
2 digital prints on billboard mesh, digital prints on aluminum / Digitaldruck
auf Netzstoff, Digitaldruck auf Aluminium
159.5 x 113.5 x 17.5 cm

Courtesy the artist / der Künstler; Galerie Buchholz, Berlin / Cologne / Köln

Aleksandra Domanović

Turbo Sculpture

Turbo Sculpture is the name given by Aleksandra Domanović to sculptures in public space in cities in Serbia, Macedonia, Croatia and Kosovo. Drawing an analogy to "Turbo Folk" (a music style from the same region) she created the term to describe monuments of Western pop icons: naturalistic statues of Rocky Balboa, Bob Marley, Tupac Shakur or Johnny Depp. In the assumption that local politicians and heroes had failed and that there was no available national story to serve as a basis for values and achievements, these figures supply symbolic identification templates from Western culture. In 2005 a monument to the Chinese-American actor Bruce Lee was set up in Mostar (Bosnia-Herzegovina) to demonstrate unity and ethnic togetherness. This makes him an alternative role model, and Western pop culture becomes an ideal that embodies principles needing to be re-established. With her *Turbo Sculptures*, Aleksandra Domanović creates a detached view of recent history that enables a critical-reflective perspective.
Her film raises the question of what constitutes collective memory and what functions can and should be fulfilled by public monuments. Do they help one to come to terms with the past? Can they function as (abstract) commentaries on various current political circumstances? Or should they help promote moral education and betterment of the population?
The video superimposes documentary photos of the sculptures, footage of them being set up and portraits of the various initiators.These images are commented by a female narrator who reads an informative text. In formal terms the work references television documentaries that aim to communication, information and education in a manner free of judgement and comment. Domanović's work comments on the supposed collective inability to come to terms with the recent history of Yugoslavia. The video compiles facts and illustrations that are not substantiated but do follow a chronological argumentation. Monotony and the superimposition of the images strengthen the impression of flat hierarchies and the asymmetries of the Internet age that lead to democratization of information. In his essay Partial Recall, Carson Chan takes up this thought when he remarks that these theories of horizontalization are applied too infrequently to contemporary forms of communication.[1] One problem resulting from this is the insufficient analysis of the current resources for recoding and communicating data as well as memories. Aleksandra Domanović undertakes both these activities in her video essay. Born in Novi Sad, she personally experienced the trauma of disintegration and new identification of the former Yugoslavian states. The confrontation with cultural developments and with a media "Balkanization" continues to influence her artistic practice. (ME)

*1981 in Novi Sad. Lives / lebt in Berlin.
www.aleksandradomanović.com

Turbo Sculpture nennt Aleksandra Domanović Skulpturen im öffentlichen Raum in Städten in Serbien, Mazedonien, Slowenien, Kroatien und dem Kosovo. Analog zum so genannten „Turbo-Folk" (einer Musikrichtung aus derselben Region) kreierte sie die Bezeichnung zur Beschreibung von Monumenten westlicher Pop-Ikonen: naturalistische Statuen von Rocky Balboa, Bob Marley, Tupac Shakur oder Johnny Depp. In der Annahme, lokale Politiker und Helden hätten versagt und es existiere keine nationale Geschichte, an deren Werte erinnert und auf deren Errungenschaften aufgebaut werden könne, liefern diese Figuren symbolische Identifikationsvorlagen aus der westlichen Kultur. Dem chinesisch-stämmigen Amerikaner Bruce Lee wurde 2005 in Mostar (Bosnien-Herzegowina) ein Denkmal gesetzt, um Einheit und ethnisches Miteinander zu demonstrieren. Er wird zum alternativen Rollenmodell und die westliche Pop-Kultur zum Ideal, welches zu re-etablierende Prinzipien verkörpert. Aleksandra Domanović gelingt mit *Turbo Sculptures* ein distanzierter Blick auf diese jüngste Geschichte, der eine kritisch-reflexive Perspektive ermöglicht.
Ihr Film wirft die Frage auf, worin kollektive Erinnerung besteht und welche Funktionen öffentliche Denkmäler erfüllen können und sollten. Dienen sie der Aufarbeitung der Vergangenheit? Können sie als (abstrahierter) Kommentar auf jeweils aktuelle politische Umstände fungieren? Oder erfüllen sie einen Bildungsauftrag zur moralischen Erziehung der Bevölkerung?
Im Video werden Dokumentationsfotos der Skulpturen, Aufnahmen von ihrer Errichtung sowie Porträts der jeweiligen Initiatoren übereinandergelegt und von einer Sprecherin kommentiert, die einen informativen Text verliest. Formal knüpft die Arbeit an Fernsehdokumentationen an, deren Ziel die wert- und kommentarfreie Vermittlung von Information und Bildung ist. Domanovićs Werk kommentiert die vermeintliche kollektive Unfähigkeit, die jüngere Vergangenheit Jugoslawiens zu verarbeiten. Das Video reiht Fakten und Abbildungen aneinander, die nicht belegt werden, aber einer chronologischen Argumentation folgen. Monotonie und Überlagerung der Bilder stützen den Eindruck flacher Hierarchien und Ungleichmäßigkeiten des Internet-Zeitalters, die zur Demokratisierung von Information führen. Carson Chan knüpft in seinem Essay Partial Recall an diesen Gedanken an, wenn er bemerkt, dass jene Thesen der Horizontalisierung bisher zu selten auf zeitgenössische Kommunikationsformen angewandt wurden.[1] Ein daraus resultierendes Problem besteht in der mangelnden Analyse heutiger Mittel zur Aufzeichnung und Vermittlung von Daten und auch Erinnerungen. Beides unternimmt Aleksandra Domanović in ihrem Videoessay. Geboren in Novi Sad, erlebte sie das Trauma vom Zerfall und die Neu-Identifikation der ehemaligen jugoslawischen Staaten mit. Die Auseinandersetzung mit kulturellen Entwicklungen und einer medialen „Balkanisierung" prägt ihre künstlerische Praxis bis heute. (ME)

Vgl. Chan, Carson: Partial Recall: A Brief Account of Aleksandra Domanović's Monuments and the Aesthetics of the Near Obsolete, in: The Avery Review Nr.1/2014, New York 2014., http://averyreview.com/issues/1/partial-recall

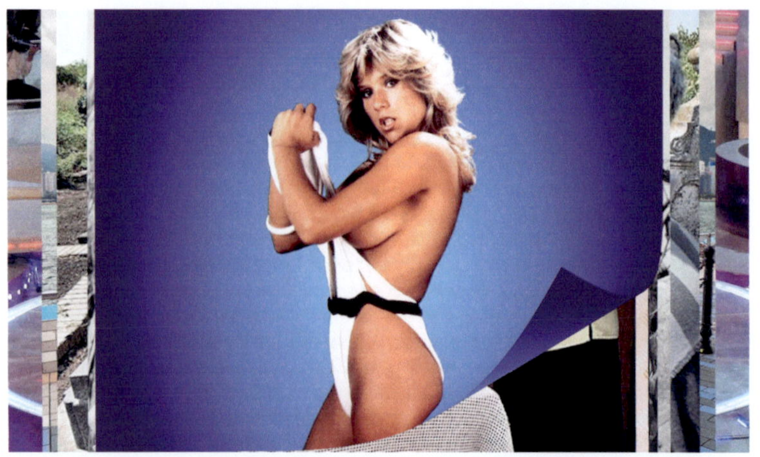

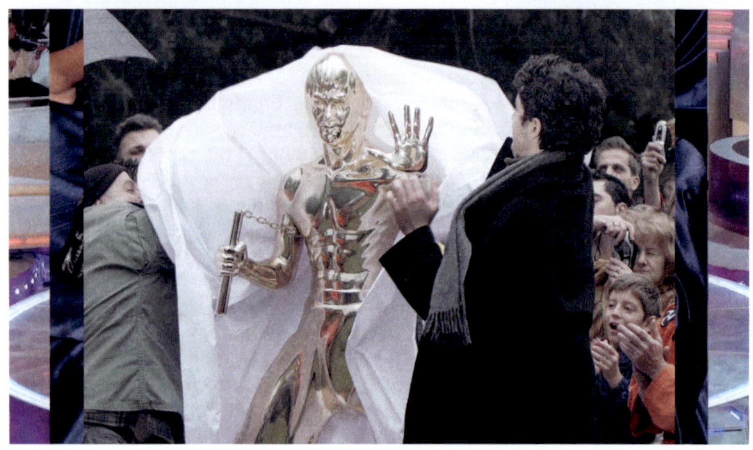

Aleksandra Domanović
Turbo Sculpture, 2010-2013
Video, 19:44 Min
Courtesy the artist / die Künstlerin; Tanya Leighton, Berlin

Dani Gal

As from Afar (Wie aus der Ferne)

"The only evidence that this conversation ever took place here is the recording, and if those recordings where altered at your discretion, then that would be the only record. The past only exists in some record of it, right? There are no facts."
This 1974 citation from American writer William S. Burroughs' conversation with the poet and filmmaker Gérard Malanga was also used as an introductory paragraph to a conversation Gal had with author and art historian René Zechlin and, most certainly, epitomizes the essence of Gal's practice.
How does an historical or political event pass into personal and *collective memory*? First coined in words by sociologist Maurice Halbwachs, the idea of *collective memory* constructs itself around multiple sources of influence and ever-evolving socio-cultural components. It is difficult to argue with Burroughs' argument that facts don't exist. In regards of the human complexity, they can only become unstable and lose their permanency. As they are recalled, re-enacted, written about, they morph into stories. Dani Gal's film and installation practice addresses these issues of perception, interpretation and the re-creation of history.
As from Afar is a fictionalized video installation based on the riveting relationship between Shoah survivor, renowned Nazi hunter Simon Wiesenthal, and Albert Speer, the Third Reich's chief architect and armaments minister. Speer was one of the rare high ranking Nazi officials to have taken responsibility for his acts, publicly admitting his shame and showing remorse for the regime's horrendous crimes while he spent twenty years in prison. After his release in 1974, Speer, in an attempt to clear his name, contacted Wiesenthal and the two established an unlikely relationship, based on correspondence and occasional meetings in Vienna. This odd friendship is the starting point of Gal's cinematic mise en scene and dialogues, which for this introspective work, originate from documentary material, interviews and the biography written by Israeli historian Tom Segev, *Simon Wiesenthal: The Life and Legends* (2010). In the first sequence of the movie, Speer and Wiesenthal stand in the workshop of a master model builder named Mr. Kuck. A survivor of the Holocaust himself, he's constructing a model of the Mauthausen concentration camp for an American film production company. He explains how the company wants railways and bigger towers, even though they didn't exist at the original site. When Speer asks Kuck how he obtained the plans for the camp, Kuck answers he built it from memory. Speer and Wiesenthal then make their way to a café, where they discuss their respective books. Several times during the video, Speer asks Wiesenthal to not publicly spread the news of their relationship for fear of the trouble it could cause Wiesenthal. The third scene finds them in front of the house designed by Ludwig Wittgenstein, a clean looking white building, where the two men randomly walk around in an almost meditative and soothing scene. Leaving Speer and Wiesenthal, the video cycles back to Kuck's workshop, where the craftsman is now building a model of that same Wittgenstein house. Accompanying the film is the narration of a short text by Austrian philosopher Ludwig Wittgenstein, based on memory and images and its relation to discourse on the Jewish Genocide. As it oscillates between fiction and facts, this heavily layered, detailed work, highlights issues linked to fictive re-creation and the multiple paths memory can take to build itself. (EL)

*1975 in Jerusalem. Lives / lebt in Berlin.

„Der einzige Beweis, dass diese Unterhaltung hier jemals stattgefunden hat, ist das Tonband, und auch wenn Sie diese Aufnahme nach Ihrem Gusto verändern würden, wäre sie der einzige Beleg. Die Vergangenheit existiert nur in Aufzeichnungen ihrer selbst, nicht wahr?

Es gibt keine Tatsachen." Dieses Zitat des amerikanischen Schriftstellers William S. Burroughs aus einem Gespräch mit dem Dichter und Filmemacher Gérard Malanga aus dem Jahr 1974 diente auch als Beginn einer Unterhaltung zwischen Dani Gal und dem Autor und Kunsthistoriker René Zechlin.

Und ganz sicher versinnbildlicht es das Wesentliche im Schaffen von Gal. Wie geht ein historisches oder politisches Ereignis ins persönliche oder *kollektive Gedächtnis* über? Das *kollektive Gedächtnis* – ein durch den Soziologen Maurice Halbwachs geprägter Begriff – speist sich aus zahlreichen Einflussquellen und sich ständig verändernden soziokulturellen Komponenten. Es ist schwierig, das Argument von Burroughs, dass es keine Tatsachen gäbe, zu entkräften. In einer komplexen menschlichen Umwelt werden Fakten instabil und verlieren jede Dauerhaftigkeit. Wenn man sich an sie erinnert, sie nachstellt oder über sie schreibt, verwandeln sie sich in Geschichten. In Dani Gals Film- und Installationsschaffen geht es um genau diese Themen – um die Wahrnehmung, Interpretation und Nachstellung von Geschichte. *Wie aus der Ferne* ist eine fiktionalisierte Video-Installation, basierend auf der fesselnden Beziehung zwischen dem Holocaust-Überlebenden und renommierten Nazi-Jäger Simon Wiesenthal und Albert Speer, dem Chefarchitekten und Rüstungsminister des Dritten Reiches. Speer war einer der wenigen hochrangigen Nazi-Funktionäre, die Verantwortung für ihre Taten übernahmen; während er eine zwanzigjährige Gefängnisstrafe verbüßte, zeigte er Reue angesichts der entsetzlichen Verbrechen des Regimes. Nach seiner Entlassung versuchte er, seinen Namen reinzuwaschen, und nahm deshalb 1974 Kontakt zu Wiesenthal auf. Es entwickelte sich eine umstrittene Beziehung, die auf einem Briefwechsel und gelegentlichen Treffen in Wien basierte. Diese ungewöhnliche Freundschaft ist der Ausgangspunkt für Gals filmische Inszenierung und für die Dialoge dieser introspektiven Arbeit. Der Wortlaut stammt aus dokumentarischem Material, aus Interviews und aus der Wiesenthal-Biografie *Simon Wiesenthal: The Life and Legends* (2010) des israelischen Historikers Tom Segev. In der ersten Szene des Films stehen Speer und Wiesenthal in der Werkstatt eines Modellbaumeisters namens Kuck. Er selbst ein Holocaust-Überlebender, konstruiert er gerade ein Modell des Konzentrationslagers Mauthausen für eine amerikanische Filmproduktionsgesellschaft. Er erklärt, dass die Verantwortlichen Eisenbahnschienen wollen und größere Türme, auch wenn diese in Wirklichkeit gar nicht existierten. Als Speer Kuck fragt, wie er an die Pläne des Lagers gekommen ist, antwortet dieser, dass er es aus dem Gedächtnis nachgebaut habe. Danach gehen Speer und Wiesenthal in ein Café, wo sie über ihre jeweiligen Bücher diskutieren. Mehrmals während des Films bittet Speer Wiesenthal, ihre Bekanntschaft nicht öffentlich zu machen – aus Angst vor den Folgen für Wiesenthal. In der dritten Szene befinden sich die beiden vor dem von Ludwig Wittgenstein entworfenen Haus: ein sauber aussehender weißer Bau, vor dem die zwei Männer auf eine beruhigende und fast schon meditative Weise ziellos umhergehen. Dann verlässt der Film Speer und Wiesenthal und geht zurück in Kucks Werkstatt, wo der Handwerker nunmehr ein Modell ebendieses Wittgenstein-Hauses baut. Den Film begleitet die Wiedergabe eines kurzen Textes des österreichischen Philosophen Ludwig Wittgenstein, in dem es um Gedächtnis und Bilder und deren Beziehung zum Diskurs über den jüdischen Genozid geht. Die vielschichtige, detaillierte Arbeit schwankt zwischen Fiktion und Fakt und lenkt die Aufmerksamkeit auf erfundene Nacherzählung und die verschiedenen Wege, die Erringung nehmen kann, um überhaupt zu wachsen. (EL)

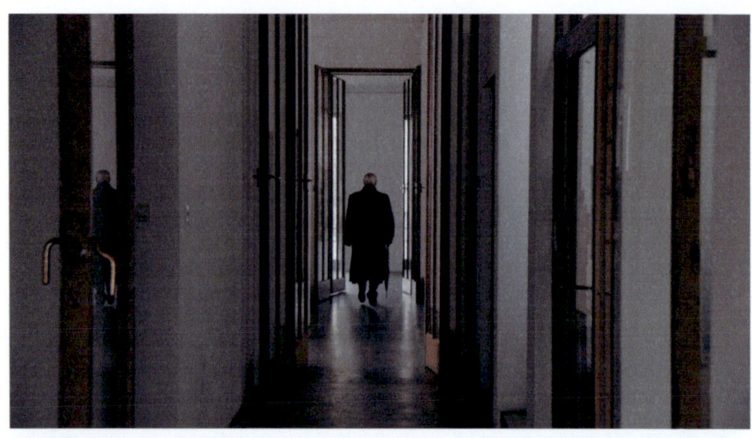

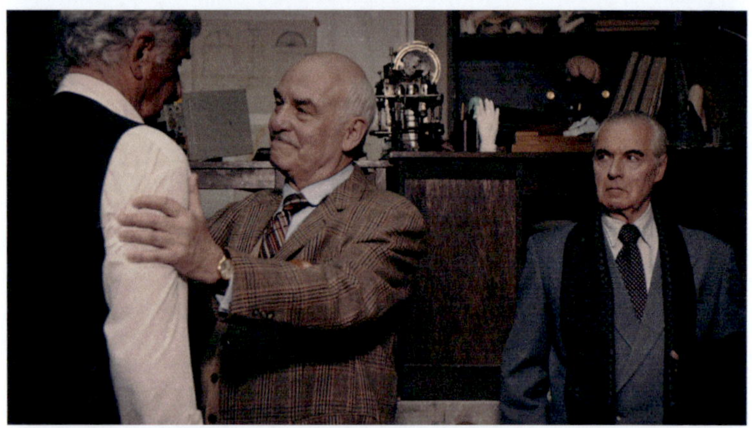

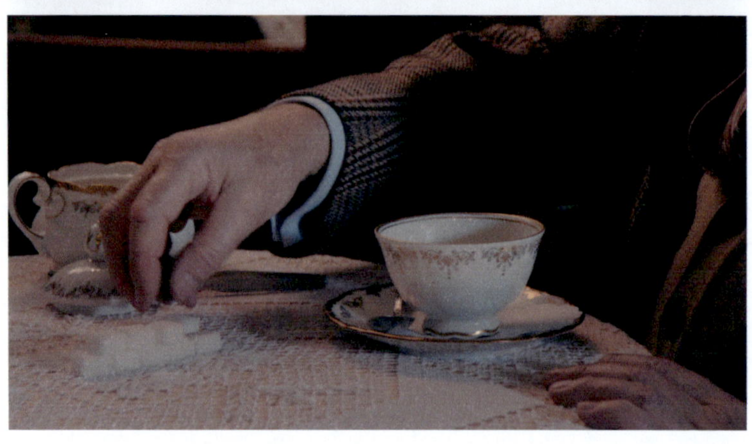

Dani Gal
As from Afar (Wie aus der Ferne), 2013.
HD video, 26 Min.
Courtesy the artist / der Künstler; Freymond-Guth Fine Arts,
Zürich / Zurich

Florian Hecker

Modulator

Florian Hecker's sound piece *Modulator* consists of an electro-acoustic composition played back through a directional loudspeaker. The acoustic signals sound atonal, segmented, and only in some sequences melodic. They unfold themselves both tonally and spatially and open up a form of perception not only in aural but also in physical, multimodal registers. The tonal spectrum of the artist's sound pieces ranges from a broad scale of synthetic sounds, which elude forms of traditional metaphoric descriptions. Hecker takes full advantage of the potential of acoustics by sequencing various auditory objects and letting them play out against each other. This modulation of perceptible sonic fluctuations and oscillations influences the listener's sensitivity to synthetic sound. So *Modulator* is more than just a challenge to, or even disruption of, the human system of perception. The noises and tones can in most cases not be attributed to familiar sounds and seem to follow a strange yet formal logic. In this way, the work uses sound performance to create a physical experience, one that remains otherwise invisible to the eye.
In another one of Hecker's works, *Modulator* served as an intermediate step: a libretto read aloud were transformed by manipulation of the speaking voices.[1] When the communication of text is disrupted, it is not only the voice of the speaker that is subjected to an alienating effect, but the information itself. The technical intervention (the modulation) can be explained in physical and corporeal terms but continues to affect the ability to communicate. If the sound installation *Modulator* determines what is and what is not language, it exposes communication practices along with influencing sensory perception. (ME)

*1975 in Augsburg. Lives / lebt in Wien / Vienna.

Florian Heckers Soundarbeit *Modulator* besteht aus einer elektroakustischen Komposition, die von einem Richtlautsprecher wiedergegeben wird. Atonal, gebrochen, nur in Segmenten melodisch klingen die akustischen Signale. Sie entfalten sich tonal wie räumlich und eröffnen eine Wahrnehmung nicht nur in akustischen, sondern auch physischen, multimodalen Volumina.

Das tonale Spektrum der Soundarbeit erreicht eine breite Skala synthetischer Sounds, die traditionelle Formen metaphorischer Beschreibung umgehen. Hecker reizt das akustische Vermögen aus, indem er verschiedene auditive Objekte aneinanderreiht und gegeneinander ausspielt. Diese Modulation von akustisch erkennbaren Schwingungen beeinflusst die menschliche Wahrnehmung von synthetischem Sound. *Modulator* ist deshalb mehr als nur eine Herausforderung oder gar Störung des menschlichen Sinnesapparates. Die Töne sind wenigen bekannten Klängen zuzuordnen und scheinen einer fremden, jedoch formalen Logik zu folgen. Die Arbeit vermittelt somit eine körperliche Erfahrung anhand einer akustischen Darstellung für das Auge unsichtbarer Signale.

In einem anderen Werk Heckers diente *Modulator* als Zwischenschritt: Ein von verschiedenen Sprechern vorgetragenes Libretto wurde durch die Abwandelung der Stimmen manipuliert.[1] Wenn die Übermittlung von Text durch die gesprochene Sprache gestört wird, verfremdet sich nicht nur die Stimme des Sprechenden, sondern auch die Information selbst. Der technische Eingriff (die Modulation) ist physikalisch und physisch erklärbar, wirkt sich jedoch weiter auf das Kommunikationsvermögen aus. Wenn die Soundinstallation *Modulator* bestimmt, was Sprache und was Nicht- Sprache ist, vermag sie nicht nur die sinnliche Wahrnehmung zu beeinflussen, sondern legt auch Praktiken der Kommunikation offen. (ME)

[1]100 Notizen – 100 Gedanken: Florian Hecker, Chimärisation, with an introduction by Chuz Martinez (Kassel: dOCUMENTA, 2012)

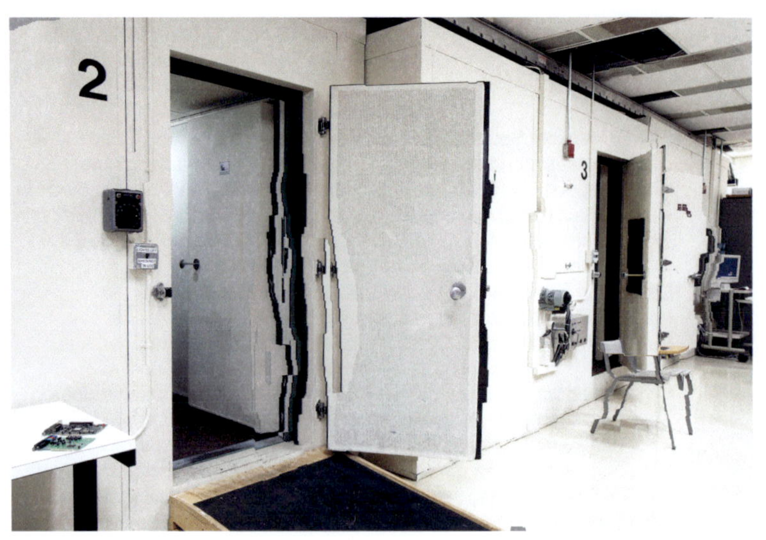

Florian Hecker
Chimerization, 2012
Processed production still / Bearbeitete Produktionsaufnahme
Original Photography / Originalfotografie © Jared Kuzia
Courtesy the artist / der Künstler; Sadie Coles HQ, London;
Galerie Neu, Berlin

Leon Kahane

19-1-2014
FRONTEX

"If there is now nothing but images, there is nothing other than the image. And if there is nothing other than the image, the very notion of the image becomes devoid of content." (Jacques Rancière)[1]

Images are now circulating in unprecedented quantities. But more important than the fact that they seem to overlay reality is the question of how we should deal with them, their circulation and the regime of visibility to which all else is subjected. What could constitute a politics of the image, and moreover what could constitute a political image? How can the aesthetic and its political analysis be correlated?

Leon Kahane's photographs and videos have a documentary look and they address themes that one could describe as political. However, they avoid the spectacular in favour of perspective that combines the work's theme with the conditions under which it becomes visible. And so, in the thirty-minute video *19-1-2014* (2014), which consists of just a single shot, we see female domestic workers in Hong Kong as they participate in a demonstration. The protestors wear headbands that express their demands; they hold up banners and wave to catch the camera's attention. Many of the women record themselves and the event with their smartphones or photograph the artist, who in turn is filming them with a camcorder. Because they stand on a downward-moving escalator, a constant stream of female demonstrators passes the static film camera. It is estimated that some 300,000 domestic workers are employed in Hong Kong, most of them women from Indonesia and the Philippines who have left behind their own families in their countries of origin. They live in a shadow economy but at the same time form the backbone of Hong Kong society. Without them, the neoliberal economy of one of the world's biggest trading powers would collapse. At their demonstration, they demand the rights that will give them the chance to be full participants in the country where they live. In this context, participation chiefly means visibility, and so the omnipresence of digital images makes helps to address socio-political deficits within processes of democratization. Kahane's *19-1-2014* provides a further visual representation of their struggle, which in turn produces visual testimonies of the protest that, in the uploading and downloading of global information flows, seek an audience and the right analysis to politically formulate the demonstrator's demands.

In contrast, Kahane's photo series *FRONTEX* (2009) dispenses with representation of those who are marginalized by the logic of a system and instead focuses on the mechanisms of the system itself. *FRONTEX* (2009) depicts offices devoid of any human presence at the Warsaw headquarters of Frontex (Agence européenne pour la gestion de la coopération opérationnelle aux frontières extérieures) the agency that coordinates external border security for the European Union. Frontex carries out risk analyses in real time, coordinates actions against migration flows, deploys border protection officials drawn from EU member states and produces evaluation reports. Mounted on large wooden boards, photographs lean against the walls in the exhibition space and evoke the physical appearance of an administrative office. The images show security cameras, diagrams on a flip chart, a row of flags of the EU member states, a conference room.

The cool and rational aesthetics of the photos stand in diametrical contrast to the media-disseminated images of streams of migrants that are often used to illustrate a dysfunctional immigration system. However, it is precisely the abstraction of these images that makes them a "resonating chamber" for the many different factors that trigger migration, flight and emigration, thus filling the crucial gap between administration and event. (VJM)

*1985 in Berlin. Lives / lebt in Berlin.

„Wenn es nur noch Bilder gibt, gibt es kein Anderes des Bildes mehr. Und wenn es das Andere des Bildes nicht mehr gibt, verliert der Begriff des Bildes selber seinen Inhalt, gibt es also kein Bild mehr." (Jacques Rancière)[1] Bilder zirkulieren in einer Menge wie nie zuvor. Wichtiger als die Tatsache, dass sie die Realität zu überdecken scheinen, ist jedoch die Frage nach dem Umgang mit ihnen, ihrer Zirkulation und dem Sichtbarkeitsregime, dem das Andere des Bildes unterworfen ist. Wie könnte eine Politik der Bilder aussehen oder aber ein politisches Bild? Wie können das Ästhetische und das Argumentative korrelieren? Leon Kahanes Fotografien und Videos sehen dokumentarisch aus und adressieren Themen, die man als politische bezeichnen könnte. Sie meiden jedoch das Spektakuläre zugunsten einer Betrachtungsweise, die sich neben dem Thema auch den Bedingungen von dessen Sichtbarwerdung widmet. So sehen wir in dem 30-minütigen, aus einer einzigen Einstellung bestehenden Video *19-1-2014* (2014) so genannte female domestic worker in Hong Kong, die an einer Demonstration teilnehmen. Die Protestierenden tragen Stirnbänder, auf denen ihre Forderungen stehen, halten Banner in die Höhe und winken Aufmerksamkeit suchend in die Kamera. Viele der Frauen nehmen sich und das Geschehen mit ihrem Smartphone auf oder aber fotografieren den Künstler, der sie wiederum mit einem Camcorder filmt. Da sie auf einer aufwärts führenden Rolltreppe stehen, zieht ein nicht abreißender Strom von Demonstrantinnen an der selbst statischen Filmkamera vorbei.
In Hong Kong arbeiten schätzungsweise 300.000 domestic worker, vor allem Frauen aus Indonesien und den Philippinen, die ihre eigenen Familien in der Heimat zurückgelassen haben. Sie leben in einer Schattenwirtschaft, bilden aber das Rückgrat der Gesellschaft. Ohne sie würde die neoliberale Ökonomie einer der größte globalen Handelsmächte kollabieren. Bei ihrer Demonstration fordern sie einen Status, der ihnen die Chance gesellschaftlicher Partizipation ermöglicht. Partizipation bedeutet in diesem Kontext primär Sichtbarkeit, und so ist auch die Omnipräsenz digitaler Bilder ein relevanter Beitrag zur Artikulation gesellschaftlich-politischer Defizite innerhalb von Demokratisierungsprozessen. *19-1-2014* liefert ein weiteres Bild der Demonstration, die ihrerseits visuelle Zeugnisse des Protests produziert, die im Up- und Download globaler Informationsverdichtung nach Adressaten und der richtigen, die Forderung politisch formulierenden Bildlegende suchen.
Kahanes Fotoserie *FRONTEX* (2009) hingegen verzichtet auf die Repräsentation jener Menschen, die von der Logik eines Systems ausgegrenzt werden und fokussiert stattdessen die Mechanismen des Systems. *FRONTEX* (2009) zeigt die menschenleeren Büros im Frontex Headquarter in Warschau: Überwachungskameras, Skizzen auf einem Flipchart, aufgereihte Flaggen von EU-Mitgliedstaaten, ein Besprechungsraum. Die auf großen Holzplatten aufgezogenen Fotografien lehnen im Raum und evozieren die physische Präsenz eines Verwaltungsbüros. Frontex (Agence européenne pour la gestion de la coopération opérationnelle aux frontières extérieures) ist eine Gemeinschaftsagentur der Europäischen Union und zuständig für die Zusammenarbeit der Mitgliedstaaten an den Außengrenzen der EU. Von ihrem polnischen Hauptquartier aus führt Frontex Risikoanalysen in Echtzeit durch, koordiniert Einsätze gegen Migrantenströme, entsendet Grenzschutzbeamte aus EU-Mitgliedstaaten und verfasst Evaluationsberichte.
Die unterkühlte Bildästhetik der Fotografien steht den medial vermittelten Bildern von Flüchtlingsströmen, die häufig für ein nicht funktionierendes Immigrationssystem vereinnahmt werden, diametral gegenüber. Gerade ihre Abstraktion macht sie jedoch zum Resonanzraum jener vielfältigen Faktoren, die Migration, Flucht und Auswanderung bewirken und füllt damit die entscheidende Leerstelle zwischen Administration und Ereignis. (VJM)

---

[1] Jacques Rancière, The Future of the Image, trans. Gregory Elliott (London: Verso, 2007), 8. / Jacques Rancière: Politik der Bilder, Berlin 2005, S. 8.1. /

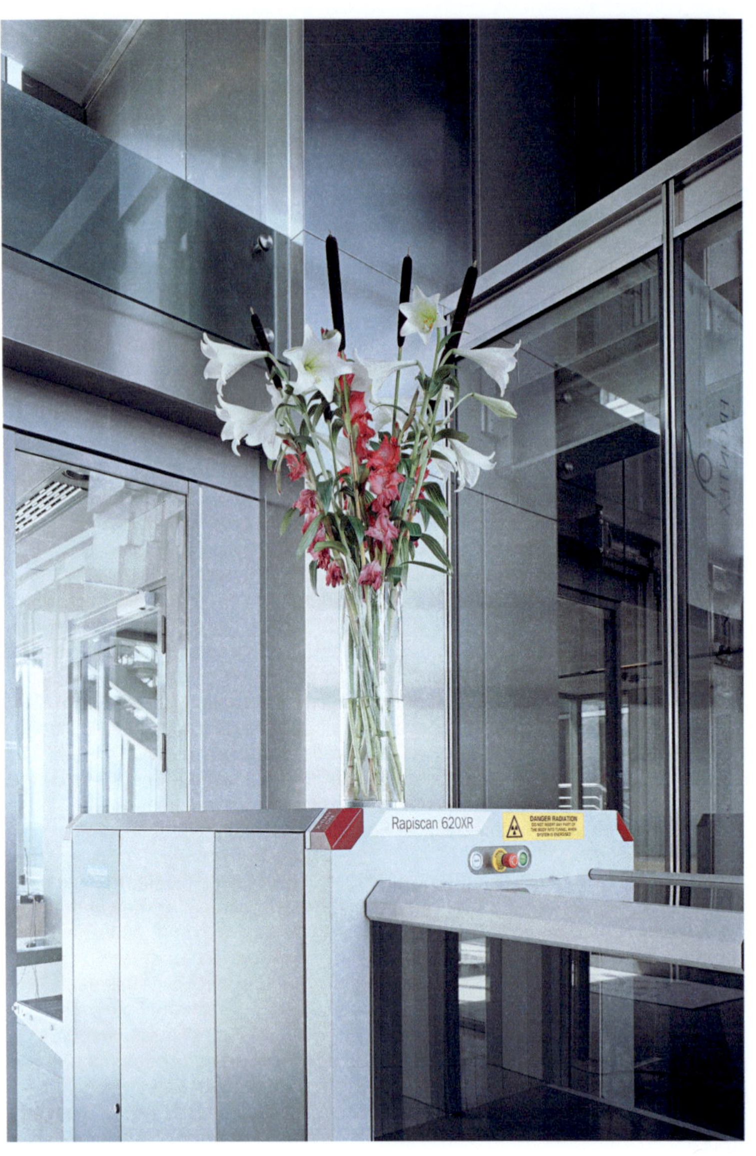
Rapiscan 620XR
DANGER RADIATION
DO NOT INSERT ANY PART OF
THE BODY INTO TUNNEL WHEN
SYSTEM IS ENERGISED

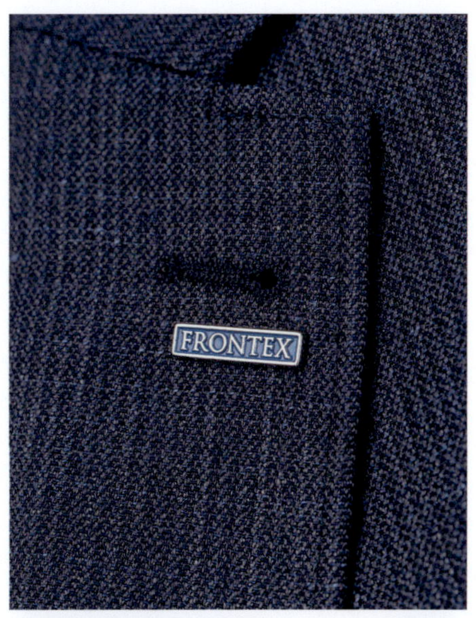

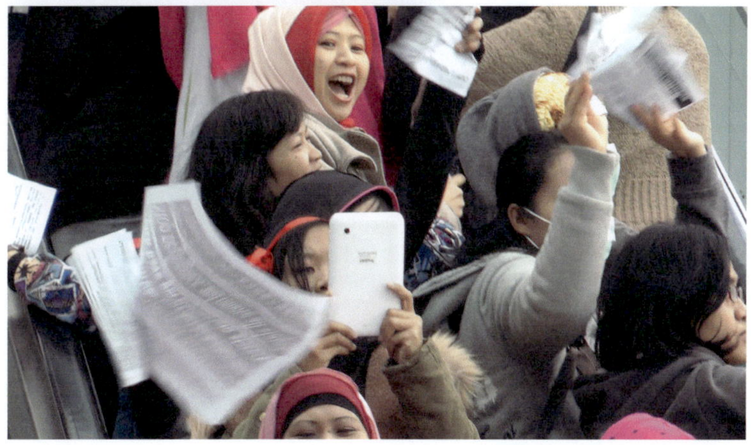

Leon Kahane
Jacket, from the series *FRONTEX*, Warsaw, 2009
Self adhesive print on pressboard / Print auf Spanplatte, 200 x 250 cm

19-1-2014, 2014
One-channel Full HD video, no sound, loop, 30'

<--   *Flowers*, from the series *FRONTEX*, Warsaw, 2009
Self adhesive print on pressboard / Print auf Spanplatte, 200 x 250 cm

Courtesy the artist / der Künstler

Daniel Keller

*Absolute Vitality Inc. Offshore Subsidiary
(Visit Beauty Atoll LTD, British Virgin Islands)
Absolute Vitality Inc. Offshore Subsidiary
(Bailouts Yet Vital LTD, Seychelles)
Absolute Vitality Inc. Offshore Subsidiary
(Blues Via Totality LTD, Belize)
Absolute Vitality Inc. Offshore Subsidiary
(Sea But Volatility LLC, Nevis)
Absolute Vitality Inc. Offshore Subsidiary
(To Value Stability LTD, Gambia)*

The term *prosumer imagineer* is a starting point to reflect on Daniel Keller's practice. Coined in the 1970's, the neologism *prosumer* is a contraction of *producer* and *consumer*. A kind of cultural modifier, the prosumer consumes material goods but also customizes them. Meanwhile, a search on the Internet reveals the word *Imagineer* to designate the engineers of the Walt Disney company. Together, the two terms inform the viewer of the subtle tongue-in-cheek approach that inflects Keller's practice.

The artist consciously develops his work by placing himself in the position of what is not so much an imaginary character, as it is an indictment of today's society of hysterical, thoughtless consumption. The central elements of Keller's practice are *Desire* and the schizophrenic cycles of mass production, consumption, and self destruction it activates. Falsely referred to as *economy*, those circles spin as fast, often according to marketing strategy. Technology facilitates this, despite predictable dramatic consequences on a human and environmental scale. Keller's critique of neo-liberal practices shapes itself into work that is densely layered and futuristic-looking. Using various outputs, such as installation, performance and digital formats, the artist highlights the sheer absurdity of capitalist corporate schemes and the empty marketing vernacular. The centrality and tyranny of technology in individual and collective life is also at stake. Works such as the *Fubu Captchas* (2013) question issues of labor and set up an imaginary countdown to the point of no return, at which point having outgrown itself with hyper-efficient machines the human race will no longer be needed. Where does it all stop?

Used specifically as a «special purpose vehicle» and a framework for an artistic project, *Absolute Vitality Inc.* is a legally registered company established in Wyoming, U.S.A. purchased by Keller and fellow artist Nic Kosmas in 2012. An invention of corporate multinationals to avoid taxes in their home countries, an offshore subsidiary is a business entity established in overseas tax havens. For *The Future of Memory*, printed shares of *Absolute Vitality Inc.'s* various subsidiaries are exhibited in hydrolock drybags, displaying the exotic names of the fiscally advantageous places they are based in, let it be Ghana or the Virgin Islands. Highlighting the triangular relationship of artist-gallery-collector, and the art market as a mechanism for commodity trading, shares in Absolute Vitality's offshore subsidiaries are to be officially acquired by collectors. These company shares offer a low risk, high reward legal investment into a conceptual art tool that according to the artist, guarantees customers (collectors) complete freedom from capricious art market trends. By buying a share, customers participate in the piece and add to the corporate sculpture, once again entering into the alienating loop of desire. (EL)

Der Ausdruck *prosumer imagineer* bildet den Ausgangspunkt der Reflexion über Daniel Kellers Schaffen. Der in den 1970-er Jahren geprägte Begriff ist eine Verschmelzung der Worte *producer* (= Produzent) und *consumer* (= Konsument). Als Modifikator konsumiert der *prosumer* materielle Güter und passt sich diese individuell an. Wenn man ihn ins Internet eingibt, bezeichnet der Begriff *imagineer* ausdrücklich die Konstrukteure und Ingenieure der Walt Disney Company und ihrer Attraktionen. Auch verdeutlicht er dem Betrachter die subtile Ironie, die in Kellers Sprache immer wieder eingestreut ist.

Er nimmt dabei selbst den Platz von etwas ein, was nicht so sehr eine imaginäre Figur ist, sondern der Inbegriff des hysterischen und blinden Konsumverhaltens von heute. Der Ausdruck spiegelt die zentralen Elemente in Kellers Schaffen unmittelbar wider: das Verlangen und die schizophrenen Zyklen der Massenproduktion, der Konsum und die Selbstzerstörung, die er auslöst. Diese fälschlicherweise als *Wirtschaft* bezeichneten Zyklen wiederholen sich so schnell und so häufig wie Marketingstrategen dies planen und wie die Technik es erlaubt – trotz vorhersehbarer dramatischer Konsequenzen im Hinblick auf Mensch und Umwelt. Kellers Kritik an den neoliberalen Praktiken nimmt in einer kompakten, futuristisch wirkenden Arbeit Gestalt an. Der Künstler nutzt verschiedene Ausdrucksmittel und beleuchtet in Installationen und Performances, aber auch auf digitaler Basis die pure Absurdität der kapitalistischen Firmensysteme und den sinnlosen Marketing-Jargon. Die herausragende Bedeutung und Tyrannei der Technik im individuellen und kollektiven Leben steht ebenfalls auf dem Spiel. Werke wie die *Fubu Captchas* (2013) befassen sich mit Fragen aus dem Bereich der Arbeit. Sie entwerfen einen Countdown bis zu jenem *point of no return*, an dem eine durch hypereffizente Maschinen sich selbst entwachsene Menschheit nicht mehr gebraucht wird. Wo hört das alles auf?

Als „Medium zur besonderen Verwendung" und als Rahmen für ein Kunstprojekt ist *Absolute Vitality Inc.* eine gesetzlich registrierte Firma in Wyoming (USA) und wurde 2012 von Keller und seinem Künstlerkollegen Nic Kosmas erworben. Eine Offshore-Niederlassung ist eine Geschäftsfiliale in einer Steueroase in Übersee, gern eröffnet von multinationalen Konzernen, die die Steuern in ihren eigenen Ländern umgehen wollen. Für die „Zukunft des Gedächtnisses" werden gedruckte Aktien der verschiedenen Niederlassungen von Absolute Vitality Inc. ausgestellt. Die exotischen Namen der steuerlich vorteilhaften Orte, an denen sich diese befinden, sind dabei sichtbar – Ghana zum Beispiel oder die Virgin Islands. Um die Dreiecksbeziehung zwischen Künstler, Galerie und Sammler sowie die Kunst als Handelsgut auf dem Kunstmarkt hervorzuheben, müssen die Aktien der Offshore-Niederlassungen von Absolute Vitality offiziell von den Sammlern erworben werden. Diese Aktien bieten ein niedriges Risiko, eine hohe Belohnung und ein legales Investment in ein Instrument der Konzeptkunst. Sie garantieren den Kunden (Sammlern) die vollkommene Freiheit von den unberechenbaren Trends auf dem Kunstmarkt. Durch den Kauf einer Aktie wirken die Kunden auch an dem Werk mit, tragen bei zu dieser gemeinschaftlichen Skulptur und treten einmal mehr in den entfremdenden Kreislauf des Verlangens ein. (EL)

*1986, Detroit. Lives / lebt in Berlin.
www.dnlklr.com

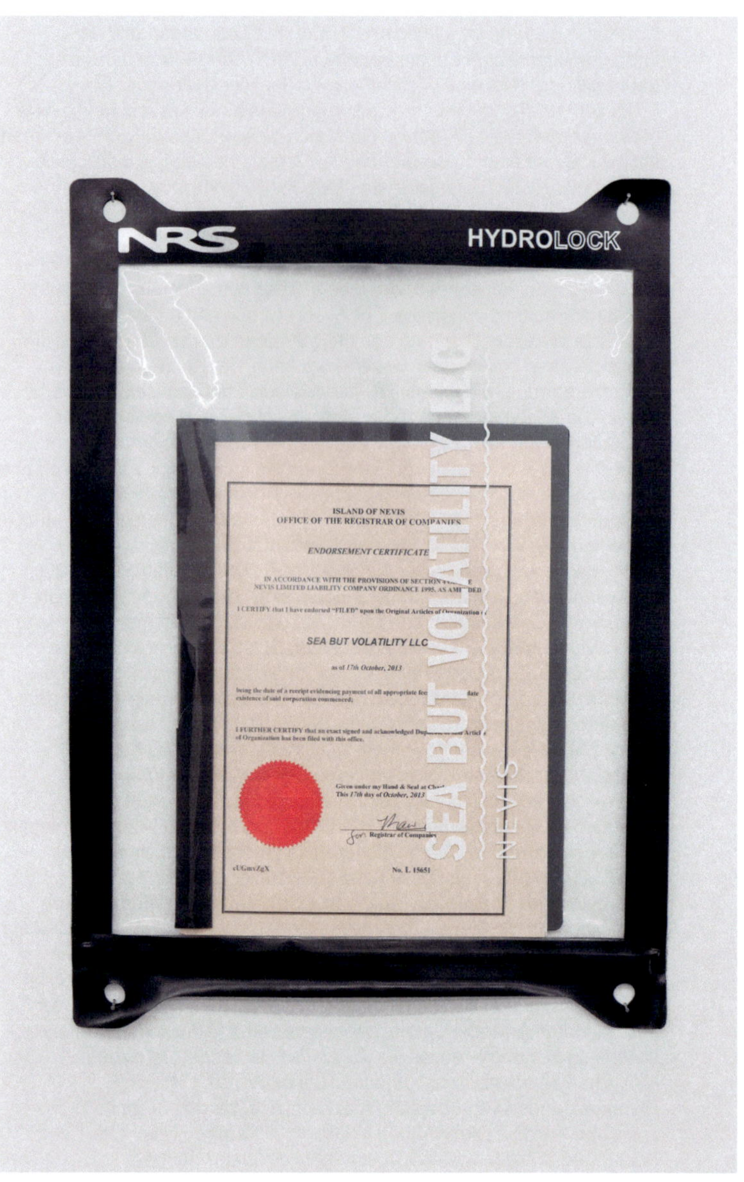
NRS
HYDROLOCK
ISLAND OF NEVIS
OFFICE OF THE REGISTRAR OF COMPANIES
ENDORSEMENT CERTIFICATE
IN ACCORDANCE WITH THE PROVISIONS OF SECTION
NEVIS LIMITED LIABILITY COMPANY ORDINANCE 1995, AS AMENDED
I CERTIFY that I have endorsed "FILED" upon the Original Articles of Organization
SEA BUT VOLATILITY LLC
as of 17th October, 2013
being the date of a receipt evidencing payment of all appropriate fees
existence of said corporation commenced;
I FURTHER CERTIFY that an exact signed and acknowledged Duplicate Original Articles
of Organization has been filed with this office.
Given under my Hand & Seal at Charlestown
This 17th day of October, 2013
Registrar of Companies
cUGmvZgX
No. L 15651
SEA BUT VOLATILITY LLC
NEVIS

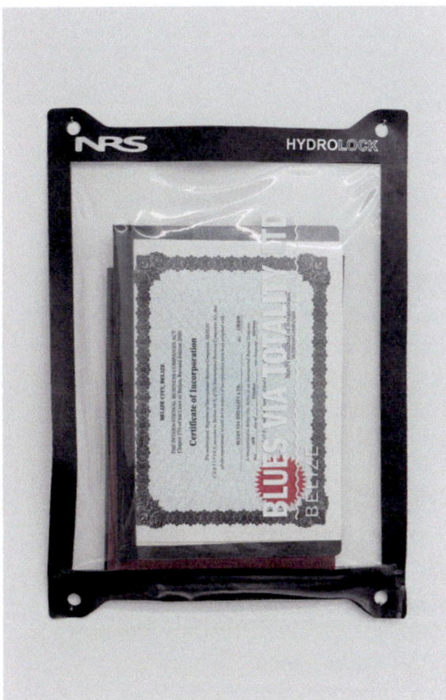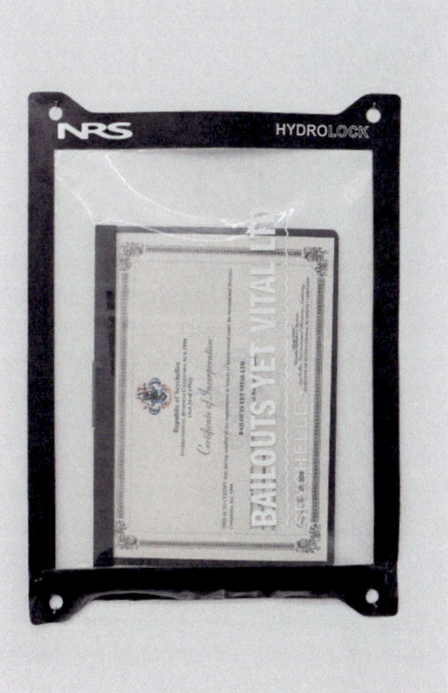

Daniel Keller
*Absolute Vitality Inc. Offshore Subsidiary (Blues Via Totality
LTD, Belize)*, 2013
*Absolute Vitality Inc. Offshore Subsidiary (Sea But Volatility
LLC, Nevis)*, 2013
Various materials / Verschiedene Materialien, 70 x 50 cm
Courtesy New Galerie, Paris; Kraupa-Tuskany Zeidler, Berlin

*Absolute Vitality Inc. Offshore Subsidiary (Bailouts Yet Vital
LTD, Seychelles)*, 2013
Various materials / Verchiedene Materialien, 70 x 50 cm
Courtesy Private Collection / Privatsammlung

Hanne Lippard

Postisms
Locus
Pandoras Cat
Beige

Hanne Lippard's medium is spoken language, in works made using sound, text and performance. Conversations, small-talk clichés, Internet postings, phrases used in an incendiary manner and everyday speech are all part of her practice. The artist uses repetition and rhythm as her main tools for recontextualizing words, sometimes causing Lippard's texts to drift into the incomprehensible. However, thanks to its basic material, her work retains the potential for recognition. Language thus becomes an instrument to create melodic refrains and the presentation of words in their aesthetic-poetic function. Lippard's investigation into speech as one of the most versatile instruments of human interaction imbues her work with a ritual character. The artist studies verbal interactions and produces communication sequences that are sometimes redundant. She confronts the listeners with countless associations and compositions that can be confusing and not resonant in semantic terms but instead possessing acoustic flow. Rules of syntax and grammar are not disregarded, but misunderstandings and phonetically similar words and syllables comprise a significant part of these acoustic works. One essential principle for understanding Lippard's practice is that a speaking person might hear him or herself in them, but in such a way that thoughts, speech and text form separate elements.

Postisms begins with an accentuation of the word "postmodernism" and varies this until it becomes unrecognizable. The prefix "post" is pushed to the point where it becomes meaningless. Without a concrete narrative thread, the piece generates a wealth of associations and provides a revealing entry point to Lippard's practice. The specific sound quality of her works is continued in *Locus*, where nonverbal, interpersonal communication is described without an active exchange between people actually taking place. Instead, the supposedly logical interaction is composed of filler words and inner rhymes. In an ironic manner, *Locus* describes a fracturing within the classical communication models of message, sender and receiver. Conversely, the confrontation between narrator and her environment by means of fragments of everyday speech is highlighted in *Pandoras Cat*, which resembles a logbook. The process of moving house, together with the organization of everyday urban life, is presented in a manner reminiscent of the blogs and digital communication of social media. In *Beige* she transforms speech sampling into a polemical treatise on the colour tone beige and its current connotation as a trivial lifestyle colour. Taking Starbucks as point of departure, the piece opens a debate about young women and social structures that is continued by Amalia Ulman. Both artists work with quotes, slogans and metaphors from text and image-based communication, the recombination of which aims to reflect an attempted self-positioning. (ME)

*1984. Lives / lebt in Berlin.
www.hannelippard.com

Hanne Lippards Medium ist die Sprache. In Ton, Text und Performance schreibt und spricht sie über das Sprechen. Dabei verwendet sie Kommentare, Versatzstücke aus Smalltalk, Posts aus dem Internet, inflationär gebrauchte Phrasen, Alltagssprache oder alltägliche Begebenheiten. Für die sorgfältige Platzierung und Re-Kontextualisierung der Wörter sind Wiederholung und Rhythmus maßgebliche Instrumente, die Lippards Texte hin und wieder ins Unverständliche abdriften lassen. Aufgrund des Ausgangsmaterials beinhalten ihre Arbeiten jedoch das Potenzial des Wiedererkennens. Sprache wird zum Instrument, das Melodie und Refrain entwickelt und die Wörter in ihrer ästhetisch-poetischen Funktion präsentiert.

Lippards Werke entwickeln rituellen Charakter, wenn das Sprechen als eines der grundlegenden, ältesten und vielgestaltigsten Instrumente menschlichen Miteinanders ausgelotet wird. Lippard studiert verbale Interaktionen und erarbeitet bisweilen redundante Kommunikationsabläufe, bei denen sie den Hörer mit zahllosen Assoziationen und verwirrenden, inhaltlich nicht stringenten, aber akustisch fließenden Kompositionen konfrontiert. Regeln von Syntax und Grammatik werden dabei nicht außer Kraft gesetzt, trotzdem haben Missverständnisse und phonetisch ähnliche Wörter und Silben einen maßgeblichen Einfluss auf die akustischen Werke. Dass eine sprechende Person sich selbst hört, Gedanken, Sprache und Text jedoch voneinander zu trennen sind, ist ausschlaggebend für das Verständnis von Lippards Arbeiten, die als Erzählerin selbst Performerin jedes ihrer Stücke ist.

Postisms beginnt mit einer Akzentuierung des Wortes „Postmodernism" und variiert dieses bis zur Unkenntlichkeit. Das Präfix „post" wird ins Nichtssagende gerückt. Ohne konkreten Erzählstrang weckt das Stück eine Vielzahl von Assoziationen und bietet einen charakteristischen Einstieg in Lippards Werk. Die spezifische Klangqualität ihrer Arbeiten setzt sich in *Locus* fort, wenn nonverbale zwischenmenschliche Kommunikation beschrieben wird, ohne dass ein aktiver Austausch zwischen Personen stattfindet. Die vermeintlich logische Beschreibung setzt sich vielmehr aus Füllworten und inneren Reimen zusammen. Ironisch wird in *Locus* ein Bruch des klassischen Kommunikationsmodells von Nachricht, Sender und Empfänger beschrieben. Die Auseinandersetzung zwischen Erzählerin und Umwelt anhand alltäglicher Sprachfetzen wiederum wird in *Pandoras Cat* deutlich, das einem Logbuch ähnelt. Ein privater Umzug sowie die Organisation von urbanem Leben und Alltag erinnern an Blogs und digitale Kommunikation über soziale Medien. In *Beige* verwandelt sich das Sprach-Sampling in eine polemische Abhandlung über den Farbton und seine aktuelle Konnotation als belanglose und universell einsetzbare Lifestyle-Farbe. Am Beispiel von Starbucks eröffnet das Stück eine Debatte über junge Frauen und soziale Strukturen, die Amalia Ulman fortführt. Beide Künstlerinnen arbeiten mit Zitaten, Slogans und Metaphern aus text- und bildbasierter Kommunikation, deren Rekombination der Versuch einer Selbstverortung in der Gegenwart spiegeln soll. (ME)

Hanne Lippard
Locus, 2012
Courtesy the artist / die Künstlerin

WITH YOUR BACK TO ME YOU STAND IN FRONT OF ME.

YOUR BACK TOWARDS WHAT MY BACK CAN SEE.

YOUR FRONT TOWARDS WHAT MY FRONT CAN SEE.

YOUR BACK IS BACK TO BACK WITH MY FRONT.

WE SHARE A DIFFERENT VIEW.

A DIFFERENT VIEW FROM THE OTHER.

YOU SEE WHAT YOU SEE.

I SEE WHAT I SEE.

OBSERVING DEMANDS A GREAT DEAL MORE THAN LOOKING, AND EVEN MORE THAN JUST NOTICING.

APPRECIATION OF WHAT IS BEING SEEN DEPENDS ON THE EXPERIENCE OF THE VIEWER.

WE SEE A CLOUD, BUT WE CAN NOT TOUCH IT.

WE ARE EQUALLY FAR AWAY FROM IT ALTHOUGH YOU ARE IN FRONT OF ME.

I TAKE ONE STEP FORWARD TOWARDS YOUR BACK.

YOUR BACK IS NOW CLOSER TO MY FRONT AND CONTINUING LIKE THIS THE TWO SIDES WILL EVENTUALLY MEET.

BACK TO FRONT.

THE QUESTION IS THEN IF YOU THEN WILL TURN AROUND AND YOUR BACK BACKWARDS WILL BE FRONT TO FRONT WITH ME.

THE QUESTION IS THEN IF I THEN WILL TURN AROUND, AND YOU WILL BE FRONT TO BACK WITH ME AGAIN.

NOW I WILL BE IN FRONT OF YOU. NOW WE WILL ONCE AGAIN BE SHARING A VIEW.

YOUR VIEW, MY VIEW, SAME VIEW BUT DIFFERENT.

OBSERVING DEMANDS ACCURACY FROM BOTH PARTS BUT THERE IS ALWAYS AN INDIVIDUAL ATTITUDE TOWARDS WHAT IS SEEN.

THERE IS ANOTHER CLOUD ON THIS SIDE OF THE SKY.

IT IS LARGER THAN THE ONE WHICH WE SAW WHEN YOUR BACK WAS TOWARDS WHAT MY BACK COULD NOT SEE.

STILL, ALTHOUGH WE HAVE CHANGED POSITIONS, IT IS EQUALLY FAR AWAY.

NEITHER OF US CAN TOUCH IT.

OUR HANDS ARE STILL TOO FAR AWAY OUR TWENTY FINGERS SLOPING DOWN THE SIDE OF OUR BODIES AT THE HEIGHT OF OUR HIPS.

RAIN STARTS TO FALL IN THE SAME LINE AS OUR HANDS.

THE CLOUD TOUCHES US AT EQUAL LENGTH.

WE ARE NOW BACK TO BACK TO BACK.

EQUALLY WET.

Deimantas Narkevičius

Books on Shelves and Without Letters

The films of Deimantas Narkevičius are about nothing less than exploring
the boundaries of filmic representation as a means to portray something
in the past. One important element in this work is the structural similarity
of image and memory as illustrations and imaginings that are permeated
by personal projections, and thus never completely realistic. And so while
Narkevičius' film is on the surface a documentary, it in fact addresses
other issues.

Books on Shelves and Without Letters shows the performance by the
band Without Letters in an antiquarian bookstore in Vilnius, amidst an
interior that looks to be thirty years old. The members of the audience
listen to the music, but also browse through the books. In other respects
too the atmosphere is relaxed, in keeping with the slightly retro-sounding
guitar band. However, the longer one watches the forty-minute video
installation, the more unclear it becomes whether this is the
documentation of a real performance by a real band or whether
everything in this film, from the location and the musicians to the
audience, have been cast by the artist for the production of the work.
In the double projection, the images alter along with the movements of
the two video cameras, changing size, and shifting forwards and
backwards. The uncut shots of the concert reproduce the perspective of
the people filming without ever being combined into a homogeneous
perspective. One senses the aesthetic of alternative music videos from
the 1980s; the fact that Narkevičius filmed with a Betacam SP, a common
video format in the 1980s, also contributes to the slightly nostalgic
impression, one that certainly has nothing of the digital precision of
today's videos. In contrast to image filters that transform digital images
into supposedly historic documents, in this work it is the material and
mechanical basis of the filmmaking itself that, through use of a different
technology and gradation, make the present seem like something far in
the past. The individual pages of the books that are read by the audience
and edited into the concert film also refer to a past that is reactivated in
the reading material. The band Without Letters is to a certain extent an
invention of Narkevičius himself: in 2010 he offered to film a video for a
group of guitar-playing guys from Lithuania. This resulted in the band's
first single, which is performed in the eponymous film *Ausgeträumt*
(Dream is Over). Since then Narkevičius has been promoting Without
Letters in the art scene and also provided a visual platform for them not
available in Lithuania elsewhere. In contrast to the possibilities provided
by social media for supplying a global community with all manner of
content, this form of collaboration harks back to the period in music
history when independent distribution channels arose that gave
musicians outside the mainstream of the entertainment industry the
chance to find their audience — a time when the category "alternative"
still implied a genuinely alternative potential. (VJM)

*1964 in Utena. Lives in Vilnius.

In den Filmen von Deimantas Narkevičius geht es um nichts weniger
als das Ausloten der Grenze der filmischen Repräsentation als
Wiedervergegenwärtigung von etwas Vergangenem. Auch die strukturelle
Ähnlichkeit von Bild und Erinnerung als von Projektionen durchzogene
und deshalb niemals ganz realistische Ab- und Einbildung spielt eine
wichtige Rolle in diesem Werk, das nur vordergründig dokumentarisch
angelegt ist.

Books on Shelves and Without Letters zeigt den Auftritt der Band Without
Letters in einer antiquarischen Buchhandlung in Vilnius, deren Interieur
aussieht wie vor dreißig Jahren. Das Publikum hört der Musik zu, blättert
aber auch immer wieder in den Büchern. Auch sonst herrscht eine
entspannte Atmosphäre, die zu der leicht retro klingenden Gitarrenband
passt. Je länger man die 40-minütige Videoinstallation betrachtet, desto
unklarer wird jedoch, ob es sich um eine Dokumentation eines realen
Auftritts einer realen Band handelt, oder ob alles an diesem Film von der
Location über die Musiker bis zum Publikum gecastet worden ist.
In der Doppelprojektion bewegen sich die Bilder mit der Bewegung
der beiden Videokameras, verändern ihre Größe, schieben sich nach
vorne und zurück. Die ungeschnittenen Konzertaufnahmen geben den
Blickpunkt der Filmenden wieder, ohne zu einer einzigen homogenen
Perspektive zusammengefasst zu werden. Es ist die Ästhetik alternativer
Musikvideos aus den 1980er Jahren, die man zu spüren meint, und
auch die Tatsache, dass Narkevičius mit Betacam SP gefilmt hat, einem
gängigen Videoformat der Achtziger, trägt zu dem leicht nostalgischen,
in jedem Fall nicht von der digitalen Präzision heutiger Videos geprägten
Eindruck bei. Im Gegensatz zu jenen farbverändernden Filtern, die
digitale Bilder in vermeintlich historische Aufnahmen verwandeln, ist es
die materielle wie mechanische Basis des Filmemachens an sich, die hier
über ihre andere Technik und Gradation die Gegenwart wie etwas weit
Zurückliegendes erscheinen lässt. Auch die vereinzelten Seiten aus den
Büchern, die das Publikum liest und die in den Konzertfilm einmontiert
sind, verweisen auf eine Vergangenheit, die sich in der Lektüre reaktiviert.
Die Band Without Letters ist zu gewissem Grad eine Erfindung von
Narkevičius selbst, der 2010 einer Gruppe Gitarre spielender Jungs aus
Litauen anbot, ein Video für sie zu drehen. Daraus entstand
die erste Single der Band, die in dem gleichnamigen Film *Ausgeträumt*
performt wird. Seitdem promotet Narkevičius Without Letters in der
Kunstszene und bietet ihr jene visuelle Plattform, die es in Litauen
nicht gibt. Im Gegensatz zu den Möglichkeiten sozialer Medien, einer
globalen Community beliebige Inhalte zur Verfügung zu stellen, knüpft
diese Form der Zusammenarbeit an jene Zeit der Musikgeschichte an,
als unabhängige Distributionskanäle aufkamen, die Musikern abseits
des Mainstream der Unterhaltungsindustrie die Möglichkeit gaben,
ihr Publikum zu finden, und die Kategorie des „Alternative" noch ein
tatsächlich alternatives Potenzial implizierte. (VJM)

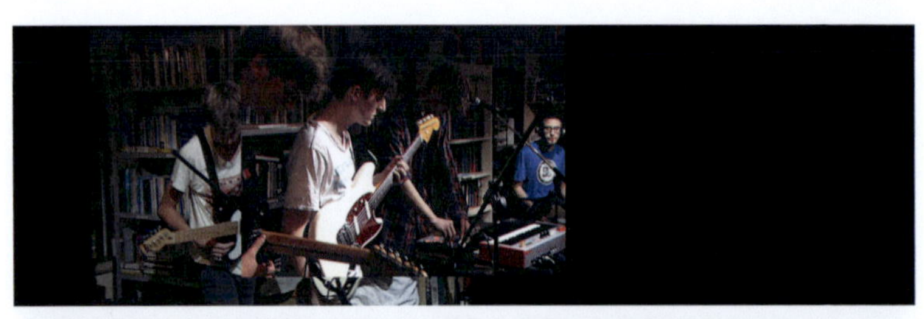

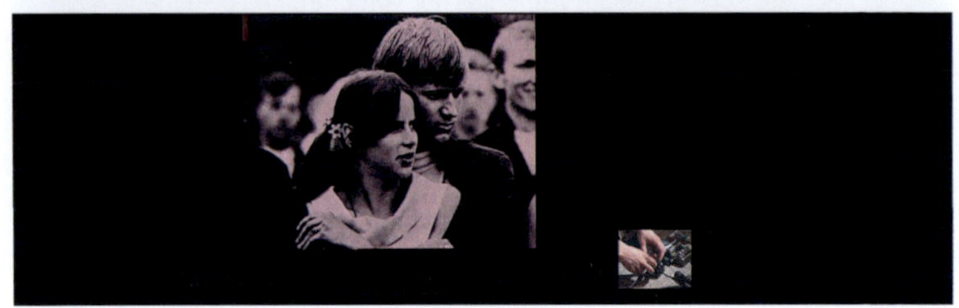

Deimantas Narkevičius
Books on Shelves and Without Letters, 2013
HD Video, 40 Min.
Courtesy the artist / der Künstler; Galerie Barbara Weiss, Berlin

Katja Novitskova

Dream Jobs 009
Special Bonds 011
Dissemination And Proliferation 012
Prediction Market 017
Dodoli de Luxe Grey

Fictitious stories of inanimate objects or images taking on a life of their own, turning into real characters in the back of their creator, have always been a staple of the entertainment world. Whether those stories are movies, cartoons, television series or books, dwelling within the genre of *family friendly* or science-fiction, it all seemed in the end an harmless *divertissement*. But what happens to images created in the digital world today? How do these elements now evolve, once removed from their initial context and distributed elsewhere? Can they also take a life of their own and a different meaning than the one originally intended? Articulating her practice around the mindboggling expansion of the Internet, Katja Novitskova explores the transformative potential of online images, which become evolutional bridges and allow for the artist to unfold thoughts on the impact of technology. Almost techno-animistic, her practice develops into a futuristic body of work based on installations, prints and sculptures, merging the digital with elements that are natural or historical in origin. In previous works, images of fauna and flora removed from the virtual world, become blown-up silhouettes mounted on aluminium panels. *Penguins (Approximation I, 2012), giraffes (Approximation II, 2012)* or *beluga whales (Approximations III, 2013)*. The slightly pixelated images cut out by the artist, are then pristinely displayed in a white gallery space, taking the shape of an immaculate and slightly terrifying digital bestiary.
Presented in *The Future of Memory*, four aluminium frames display digital prints of cute animals: a baby panda, a baby koala sitting on a laptop, a monkey and a porcupine mother and her newborn. The works continue Novitskova's core practice of creating embodiments for online images. The works are printed on papyrus to create both an opposition of two time periods (*ancient and contemporary*) and a superposition of different aspects of human communication (*writing and the computer*). The artist also evokes a frightening yet plausible aspect of the future in which, looking at these animals on papyrus the way an archaeologist looks at Egyptian hieroglyphs, people will try to imagine what those creatures were like in reality. If Novitskova is drawing parallels between the cycles of evolution and technology, *Dodoli de Luxe Grey* (2014), a completely new piece, represents therefore a natural evolution, expanding her artistic practice further into robotic aesthetics. The work presents the naked structure of an ordinary electric baby swing, which the artist has stripped of its material and decoration, revealing a scary-looking structure underneath. This machine can reproduce the heartbeat of the mother or sing children songs and thus posits a potential future for humanity of robot companionship (and more). This scenario, no longer simply an odd science fiction tale, would seem to make Novitskova ponder on this thought: Is this all just part of natural selection? (EL)

*1984 in Tallin. Lives / lebt in Amsterdam.
www.katjanovi.net

Erfundene Geschichten von unbelebten Objekten oder Bildern, die ein Eigenleben beginnen und sich hinter dem Rücken ihrer Schöpfer in echte Gestalten verwandeln, waren schon immer ein Haupterzeugnis der Unterhaltungswelt. Ob als Filme, Cartoons, Fernsehserien oder Bücher, angesiedelt im familienfreundlichen Entertainment oder im Science-Fiction-Bereich – letztlich ging es immer um harmlose Zerstreuung. Aber was passiert mit den Bildern, die heute in der digitalen Welt erschaffen werden? Wie entwickeln sich diese Elemente, wenn sie ihrem ursprünglichen Kontext einmal entnommen wurden und sich anderswo verbreitet haben? Können auch sie ein Eigenleben annehmen und eine andere Bedeutung als die ursprünglich beabsichtigte?

Katja Novitskova beschäftigt sich in ihrer Arbeit mit dem erstaunlichen Wachstum des Internets. Sie erforscht das transformative Potential von Online-Bildern, die zu Brücken der Entwicklung werden und es der Künstlerin ermöglichen, Gedanken über die Auswirkungen von Technik zu entwickeln. Sie erschafft futuristische Werke (Installationen, Drucke und Skulpturen), in denen digitale mit natürlichen oder ihrem Ursprung nach historischen Elementen in beinah techno-animistischer Weise verschmelzen. In früheren Arbeiten entstanden aus Bildern von Flora und Fauna, die der virtuellen Welt entnommen wurden, vergrößerte Silhouetten auf Aluminiumplatten. Die von der Künstlerin ausgeschnittenen, etwas pixeligen Bilder von Pinguinen (*Approximation I, 2012*), Giraffen (*Approximation II, 2012*) oder Belugawalen (*Approximation III, 2013*) waren unverfälscht in einem weißen Galerieraum zu sehen und wurden so zu einem makellosen und etwas furchteinflößenden Bestiarium.

In *The Future of Memory* werden in vier Aluminiumrahmen Digitalfotos von putzigen Tieren gezeigt: ein Baby-Panda, ein Baby-Koala, der auf einem Laptop sitzt, ein Affe und eine Stachelschweinmutter mit ihrem Neugeborenen. In diesen Arbeiten setzt sich Novitskovas wichtigste künstlerische Praxis fort, die darin besteht, Darstellungsformen für Online-Bilder zu erschaffen. Die Fotos sind auf Papyrus gedruckt – auf diese Weise entsteht sowohl ein Gegensatz zwischen zwei Zeitperioden (Altertum und Heute) als auch eine Überlagerung verschiedener Aspekte menschlicher Kommunikation (Schrift und Computer). Auch beschwört die Künstlerin eine beängstigende und doch plausible Zukunftsvision herauf: Wie die Archäologen die ägyptischen Hieroglyphen werden die Menschen der Zukunft diese Tiere auf Papyrus betrachten und versuchen sich vorzustellen, wie diese Kreaturen wohl in Wirklichkeit gewesen sind. Novitskova zieht Parallelen zwischen den Zyklen von Evolution und Technologie. Ihr neues Werk *Dodoli de Luxe Grey* (2014) stellt von daher eine natürliche Entwicklung dar und dehnt ihr künstlerisches Schaffen zugleich weiter in Richtung einer Roboter-Ästhetik aus. Die Arbeit zeigt die nackte Konstruktion einer üblichen elektrischen Babyschaukel. Die Künstlerin hat Material und Dekoration entfernt und enthüllt die unheimlich wirkende Struktur darunter. Die Maschine kann den Herzschlag der Mutter nachahmen oder Kinderlieder singen und postuliert auf diese Weise für die Menschheit eine mögliche Zukunft in Begleitung von Robotern (und mehr). Dieses Szenario, das nicht mehr nur eine skurrile Science-Fiction-Erzählung wäre, würde Novitskova möglicherweise über diesen Gedanken nachsinnen lassen: Ist dies alles nur Teil der natürlichen Auslese? (EL)

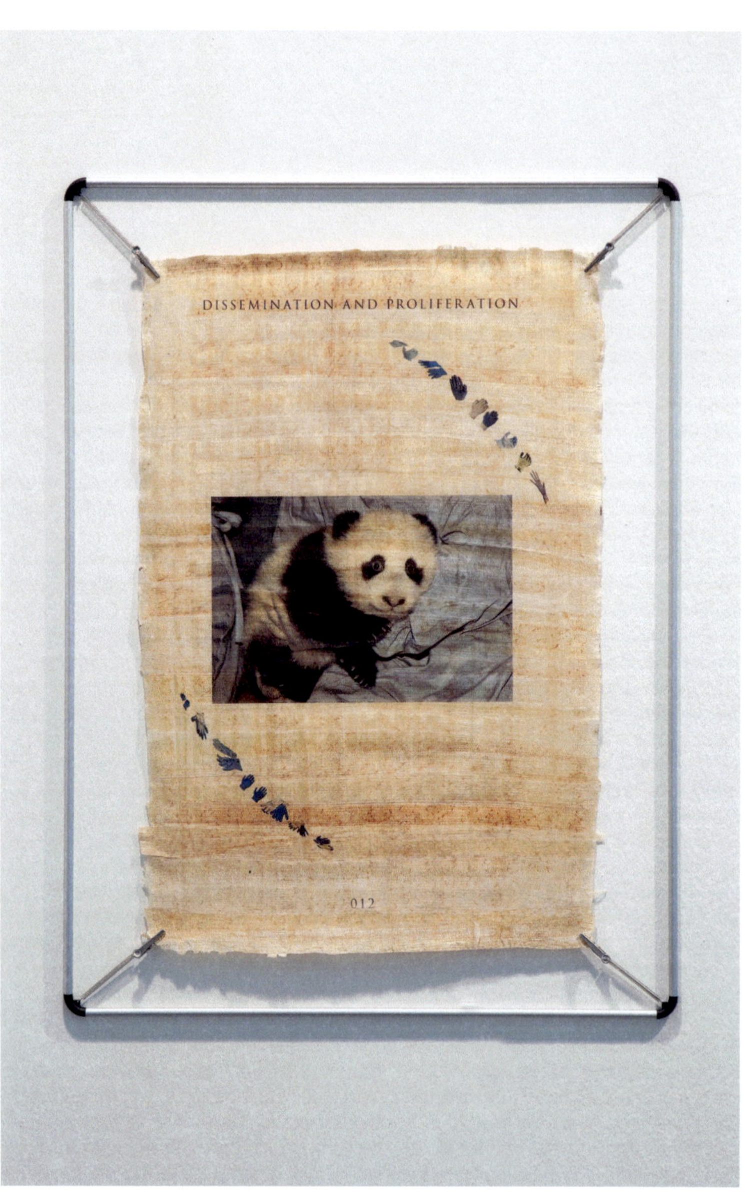
DISSEMINATION AND PROLIFERATION
012

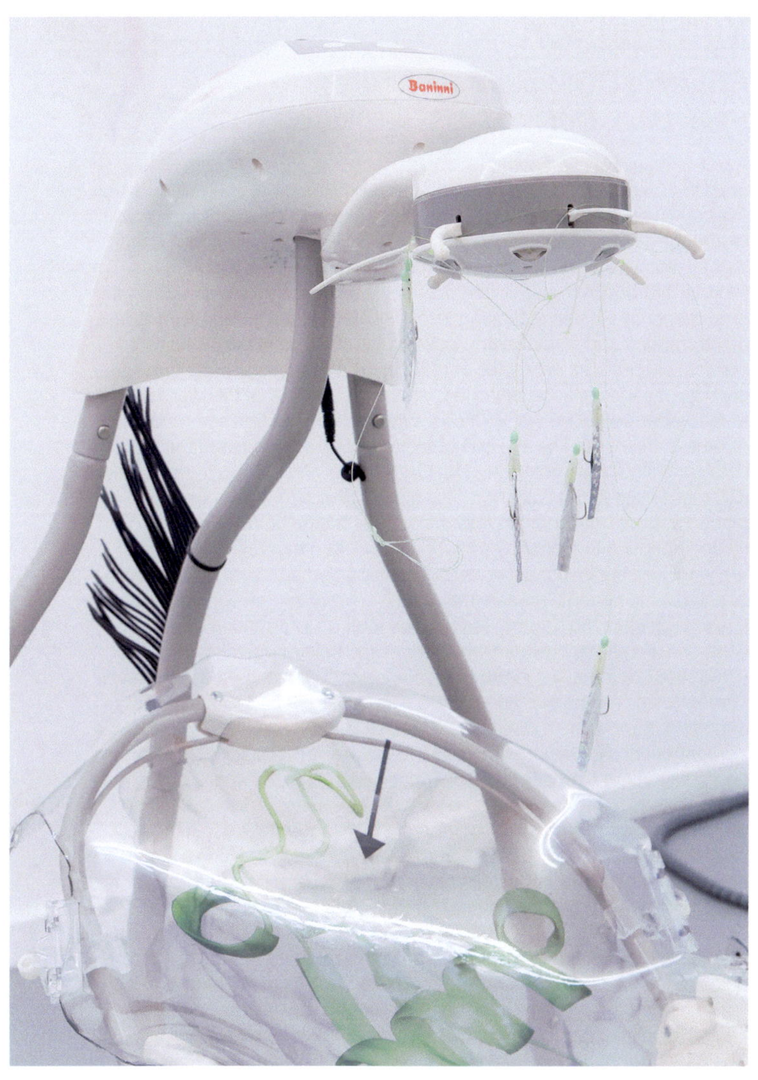

Katja Novitskova
Dodoli de Luxe Grey, 2014
Elektrische Babywiege / Electronic baby swing
110 x 100 x 90 cm

<—   *Dissemination And Proliferation 012*, 2013
Digital print on Papyrus, 72 x 55 cm
(Part of the Papyrus Series)

Courtesy the artist / die Künstlerin; Kraupa-Tuskany Zeidler, Berlin

Yuri Pattison

RELiable COMmunications
Pale_Blue_Dot

A pre-Internet Russian communication network, RELCOM was widely used to spread news of the event during the 1991 Soviet coup d'état when the putschists, looking to control the country and take down President Gorbachev, suppressed broadcast mediums. Partly bearing its name, Yuri Pattison's work *RELiable COMmunications* (2013) is a website archive that brings together that political event and the leak of US military documents by Chelsea Manning in 2010. Displayed in a frenetic mashup of information and visual layers, it draws parallels between those two political chapters as examples of resistance. The website's front page displays a series of subdirectories, which open tabs that then reveal links to time-stamped postings, IRC logs, email addresses and scanned photos of the coup. The site combines a collage of pictures of the Chelyabinsk Oblast meteorite, The Crypto Anarchist Manifesto and other IRC logs linked to the Gulf War. This disjunctive, non-linear narrative, placed into a virtual context, flattens out any notion of time, instead calling attention to digital surveillance and data control. The layering of the work and the incessant scrolling, clicking and tab opening necessary to access the material reflects the research process Pattison underwent. It also highlights the fragmented way we look up information online. Chat conversations between whistleblower Chelsea Manning (Bradass87) and hacker Adrian Lamo appear on the screen as the viewer scrolls down. The page color evolves into pixilated shades of blue-gray, exposing the texture of *Pale_Blue_Dot* (2013), both a separate work and a component of the website. An image taken at the request of astronomer and philosopher Carl Sagan by the spacecraft Voyager when leaving our solar system, it depicts earth as a pale blue pixel dot. When Manning declassified secret US war documents, it subsequently led to her arrest as she was turned in by Lamo, whom she had confessed to in a series of chat exchanges, now considered part of the Iran War and Afghan War logs, or classified military material Manning had made public. To try explaining the reasons for her actions and depict her troubled mindset, Manning had sent Lamo a link to an image of the Pale Blue Dot. After discovering the URL Manning sent was dead, Pattison decided to restore it and bought the domain to host a new work on the file path, directly linking it with the original historical record.

The name *Bahnhof* is the last element on the site, appearing at the bottom. It comes as a final question mark, if not as a possible answer, to the issues informing Pattison's work: the sometimes dangerous evolution of the Internet and the physical consequences of our online actions. Indeed, the Swedish independent Internet provider *Bahnhof* notoriously hosts The Pirate Bay and Wikileaks. (EL)

*1986 in Dublin. Lives / lebt in London.
www.yuripattison.com

Das russische Netzwerk RELCOM von 1990 (also aus der Zeit vor dem Internet) wurde während des sowjetischen Staatsstreichs im Jahr 1991 stark genutzt, denn bei dem Versuch, das Land unter ihre Kontrolle zu bringen und Präsident Gorbatschow abzusetzen, unterdrückten die Putschisten jede mediale Berichterstattung. Yuri Pattisons Arbeit *RELiable COMmunications* (2013), die zum Teil den Namen des Netzwerks trägt, ist ein Webarchiv zu diesem politischen Ereignis, aber auch zu der Weitergabe amerikanischer Militärdokumente durch Chelsea Manning im Jahr 2010. In einer wilden Mischung aus Informationen und visuellen Ebenen zieht die Arbeit Parallelen zwischen den beiden politischen Ereignissen und dem Widerstand als solchem. Die Website zeigt zunächst eine Reihe von Unterverzeichnissen, über die man zu Tabs und danach zu Links gelangt. Diese wiederum führen zu zeitlich markierten Postings, zu Chatprotokollen, E-Mail-Adressen und gescannten Fotos vom Staatsstreich. Eine Bildcollage zum Meteoriteneinschlag in der Oblast Tscheljabinsk trifft auf das Krypto-Anarchistische Manifest und weitere Chatprotokolle zum Golfkrieg. Diese aufgelöste, nicht-lineare Erzählung in einem virtuellen Kontext ebnet jeden Zeitbegriff ein und lenkt die Aufmerksamkeit stattdessen auf digitale Überwachung und Datenkontrolle. Die verschiedenen Schichten der Arbeit, das ständige Scrollen, Klicken und Öffnen neuer Seiten, um zum Material zu gelangen, spiegelt den Rechercheprozess wider, dem Pattison sich unterzogen hat. Auch beleuchtet das Werk die fragmentierte Art und Weise, in der wir online nach Informationen suchen.

Chatgespräche zwischen der Whistleblowerin Chelsea Manning (Bradass87) und dem Hacker Adrian Lamo erscheinen auf dem Bildschirm, wenn der Betrachter weiter herunter scrollt. Die Bildschirmfarbe ändert sich zu pixeligen Schattierungen von Blau-Grün nach Art des Fotos *Pale_Blue_Dot* (2013), das somit ein eigenes Werk und zugleich ein Teil der Website ist. Auf Bitten des Astronomen und Philosophen Carl Sagan wurde das Foto von der Raumsonde Voyager gemacht, als diese unser Sonnensystem verließ; es zeigt die Erde als blassblauen Pixel. Als Manning geheime US-Kriegsdokumente freigab, führte dies in der Folge zu ihrer Verhaftung, da sie von Lamo den Behörden gemeldet wurde. Sie hatte sich ihm gegenüber in mehreren Chats offenbart, die jetzt als die Kriegsprotokolle bekannt sind. Um die Gründe für ihre Taten versuchsweise zu erklären und ihren verwirrten Zustand zu verdeutlichen, hatte Manning den Link zu einer Abbildung des Pale_Blue_Dot an Lamo geschickt. Nachdem Pattison herausgefunden hatte, dass die Webadresse, die Manning verschickt hatte, nicht mehr existierte, entschied er sich, sie wiederherzustellen, und kaufte die Domain, um eine neue Arbeit auf dem Zielpfad zu hosten und sie direkt mit dem ursprünglichen historischen Inhalt zu verbinden.

Der Name *Bahnhof* erscheint als letztes Element ganz unten auf der Seite. Er ist ein letztes Fragezeichen oder die mögliche Antwort auf die Fragen, die Pattisons Arbeiten dauerhaft beeinflussen – nach der anomalen Entwicklung des Internets und den physischen Folgen unserer Online-Aktivitäten. Tatsächlich hostet der unabhängige schwedische Internetprovider *Bahnhof* bekanntermaßen auch The Pirate Bay und Wikileaks. (EL)

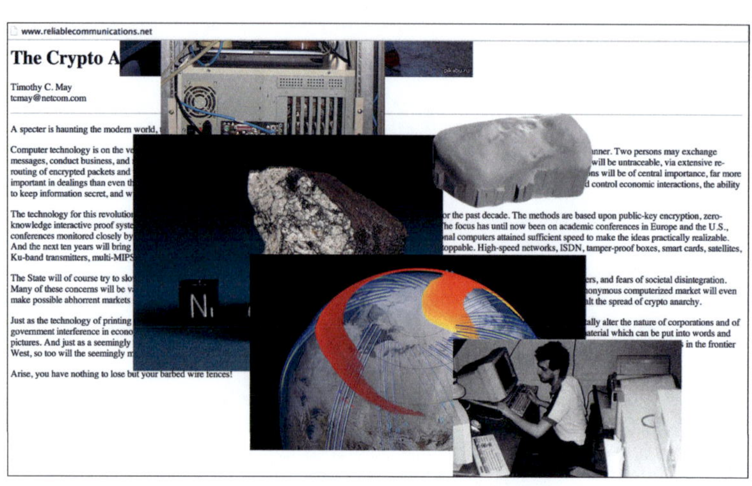

The Crypto A

Timothy C. May
tcmay@netcom.com

A specter is haunting the modern world,

Computer technology is on the ve... nner. Two persons may exchange
messages, conduct business, and ... will be untraceable, via extensive re-
routing of encrypted packets and ... ns will be of central importance, far more
important in dealings than even th... d control economic interactions, the ability
to keep information secret, and w...

The technology for this revolution ... or the past decade. The methods are based upon public-key encryption, zero-
knowledge interactive proof syste... he focus has until now been on academic conferences in Europe and the U.S.,
conferences monitored closely by ... nal computers attained sufficient speed to make the ideas practically realizable.
And the next ten years will bring ... oppable. High-speed networks, ISDN, tamper-proof boxes, smart cards, satellites,
Ku-band transmitters, multi-MIPS...

The State will of course try to slo... ers, and fears of societal disintegration.
Many of these concerns will be va... onymous computerized market will even
make possible abhorrent markets ... lt the spread of crypto anarchy.

Just as the technology of printing ... ally alter the nature of corporations and of
government interference in econo... aterial which can be put into words and
pictures. And just as a seemingly ... s in the frontier
West, so too will the seemingly m...

Arise, you have nothing to lose but your barbed wire fences!

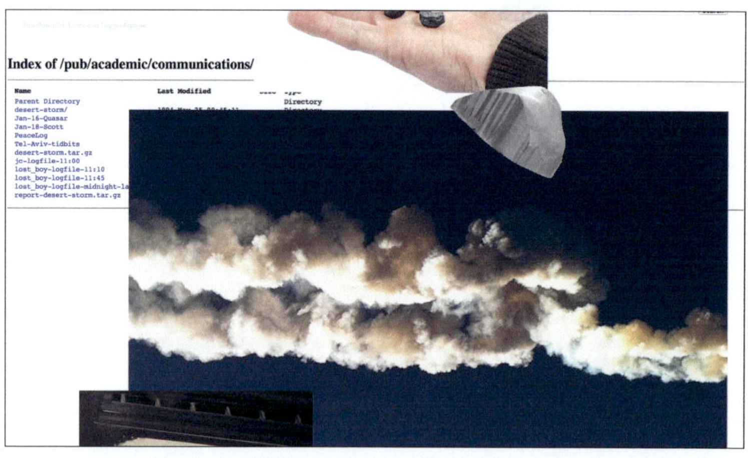

Index of /pub/academic/communications/

Name	Last Modified		Type
Parent Directory			Directory
desert-storm/	1994-Nov-25-08:45:11		Directory
Jan-16-Quasar			
Jan-18-Scott			
PeaceLog			
Tel-Aviv-tidbits			
desert-storm.tar.gz			
jc-logfile-11:00			
lost_boy-logfile-11:10			
lost_boy-logfile-11:45			
lost_boy-logfile-midnight-la			
report-desert-storm.tar.gz			

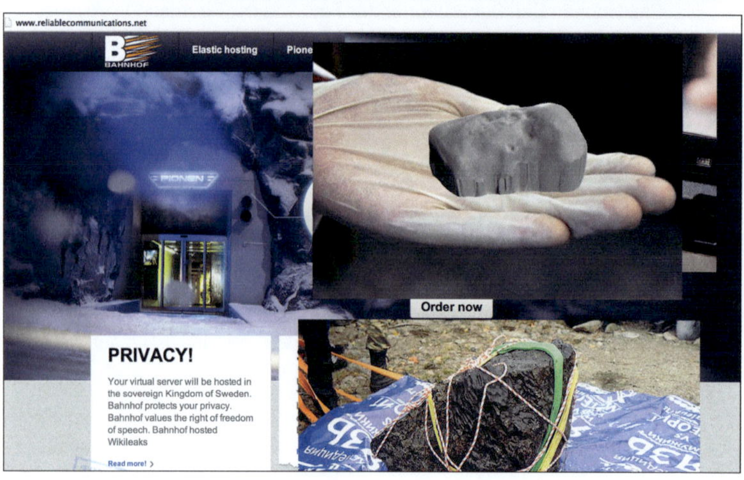

Yuri Pattison
Pale_Blue_Dot, (http://www.kxol.com.au/images/pale_blue_dot.jpg), 2013
Hyperlink & jpeg Image / c-type print,
dimensions variable / Hyperlink & jpeg
Bild / C-Print, Größe variabel

<--   *RELiable COMmunications (http://reliablecommunications.net),* 2013
webpage (html, css, javascript, php, jpeg, gif & png)
Commissioned by Legion TV, London; co-presented with the New
Museum, New York / Auftragswerk für Legion TV, London;
co-präsentiert mit New Museum, New York

Courtesy the artist / der Künstler

Jon Rafman

Mainsqueeze

Entirely made of footage found online while exploring the deep Internet, *Mainsqueeze* carries forward Rafman's exploration of the digital world in constructing contemporary alienation and isolation. This video discernibly departs from Rafman's previous works, which contain what the artist describes as a "flaneur-gaze", images somehow possessing a contemplative romantic quality to them. By comparison, the seedy corners of the dark web composing this narrative have none of that. Images of passed out drunk people, an angry salaryman and screenshots from Tumblr accounts alternate with sequences of a bodybuilder crushing a watermelon between his thighs, manga pornography and bondage games. A spinning washing machine, opening the first sequence, reappears as a motif throughout the work and physically embodies the endless loop of tension and release that structures the video. Feverishly accelerating the narrative, spinning faster and faster, it reaches the final point of explosion, epitomizing the self-destruction that comes with obsession. Tying together those frenetic sequences, a synthetic voice narrates, hovering between hateful, self-deprecating comments taken from various message boards, and modified quotes from literature baring an empty, almost meditative feeling.

The graphic scene of a young girl playing with a crawfish pet, then slowly crushing and killing it in front of the camera sums up the work's cycle of building frustration and the violent outlets of its release. In the background, the voice recounts a story of anger: "I'm a caregiver to my mother and it is not an easy job. I feel so frustrated at times. Don't get me wrong, I love my mother so much but sometimes, it just takes my breath away at what it takes to take care of her. She's 78 years old and diabetic and blind. Mum really does tries to be independent but it's so hard for her sometimes that it just makes me want to break down and cry. I also try to work outside of my home, I don't have to do this but I just need a break sometimes. All I hear about is her health problems and I don't have any answers for her. I would just once like someone to be concerned about me, ask me how my day went or how I feel. I know that it sounds selfish but I'm really not."

Mainsqueeze provides an overwhelming glimpse into places where hidden obsessions, identity issues and loneliness exist in abundance. Jon Rafman extracts fragments from this morass to assemble a hellish yet poetic mise en abyme of modern alienation. Like an anthropologist or a crime photographer, the artist observes and documents those online subcultures but never judges or makes a moral statement, instead leaving the viewer room to ponder their own sense of entrapment. To the question "Are we all doomed?" the last sequence of the video seems to answer with a detached "yes" and an ironic thumb in the air. Hundreds of people, floating together in a swimming pool, moving all along to a mechanically induced wave, resemble a human and voiceless web of flesh. (EL)

*1981, Montréal. Lives / lebt in Montréal.
www.jonrafman.com

Diese Arbeit ist ausschließlich aus Filmmaterial entstanden, das online auf Erkundungstouren durch die Tiefen des Internets gefunden wurde. Mit *Mainsqueeze* setzt Rafman seine Erforschung der digitalen Welt in einer Konstruktion zeitgenössischer Entfremdung und Isolation fort. Dieses Video unterscheidet sich von Rafmans früheren Arbeiten, die etwas enthalten, was der Künstler den „Flaneur-Blick" nennt: Bilder, die gewissermaßen eine kontemplative, romantische Qualität in sich tragen. Die miesen und dunklen Ecken des Internets, aus denen sich die Erzählung von *Mainsqueeze* speist, haben nichts davon an sich. Bilder von ohnmächtigen Betrunkenen, ein wütender Angestellter und Aufnahmen aus Tumblr Accounts alternieren mit Szenen, in denen ein Bodybuilder eine Wassermelone zwischen seinen Schenkeln zerdrückt, mit Manga-Pornografie und Fesselspielen. Eine schleudernde Waschmaschine, die die erste Szene eröffnet, taucht als Motiv immer wieder auf und verkörpert die Endlosschleife virtueller Spannung und Erlösung, die das Video strukturiert. Fieberhaft beschleunigt sich die Erzählung, dreht sich schneller und schneller, erreicht den Endpunkt der Explosion und versinnbildlicht damit die Selbstzerstörung, die mit Besessenheit einhergeht. Ein synthetischer Erzähler verbindet diese infernalischen Sequenzen. Er wechselt dabei zwischen hasserfüllten, herabwürdigenden Kommentaren aus verschiedenen Message Boards und nichtssagenden, beinah meditativen, veränderten Literaturzitaten. Die drastische Szene, in der ein junges Mädchen mit einem Krebs spielt, ihn dann zerdrückt und vor der Kamera tötet, fasst den Zyklus aus Frustration und befreiendem Gewaltakt zusammen. Im Hintergrund erzählt die Stimme eine Geschichte über Wut: „Ich pflege meine Mutter, und das ist keine einfache Arbeit. Ich bin manchmal so frustriert. Verstehen Sie mich nicht falsch, ich liebe meine Mutter sehr, aber manchmal nimmt es mir den Atem, so anstrengend ist es, sie zu pflegen. Sie ist 78 Jahre alt, hat Diabetes und ist blind. Sie versucht wirklich, unabhängig zu bleiben, aber manchmal ist es so schwer für sie, dass ich weinend zusammenbrechen möchte. Ich versuche auch, außer Haus zu arbeiten, ich muss das nicht, aber ich brauche ab und zu eine Pause. Alles, wovon ich höre, sind ihre gesundheitlichen Probleme, und ich habe keine Antworten für sie. Ich hätte nur gern einmal, dass jemand um mich besorgt ist, mich fragt, wie mein Tag war oder wie ich mich fühle. Ich weiß, das klingt selbstsüchtig, aber das bin ich wirklich nicht."
Mainsqueeze bietet einen überwältigenden Blick auf Orte, an denen versteckte Obsessionen, Identitätsfragen und Einsamkeit reichlich vorhanden sind. Jon Rafman extrahiert Fragmente davon und versammelt sie zu einer höllischen, aber poetischen Mise en abyme moderner Entfremdung. Wie ein Anthropologe oder ein Kriminalfotograf beobachtet und dokumentiert der Künstler diese Online-Subkulturen, urteilt aber nie oder trifft eine moralische Aussage. Stattdessen lässt er dem Zuschauer Raum, über sein eigenes Gefühl, in der Falle zu sitzen, nachzudenken. Auf die Frage „Sind wir alle verdammt?" antwortet die letzte Sequenz des Videos mit einem gelösten „Ja" und einem ironischen Daumen nach oben. Hunderte von Leuten, die zusammen in einem Swimmingpool treiben und sich im Rhythmus einer mechanisch erzeugten Welle bewegen sehen aus wie ein Netz aus menschlichen Leibern ohne Stimme. (EL)

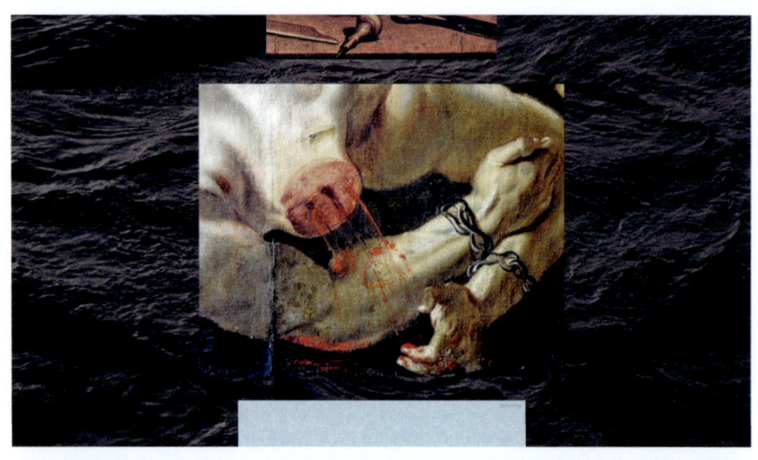

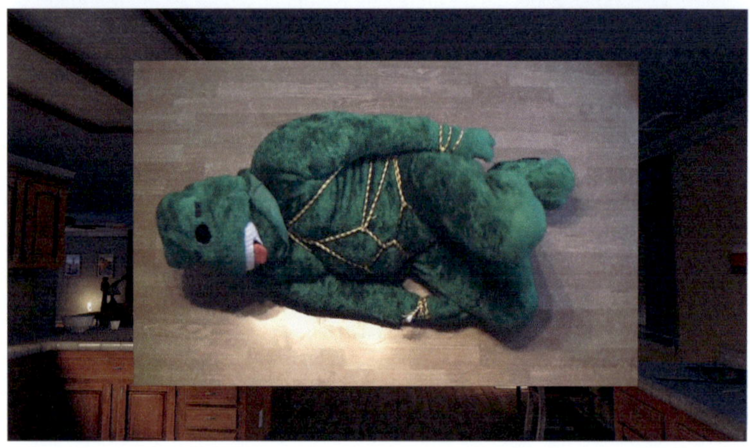

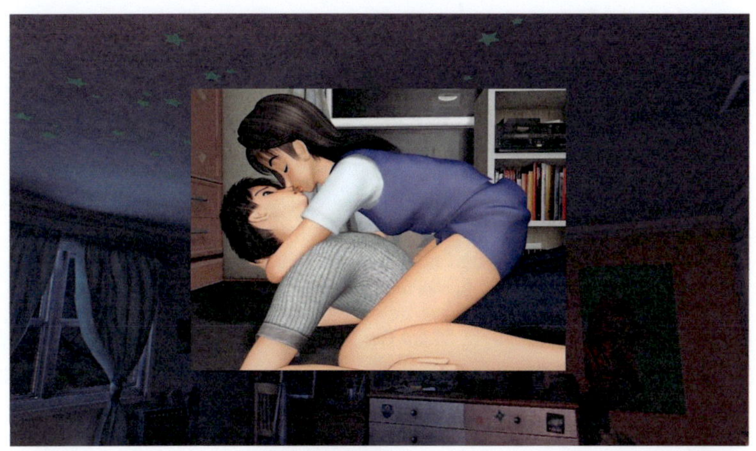

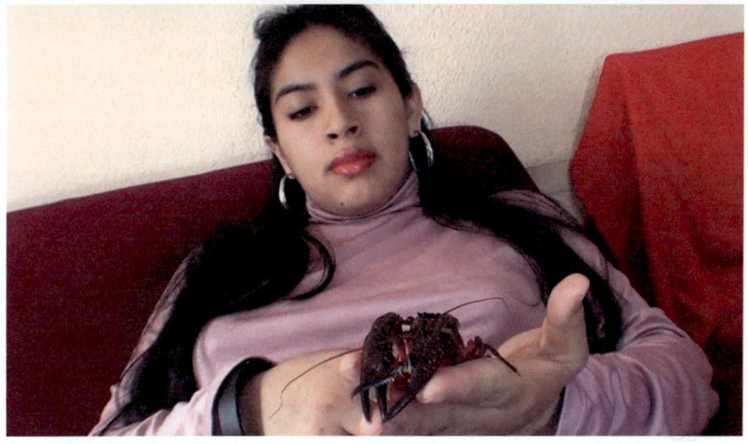

Jon Rafman
Mainsqueeze, 2014
HD Video, 7:23 Min.
Courtesy the artist / der Künstler

Adriana Ramić

*The Return Trip is Never the Same (After
Trajets de Fourmis et Retours au Nid,
M. Victor Cornetz, 1910)*

Adriana Ramić's *The Return Trip is Never the Same* arose from an intensive
process of research: Ramić studied interdisciplinary data processing and liberal
arts in California and is interested in animals. Prompted by a stay at the Google
Cultural Institute in Paris in 2014, she met with etymologists and beetle specialists
and consequently acquired the book Trajets de fourmis et retours au nid (Ant
Paths and Return to the Nest) by Victor Cornetz, written in 1910. The French
researcher was interested in the eusociality of ants and studied their paths, which
he recorded in sketches contained in the aforementioned book. After Ramić had
also read scientific publications by researchers at the Netherlands Institute of
Ecology and writings by the media theorist Jussi Parikka on the communication
strategies of insects[1], she concentrated these sources of inspiration into *The
Return Trip is Never the Same*. Each page of this eighty-two page e-book consists
of three levels. The topmost colour motif corresponds to the ant paths
documented by Cornetz, and can be traced in glowing colour using a finger. On
the first level, a text section is mostly covered and contains combinations of letters
that can hardly be discerned. It was created when the artist traced the insect paths
over a Swype keyboard ((2 - footnote)), which autocorrected the words into a
semi-discernible text in various languages. The second text section is a translation
created with Google's automatic service. Within the text are words that had
previously been frequently used in the artist's computer and thus constitutes a
document of her own digital traces.
Recent scientific insights into the communication strategies of ants and other
insects show that these animals leave traces in the natural environment. These
can be read by members of the same species and are stored by means of plants
to be passed on to other species and generations.[3] Chemical traces in the soil and
in plants thus give information to other living creatures about optimal or deficient
living environments. The organization of ant colonies into communities is based on
a form of internal communication using pheromones. This not only enables
communication about paths to food and to the colony, but also creates and
preserves internal structures. Ant communities function on principles of internal
intelligence based on decentrally-organized mechanisms. These forms of
behaviour, also known as stigmergy, take place in a manner equivalent to the
collective treatment of data volumes in the Internet. Here the organism puts trust
in the behaviour of the network's participants and adjusts to these in a flexible way.
Sharing processes, peer-to-peer exchange and anonymous communication
between many parties is conducted in a similar manner in the World Wide Web.
The individual participant does not play a specific role, but instead contributes to
the intelligence of the group and in doing so influences the process and its result.
The system remains alive, one might say, through the constant participation of its
users. Thanks to such strategies, databanks are able to respond to the user and to
modify themselves. This form of self-organization is based on reciprocal
awareness and leads to complex structures that hinge on the border between
remembering and forgetting. (ME)

*1989 in Chicago. Lives / lebt in New York.
www.adrianaramic.com

Der Entstehungsprozess von Adriana Ramićs *The Return Trip is Never the Same* ist Resultat einer intensiven Recherche: Ramić studierte Interdisziplinäre Elektronische Datenverarbeitung und freie Kunst in Kalifornien und interessiert sich für Tiere. Anlässlich eines Aufenthalts im Google Kulturinstitut in Paris 2014 gelangte sie über Treffen mit Insektenforschern und Käferspezialisten in den Besitz des Buches Trajets de fourmis et retours au nid (Ameisenwege und Rückkehr zum Nest) von Victor Cornetz aus dem Jahr 1910. Der französische Forscher beschäftigte mit der Eusozialität von Ameisen und studierte deren Pfade, die er in Skizzen festhielt, die in besagtem Buch versammelt sind. Nachdem Ramić sich zusätzlich mit wissenschaftlichen Publikationen von Forschern des Niederländischen Instituts für Ökologie und Schriften des Medientheoretikers Jussi Parikka zu Kommunkationsstrategien von Insekten[1] vertraut gemacht hatte, verdichtete sie diese Impulse in *The Return Trip is Never the Same*. Die Seiten des 82-seitigen E-Books bestehen jeweils aus drei Ebenen. Das oberste farbige Motiv entspricht den von Cornetz dokumentierten Ameisenpfaden, die mit einem Finger und leuchtender Farbe nachgezeichnet sein könnten. Darunter ist jeweils ein nahezu zusammenhangloser Text zu erkennen. Ein zweiter Textkörper in der hinteren Ebene wird größtenteils überdeckt und enthält kaum entzifferbare Buchstabenkombinationen. Er entstand, indem die Künstlerin die Insektenpfade über eine Swype-Tastatur[2] fahren ließ. Ein Autokorrekturprogramm erstellte anschließend den zweiten lesbaren Text in unterschiedlichen Sprachen. Dieser wiederum enthält Wörter, die im Computer der Künstlerin zuvor häufig benutzt worden waren und damit eine Dokumentation ihrer eigenen digitalen Spuren.

Neuere wissenschaftliche Erkenntnisse über die Kommunikationsstrategien von Ameisen und anderen Insekten zeigen, dass diese Tiere Spuren in der Natur hinterlassen, die für Artgenossen lesbar sind und über das Pflanzenreich gespeichert und an andere Arten und Generationen weitergegeben werden.[3] Chemische Spuren im Erdboden und an Pflanzen übermitteln somit anderen Lebewesen Hinweise zu optimalen oder mangelhaften Lebensräumen. Die Organisation von Ameisenvölkern in Staaten basiert auf einer internen Verständigung über Pheromone. So werden nicht nur Wege zu Nahrung und zur Kolonie vermittelt, sondern auch interne Strukturen geschaffen und bewahrt. Ameisenstaaten funktionieren nach Prinzipien kollektiver Intelligenz, anhand von dezentral organisierten Mechanismen. Diese Handlungsweise, auch als Stigmergie bezeichnet, verläuft äquivalent zum kollektiven Umgang mit Datenmengen im Internet. Der Organismus vertraut dabei auf das Verhalten seiner Teilnehmer und richtet sich flexibel an ihnen aus. Sharing-Prozesse, Peer-to-Peer-Austausch und eine anonyme Kommunikation Vieler verlaufen im World Wide Web nach ähnlichen Prinzipien. Der einzelne Teilnehmer nimmt keine spezifische Rolle ein, sondern trägt zur Intelligenz der Gruppe bei und beeinflusst so den Prozess und das Ergebnis. Das System hält sich sozusagen über die stetige Beteiligung seiner Nutzer am Leben. Datenbanken sind aufgrund solcher Strategien in der Lage, auf den Benutzer zu reagieren und sich zu modifizieren. Diese Form der Selbstorganisation basiert auf wechselseitigem Bewusstsein und führt zu komplexen Strukturen im Grenzbereich zwischen Speichern und Vergessen. (ME)

[1] Jussi Parikka, Insect Media. An Archaeology of Animals and Technology, (Minneapolis: University of Minnesota Press, 2010)
[2] This is a keyboard for data entry on touchscreens, in which the finger does not need to physically touch the screen.
[3] Olga Kostenko, et al: "Legacy effects of aboveground–belowground interactions," Ecology Letters no.15/2012 (August 2012) 813–821.

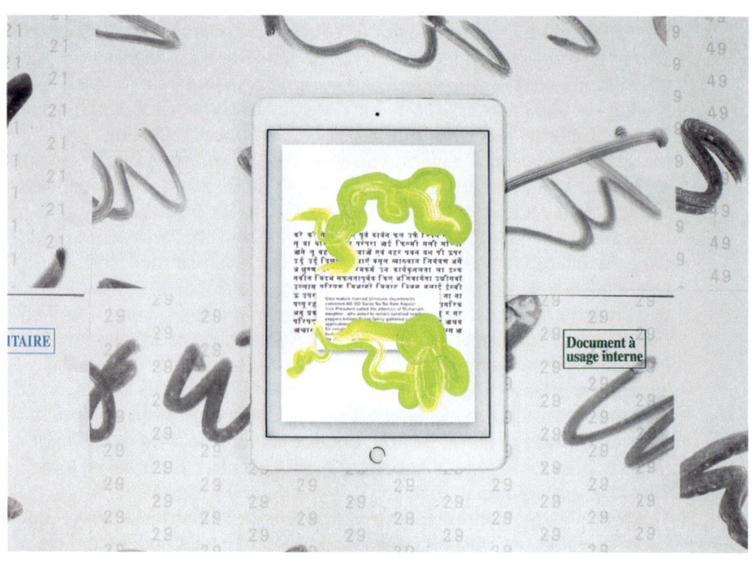

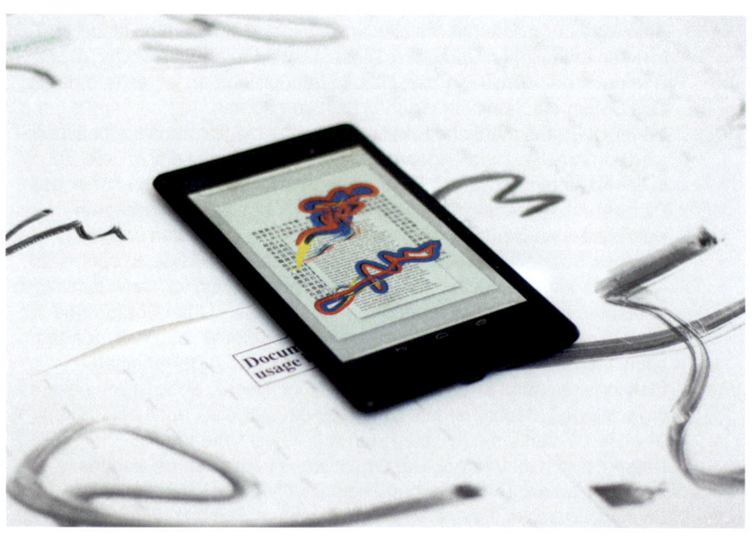

Adriana Ramić
*The Return Trip is Never the Same (after Trajets de Fourmis
et Retours au Nid by Victor Cornetz)*, 2014
E-Book, 82 pages / Seiten
Installation view with / Ausstellungsansicht mit Nobody
Messages from Nautilus
PDF, tablet, ink, A3 paper / PDF, tablette,tinte,A3 Papier
Courtesy the artist / die Künstlerin
Images / Bilder: Derek Paul Boyle

Antoine Renard

1110533_Capture Name (Bob)
2553418_Why do cats sleep on the newspaper (何故、猫は新聞に乗るのか?)

The sculptures of Antoine Renard are hard to decode and at the same time can be read intuitively. When does an abstract form become recognisable as a cat? The moment is in the eye of the beholder. But once the motif has been discerned it triggers a chain of intuitive associations that, for those familiar with the Internet, seems never-ending: the cat is by far the most popular Internet motif. It is the best-loved pet animal on the World Wide Web and users love to create, post, comment on and share videos, comics and images of cats. This attitude to felines seems symptomatic of the democratization of online content described as *The Long Tail* by the artist Mark Leckey and the journalist Chris Anderson. The "long tail" actually refers to the long-term, low-level earnings to be made through digital sales channels, which conversely means that niche products too will, in the long run, find their buyers and public. Leckey expands this idea with respect to the Internet and the way it fosters creative approaches to the production of content. So the "long tail" refers to the potential of each individual to become a transmitter and to share his thoughts with an undefined general public. Amateurs become Internet presenters and editors when they are able to select content subjectively. The video platform YouTube is one embodiment of this theory and thus forms an antithesis to the programmes of public service radio and television. In the thinking behind Renard's work, the popularity of YouTube and of the Internet itself transforms anonymous objects into collective icons.

The potentially endless number of people who consume *Grumpy Cats, Lolcats*, cute cat photos and videos converts a seemingly random motif into a contemporary symbol. The passion for images and other digital content is either shared or not – this essential principle regulates the popularity of digital contents. The motif of Renard's sculptures is based on a recently taken photo of a real cat. Its owners published photos of the animal and the artist used these to create the sculptures in the exhibition. The non-hierarchical principle is adapted once more because Renard not only uses source material that is accessible to all, but equally accessible technical resources as well: the found cat photos are scanned by online software that creates three-dimensional model sketches of the image. These sketches are then produced by a 3D printer that forms the sculptures from polystyrene and thus creates a tangible representation of the motif. The artworks in the exhibition space can, in this sense, be regarded more as representations of data and information that are transferred from a digital to a physical level. (ME)

*1984 in Paris. Lives / lebt in Berlin.
www.antoinerenard.net

Die Skulpturen von Antoine Renard sind schwer zu entziffern und zugleich intuitiv lesbar. Wann die abstrakte Form als Katze zu erkennen ist, liegt im Auge des Betrachters. Ist das Motiv jedoch einmal erkannt, setzt sich eine intuitive Assoziationskette in Gang, die für Personen, die mit dem Internet vertraut sind, unabschließbar erscheint: Die Katze ist das mit Abstand beliebteste Motiv im Internet. Sie ist das populärste Haustier des World Wide Web, und die User lieben es, Videos, Comics und Bilder von Katzen zu erstellen, zu posten, zu kommentieren und zu teilen. Dieser Umgang mit Katzen scheint symptomatisch für jene Demokratisierung von Online-Inhalten, die der Künstler Mark Leckey und der Journalist Chris Anderson als *The Long Tail* bezeichnen. „The Long Tail" (der lange Schwanz) beschreibt eigentlich langfristig geringe Umsätze bei digitalen Vertriebswegen, was im Umkehrschluss bedeutet, dass auch Nischenprodukte auf lange Sicht Käufer und Publikum finden. Leckey erweitert den Gedanken in Hinblick auf das Internet und den dortigen (kreativen) Umgang mit Inhalten und deren Erstellung. Der „Long Tail" beschreibt dann das Potenzial jedes Einzelnen, zum Sender zu werden und seine Gedanken mit einer unbestimmten Öffentlichkeit zu teilen. Amateure werden zu Moderatoren und Redakteuren des Internets, wenn sie Inhalte subjektiv auswählen können. Die Videoplattform YouTube steht stellvertretend für diese Theorie und bildet damit einen Gegenpol zu den Programmen des öffentlichen Rundfunks und Fernsehens.

Ihre Popularität und die des Internets insgesamt machen aus anonymen Objekten kollektive Ikonen, so der Gedanke hinter Renards Werk. Die potenziell unendliche Menge von Menschen, die *Grumpy Cats, Lolcats*, niedliche Katzenfotos und -videos konsumiert, verwandelt ein scheinbar beliebiges Motiv in ein zeitgenössisches Symbol. Die Leidenschaft für Bilder und andere digitale Inhalte wird geteilt oder nicht – dieses grundlegende Prinzip reguliert die Popularität digitaler Inhalte. Das Motiv der Skulpturen von Renard basiert auf dem erst vor kurzem aufgenommenen Bild einer tatsächlichen Katze. Deren Besitzer haben Fotos von dem Tier veröffentlicht, und der Künstler hat daraus die Skulpturen in der Ausstellung gemacht. Das non-hierarchische Prinzip wird nochmals adaptiert, wenn Renard sich nicht nur eines Ausgangsmaterials, sondern auch technischer Mittel bedient, die für jedermann zugänglich sind: Die gefundenen Fotografien von Katzen liest eine Online-Software, die dreidimensionale Modell-Skizzen der Abbildung erstellt. Diese Skizzen werden dann von einem 3D-Drucker produziert, der die Skulptur aus Styropor und damit ein greifbares Abbild des Motivs formt. Die Kunstwerke im Ausstellungsraum sind in diesem Sinn eher Repräsentationen von Daten und Informationen, die von einer digitalen auf eine physische Ebene übertragen werden. (ME)

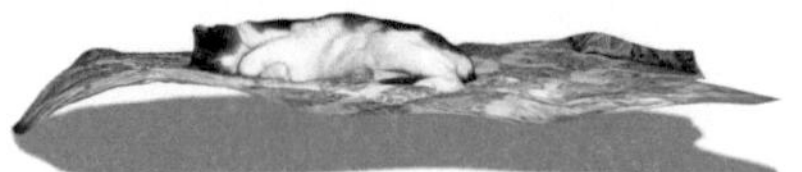

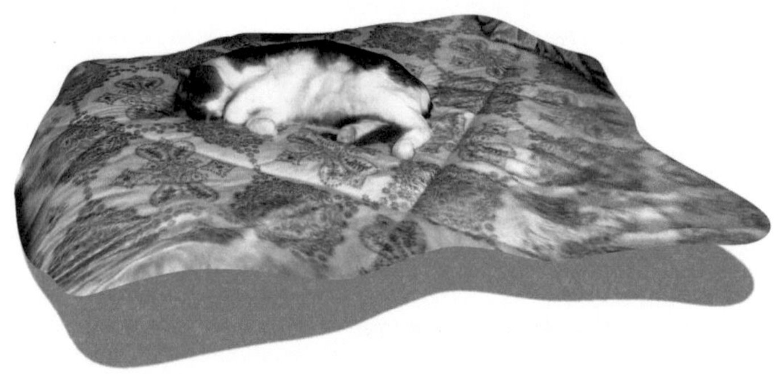

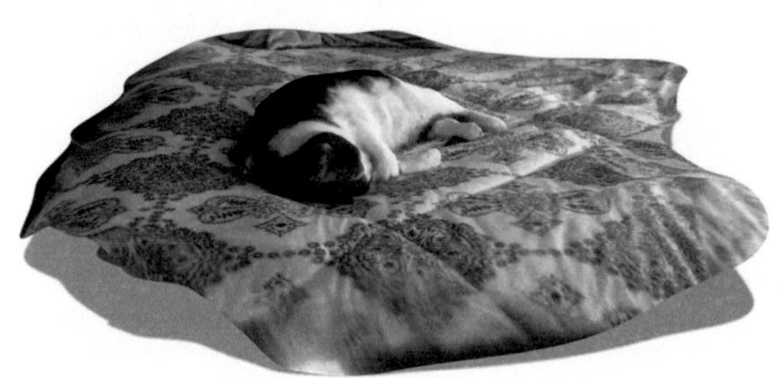

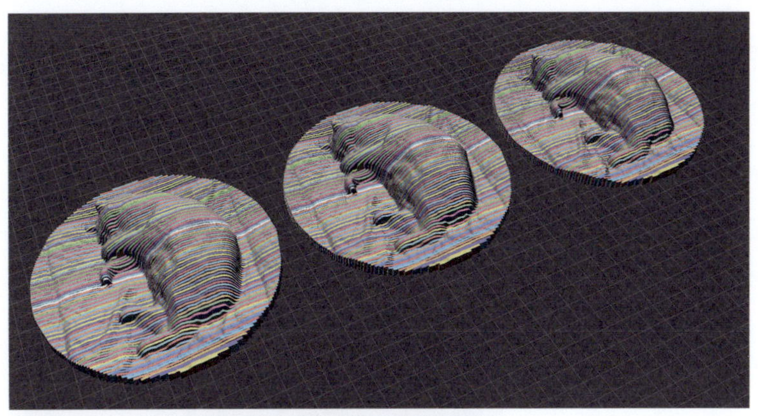

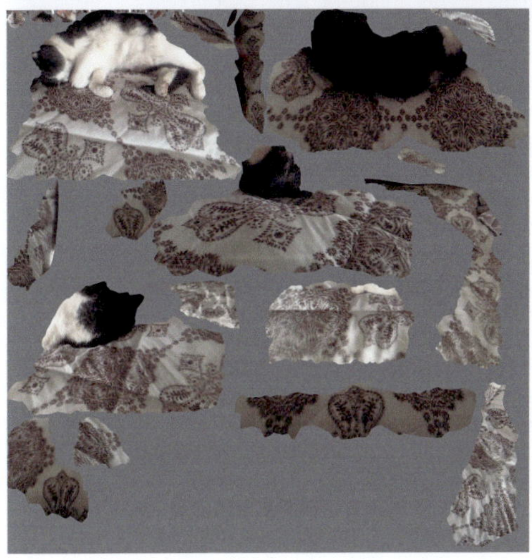

Antoine Renard
1110533_Capture Name (Bob), 2015
SYNTHOS XPS PRIME S 30
65 x 205 x 12 cm
Courtesy the artist / der Künstler

Mandla Reuter

City

"Seeing comes before words. (…)The relation between what we see and what we know is never settled. Each evening we see the sun set. We know that the earth is turning away from it. Yet the knowledge, the explanation, never quite fits the sight."

As John Berger wrote in his book, *Ways of Seeing* (1972), perception and interpretation morph because of multiple factors, including the viewer's environment and biography. As we understand more and more online, fiction and reality can be altered or obstructed to the point that the two become confused. Multifaceted and baring minimalistic aesthetics, Mandla Reuter's practice shifts in its form and meaning according to its setting, pushing the viewer to expand his or her thoughts beyond what they can immediately look at. Within the context of a gallery's blank space or inside museum walls, Mandla Reuter's performances and installations remain autonomous enough to avoid loss of any possible layers of interpretation. Creating an almost psychedelic three-dimensional mind expansion, circles of possible interpretation interconnect. His installations let different narratives unfold without directly pointing at or resolving to a definitive meaning. A motif in Reuter's work is a sort of lifting of the curtain, placing the viewer inside the frame containing and so-called reality. In past exhibitions, Reuter has blocked the regular entrances of museums to force visitors to use alternative doors to view his artworks. The artist has also doubled exhibitions, juxtaposing two similar shows at the same time in the same city. Yet, they ended up being completely different because of differences in their respective settings in different places. The viewer is not passive when he or she looks at Reuter's work. He or she becomes an integral part of a twisted reality.
Exhibited in *The Future of Memory*, the installation *City* (2014), which was first presented as part of Reuter's show *Armilla*, is high perched on a pallet mounted on scaffolding. A blue water tank fitted with a pump is filled with Evian "spring water". Emerging from the tank is a black tube snaking down on to the floor and throughout the space, including through rough perforations in the walls. Closing the circle, the tube circumvents stacked packages of Evian bottles and comes back to its source, the blue plastic tank. Mirroring an industrial cycle of water treatment, *City* makes visible what lies beneath the surface, putting the idea of the purity of the water into opposition with the reality of its processing. The artist makes the fancy water evaporate. What is left is dirt, both physical and ideological. (EL)

*1975 in Nqutu. Lives / lebt in Berlin.

„Das Sehen kommt vor den Worten. (…) Die Beziehung zwischen dem, was wir sehen, und dem, was wir wissen, ist niemals endgültig. Jeden Abend sehen wir den Sonnenuntergang. Wir wissen, dass die Erde sich von ihr wegdreht. Aber das Wissen, die Erklärung passt nie ganz zum Anblick.“

Wie John Berger in seinem Buch *Ways of Seeing* (1972) geschrieben hat, ändern sich Wahrnehmung und Interpretation aufgrund zahlreicher Faktoren, unter anderen der Umgebung und der Biographie des Betrachters. Wie wir gerade online zunehmend beobachten, können Fiktion und Realität bis zur völligen Verwirrung verändert oder blockiert werden. Mandla Reuters facettenreiches, von minimalistischer Ästhetik geprägtes Kunstschaffen ist wandlungsfähig in Form und Bedeutung: Es drängt den Betrachter dazu, weiter zu blicken und das Gesamtbild zu erfassen. In einer leeren Galeriearchitektur oder umgeben von Museumswänden nutzen Reuters Performances und Installationen den Raum, bleiben aber unabhängig genug, um nicht zuzulassen, dass ebendieser Raum etwaige Interpretationsansätze untergräbt.
Auf einer fast psychedelischen, dreidimensionalen Gedankenreise verbinden sich zahllose Kreise an Möglichkeiten und Gedanken. Seine Installationen legen verschiedene Erzählungen offen, ohne dass sie direkt auf eine davon verweisen oder eine benennen. Ein Motiv von Reuters Arbeiten ist allerdings eine Art Blick hinter den Vorhang: Der Betrachter befindet sich hinter dem Rahmen, der die sogenannte Realität enthält. In früheren Ausstellungen hat Reuter die regulären Museumseingänge blockiert und die Besucher gezwungen, andere Wege und Türen zu finden, um seine Kunst zu sehen. Der Künstler hat auch Ausstellungen verdoppelt, d.h. zwei ähnliche Schauen einander exakt zur gleichen Zeit gegenübergestellt. Allerdings waren sie letztlich aufgrund verschiedener Schauplätze und Örtlichkeiten doch völlig unterschiedlich. Der Besucher bleibt nicht passiv, wenn er Reuters Arbeiten betrachtet. Er wird zu einem wesentlichen Bestandteil der verschiedenen Ebenen einer verzerrten Realität.
In *The Future of Memory* ist die Installation *City* ausgestellt, die in der Ausstellung *Armilla* erstmals zu sehen war. Die Installation befindet sich hoch oben auf einer Palette, die von einer Metallkonstruktion gehalten wird. Ein mit einer Pumpe versehener blauer Wassertank ist mit Spring Water von Evian gefüllt. Aus dem Tank taucht ein schwarzer Schlauch auf, schlängelt sich hinunter auf den Fußboden, verläuft durch den Raum und durchbricht dabei grob die Wände. Der Schlauch umrundet einige gestapelte Kästen mit Evian-Flaschen und verläuft dann zurück zu ihrer Quelle, dem blauen Plastiktank. Hier schließt sich der Kreis. Indem sie den industriellen Zyklus der Wasseraufbereitung reflektiert, hebt die Installation *City* hervor, was unter der Oberfläche liegt, und konfrontiert Gedanken an Luxus und Reinheit mit der Realität. Sie lässt das angesagte Wasser verdampfen. Übrig bleibt Schmutz – sowohl materieller als auch ideologischer Art. (EL)

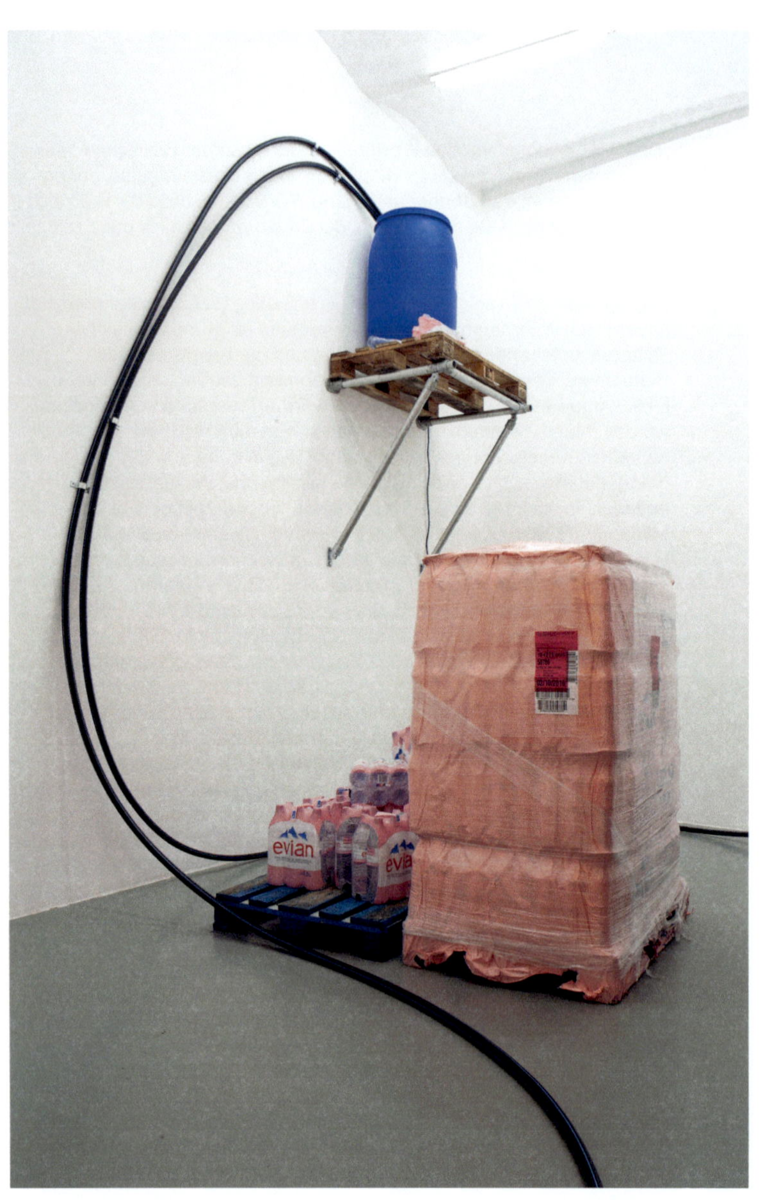

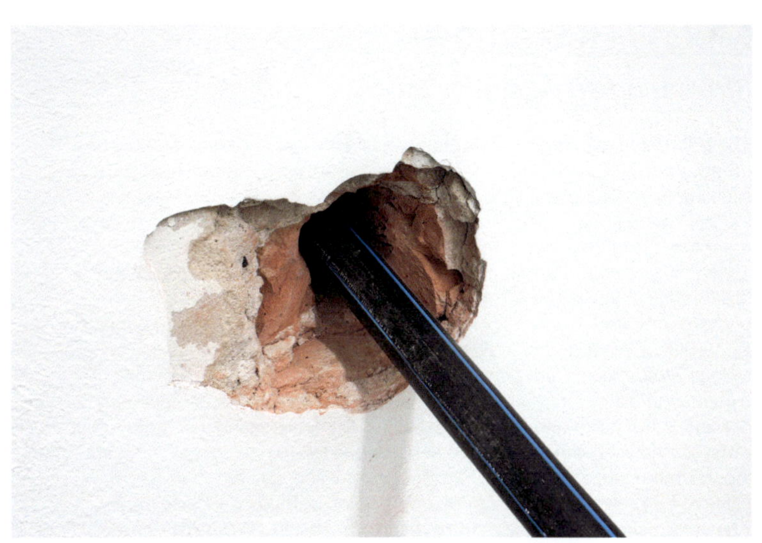

Mandla Reuter
City, 2014
Holz, Stahl, PE Druckschlauch, Pumpe, Evian Wasser,
andere Materialien; Maße variabel / Wood, steel, PE water pipe,
pump, Evian water, other materials; dimensions variable
Courtesy the artist / der Künstler; Galerie Mezzanin, Wien / Vienna.
Bilder / Images: Robert Gruber

Meggy Rustamova

L'invitation au voyage

The referent of (analogue) photography has a different character to that of other forms of representation, writes Roland Barthes in Camera Lucida, a book of his "reflections on photography." What we see in a photograph is indeed located at that place that lies between infinity and the *spectator*. The meaning, the *noema*, of photography corresponds to "this has been": something real happened and is stored as a presence detached from the flow of time in the image of the past. And so, since the invention of photography "the past is as certain as the present; what we see on paper is as certain as what we touch."[1]

Meggy Rustamova's film *L'Invitation au voyage* exploits this trust in the evidence of the photographic, our belief that something has been directly present in the world and now addresses us, the observer, in a photograph. It presents viewers with a sequence of black and white photographs that are incorporated into a narrative by an off-screen voice; this narrative tells the story of a woman who has disappeared and left behind only these photos. The pictures are addressed to the man whom she left. Slowly the camera approaches these static testimonies to the past while a female voice comments on the images and tries to reconstruct the past of the vanished woman, as well as the man's journey into the past recorded by in the images that have been left behind for him. *L'invitation au voyage* — the title is taken from a poem by Baudelaire — is a suggestive approach to the potential of photography to tell more than one story and for melding together fact and fiction, until the fuzziness of the tones that make up each photograph have expanded to include the narrative too. Yellow Post-Its on selected photos promise an explanation, but the pencilled-in words have been erased and the path back to the time when they were written is now blocked. It is the camera that guides us through the life story of the woman: her childhood, her time as a student, her relationships. It zooms in on the photographs until the image becomes grainy, focusing on details, navigating between the material level of the image and the content this conveys. But are we really seeing testimonies to a lived past, coherent images that, taken together, recount a biography? Or is it in fact their specificity, and simultaneously their universal quality, that predestines them as witnesses to a story that could be completely invented? Is the spoken text a parallel narrative following the coordinates of the images? Or is it instead an autonomous element that has been superimposed on the photographs?

Nothing in the spoken narrative is reflected directly in the images. In fact, the text behaves more like a transparent sheet laid over the individual photos. The image is still there, but its clarity is diminished in favour of the context in which it is placed. Barthes' concept of the *studium* is still valid: the cognitive apprehension of a photograph that enables one to draw conclusions of a cultural and socio-historical nature about the depicted elements and, as part of this cultural perspective, allows the information contained in the image to find its way into our consciousness. Otherwise we would not be convinced that we can find traces of the spoken narrative in the images. In this work by Rustamova, the decisive aspect of the "*this has been,*" an inalienable connection between the photograph and its referent, slowly but surely dissolves during this imaginary journey into the past. (VJM)

*1985 in Tiflis. Lives / lebt in Brussels & Ghent.
www.meggyrustamova.com

Der Referent der (analogen) Fotografie ist nicht von der gleichen Art wie der von anderen Darstellungssystemen, schreibt Roland Barthes in Die helle Kammer, seinen „Bemerkungen zur Photographie". Das, was wir auf einer Fotografie sehen, befand sich tatsächlich an jenem Ort, der zwischen Unendlichkeit und dem wahrnehmenden Subjekt, dem *spectator*, liegt. Der Sinngehalt, das *noema*, der Fotografie ist entsprechend das „*Es-ist-so-gewesen*": etwas Reales hat sich ereignet und als aus dem Lauf der Zeit abgesonderte Präsenz in das Bild der Vergangenheit eingelagert. Und so ist seit der Erfindung der Fotografie „die Vergangenheit so gewiss wie die Gegenwart, ist das, was man auf dem Papier sieht, so gewiss wie das, was man berührt."[1]

Meggy Rustamovas Film *L'Invitation au voyage* macht sich dieses Vertrauen in die Evidenz des Fotografischen, etwas habe eine unmittelbare Präsenz in der Welt gehabt, die sich nun an uns, die Betrachter richte, zunutze. Er präsentiert uns eine Abfolge von Schwarz-Weiß-Fotografien, die über eine Stimme aus dem Off in ein Narrativ eingebunden werden, das uns die Geschichte einer Frau erzählt, die verschwunden ist und lediglich die Fotografien hinterlassen hat. Adressat der Bilder ist jener Mann, den sie verlassen hat. Langsam nähert sich die Kamera den statischen Zeugnissen der Vergangenheit, während eine Frauenstimme die Bilder kommentiert und die Vergangenheit der verschwundenen Frau ebenso zu rekonstruieren sucht wie die Reise des Mannes in die ihm überlassene, bildlich festgehaltene Vergangenheit. *L'invitation au voyage* – der Titel ist einem Gedicht Baudelaires entlehnt – ist eine suggestive Annäherung an das Potenzial der Fotografie, Geschichte(n) zu erzählen und Fakt und Fiktion einander anzunähern, bis die Unschärfe der jeder Aufnahme zugrunde liegenden Bildpunkte auch die Erzählung erfasst hat. Gelbe Post-Its Text eine parallele auf ausgewählten Fotos versprechen eine klärende Zuordnung, doch die Bleistiftschrift ist ausradiert und der Weg zurück in die Zeit ihrer Entstehung versperrt. Es ist die Kamera, die uns Zuschauer durch die Lebensgeschichte der Frau, ihre Kindheit, ihr Studium, ihre Partnerschaften leitet. Sie zoomt in die Fotografien hinein, bis das Bild körnig wird, fokussiert Details und navigiert zwischen der materiellen Ebene des Bildes und dem Inhalt, den diese transportiert. Doch sind es wirklich Zeugnisse einer gelebten Vergangenheit, kohärente Bilder, die in ihrer Addition eine Biografie nacherzählen? Oder ist es gerade das Besondere und zugleich Allgemeingültige, das sie zu Zeugen einer Erzählung, die selbst vollständig erfunden sein könnte, prädestiniert? Ist der gesprochene Text eine parallele Erzählung entlang bildlicher Koordinaten oder eine autonome Ebene, die lediglich über diese geblendet wurde?

Nichts von dem, was gesagt wird, ist in den Bildern selbst direkt lesbar. Der Text verhält sich eher wie eine durchsichtige Folie, die sich über die einzelnen Fotografien legt. Das Bild ist noch immer da, aber seine Schärfe nimmt ab zugunsten des Kontextes, in den es tritt. Was Barthes das *studium* genannt hat, den wissenden Zugang zu einer Fotografie, der aus dem Abgebildeten Rückschlüsse kultur- und sozialhistorischen Charakters zu ziehen vermag und die in dem Bild angelegten Informationen im Zuge dieser kulturellen Wahrnehmung ihren Weg ins Bewusstsein bahnen lässt, gilt noch immer. Ansonsten wären wir nicht überzeugt davon, Spuren des Gesagten in den Bildern zu finden. Doch das für ihn noch entscheidende „*Es-ist-so-gewesen*" einer unabdingbaren Verbindung der Fotografie zu ihrem Referenten löst sich in der imaginären Reise in diese Vergangenheit sukzessive auf. (VJM)

---

[1] Roland Barthes: Die helle Kammer. Bemerkungen zur Photographie, Frankfurt am Main 1989, S. 86f und S. 97. / Roland Barthes, Camera Lucida. Reflections on photography, (New York: Farrar, Straus and Giroux, 1981), 86f and 97.

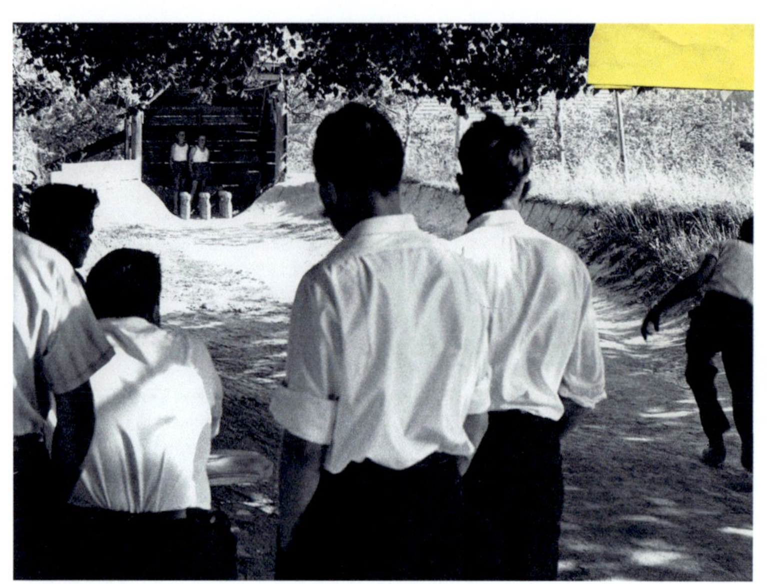

Meggy Rustamova
L'invitation au voyage, 2014
HD Video, 13 Min.
Courtesy the artist / die Künstlerin

Augustas Serapinas

Marie

Creating context-based installations, Augustas Serapinas develops his practice around the alteration and manipulation of architectural spaces. Identifying forgotten or hidden places within the walls of art institutions or from his direct environment, Serapinas turns these concealed spots into artworks. Dismantling what is officially regarded as art in the museum, the young artist therefore continues the tradition of institutional critique. For *The Future of Memory*, the artist opens a hidden door in the exhibition room, revealing a "space-in-between". Serapinas has installed a desk and chair in the space, as well as items he found in the museum's offices. At times, *Marie*, a curatorial assistant at Kunsthalle Wien, will work there, using a sign to indicate when she is away or in a meeting. Kunsthalle Wien consists of a number of locations, with offices separate from exhibition spaces. By transposing one of the employees into the show, the artist symbolically moves the working area directly into the exhibition hall, revealing what goes on behind the curtains or, in this case, the neat white walls.

By extension, Serapinas also questions what is presented as "reality". Beyond the modification of the Kunsthalle space, a mind game infuses the artist's practice, reminiscent of that of chess. In the genre of Heroic Fantasy cartoons and literature, destiny is sometimes physically embodied as a ghost playing chess with elements on earth, moving pawns around to see what this generates, changing their paths, endlessly disrupting their narrative. This is clearly an extrapolation, yet the metaphor still applies. Serapinas manipulates the exhibition plot to alter thoughts. The emotional reactions and the shift of perception that might be triggered in the viewer by the artist's interference with the space is what fuels Serapinas' process.

The exhibition venue becomes a platform for different narratives, issues and questions to unfold. These are directly linked to the place of art in the museum, and also touch on questions at a broader, societal level. Does this reality provoked by the artist exist, or is it only exacerbated within the art sphere? Or is it possible that, in a twist, the art context will instead diminish the message conveyed by that reality? While visitor reactions will probably remain an enigma for Serapinas, each one still gets to decide on these questions for themselves. (EL)

*1990 in Vilnius. Lives / lebt in Vilnius.

Augustas Serapinas kreiert kontextspezifische Installationen, in seiner Kunst geht es um die Veränderung und die Manipulation von Architekturräumen. Er entdeckt vergessene oder versteckte Orte in den Wänden von Kunstinstitutionen oder in seiner direkten Umgebung und macht diese verborgenen Stellen zu seinen Kunstwerken. Indem er das, was offiziell als Kunst im Museum gilt, dekonstruiert, schließt der junge Künstler an eine etablierte Tradition der Institutionenkritik aus den Neunziger Jahren an.

Für *The Future of Memory* öffnet der Künstler eine verborgene Tür in der Ausstellung und macht einen „Zwischenraum" sichtbar. Serapinas hat einen Schreibtisch nebst Stuhl in die Mitte gestellt, außerdem Dinge, die er in den Büroräumen des Museums gefunden hat. Gelegentlich kommt *Marie*, eine Ausstellungsassistentin der Kunsthalle Wien, und arbeitet hier. Durch ein Zeichen signalisiert sie, dass sie weg ist oder in einem Meeting. Die Kunsthalle Wien hat zwei Adressen. Indem er eine der Angestellten in die Ausstellung transferiert, überführt der Künstler auf metaphorische Weise den Arbeitsbereich direkt in die Ausstellungshalle und macht sichtbar, was sich hinter dem Vorhang (oder in diesem Fall hinter den sauberen weißen Wänden) abspielt.

Im Umkehrschluss stellt Serapinas die Frage, was uns als Realität präsentiert wird. Ein Gedankenspiel, das an ein Schachspiel erinnert, durchzieht die Arbeit des Künstlers und legt sich über die architektonische Veränderung. Im Comic- und Literaturgenre der Heldengeschichte nimmt das Schicksal bisweilen Gestalt an – als eine Art Geist, der mit den irdischen Elementen Schach spielt, der Figuren verschiebt, um zu sehen, wohin das führt. Der ihren vorgegebenen Weg ändert und ständig ihre Geschichte unterbricht. Dies ist sicherlich zu weit gedacht, aber die Metapher passt trotzdem. Serapinas manipuliert die Handlung, um die Gedanken zu bewegen. Die emotionalen Reaktionen und die veränderte Wahrnehmung, die der Eingriff des Künstlers in den Raum beim Betrachter auslösen könnte – das ist es, was den Schaffensprozess von Serapinas anregt.

Der Raum wird zur Bühne, auf der sich verschiedene Erzählungen, Themen und Fragen entfalten können. Diese sind entweder direkt mit der Stellung der Kunst im Museum verbunden, können aber auch eine umfassendere, gesellschaftliche Ebene berühren. Existiert diese vom Künstler verursachte Realität oder wird sie nur durch die Sphäre der Kunst ermöglicht? Ist es umgekehrt denkbar, dass der Kunstkontext die Botschaft schmälert, die diese Realität vermittelt? Auch wenn die Reaktion des Betrachters für Serapinas ein Rätsel bleiben wird, ist die Botschaft doch zumindest in der Welt. (EL)

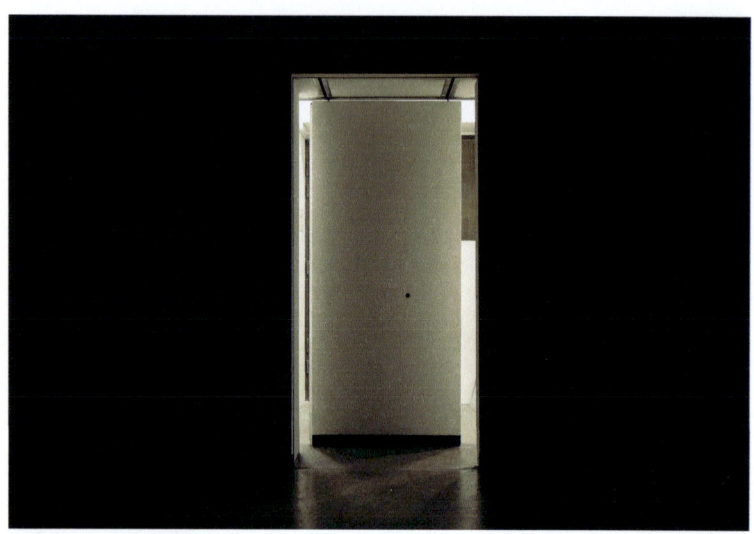

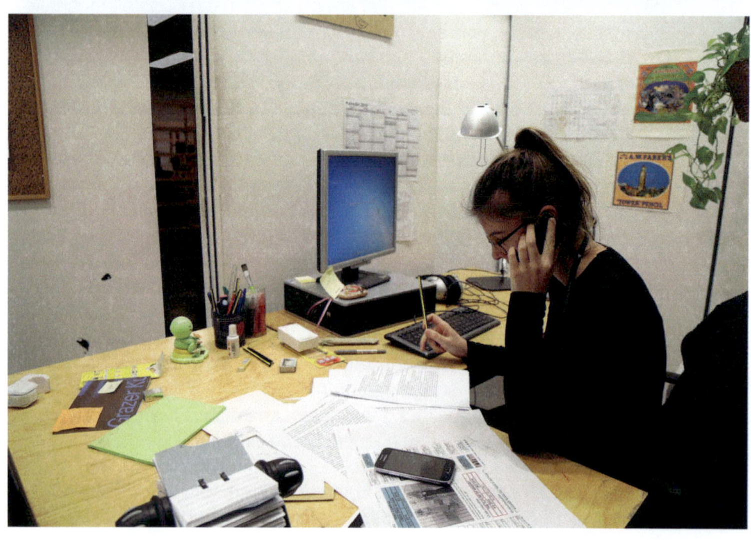

Augustas Serapinas
Marie, 2015
Installation / Performance
Courtesy the artist / der Künstler

Michael Staniak

DATA_901 (VLSR)
DATA_012 (1128GB)
DATA_760 (1081GB)

The 2013 Simon Klose documentary TPB AFK recalls the story of one of the world's largest filesharing websites, The Pirate Bay. In one sequence, Peter Sunde, one of the founding members of the site, allows the camera inside a small, secret room. There, he presents what looks like a medium sized box he can hold in his two hands. This little black box tracks the largest volume of BitTorrent traffic in the world and coordinates 50 percent of it. The amount of material, and the nature of the information this tiny plastic device processes, can hardly be imagined. Expanding the thought and turning this sentence into a question: is it reasonable and safe to place this amount of information on a fragile piece of hardware? Informed by the act of surfing the web, Michael Staniak makes experimental, digital media-inspired paintings. The three pieces presented by the artist in *The Future of Memory* are part of his *DATA_ series* (2014), which explore issues linked to the mutability and instability of the devices that physically contain our data. Parallel to these problematics, the series questions how secure our data is and what the consequences are of potential security failures. Can these devices last, and for how long? The constant upgrading all electronic material is subject to seems to imply it's not secure enough yet. The "cloud" and the Internet currently seem to be the only safe places to conserve information — what goes on the Net stays there forever. This last statement obviously adds complication to our ability to think about this problem.
While Staniak's work clearly makes reference to digital aesthetics, it also seamlessly manages to combine both analog and digital attributes. Each work is made using a type of paint the artist develops from different forms of digital storage media that have been pulverized into small granules. DVD's, M-Disc's and silicon wafers, each with the capacity to resist time for a period ranging from five to one thousand years, are in these works reduced to a material. Once images of the paintings are uploaded to the web, they start floating around within various search engine databases and Google's infinite sea of images. Similar to the cycles of information preservation, the digital hardware turns into a simple picture and an integral part of the permanent universe it was once meant to store. (EL)

*1982 in Melbourne. Lives/lebt in Melbourne.
www.michaelstaniak.tumblr.com

Simon Kloses Dokumentation TPB AFK erzählt die Geschichte von einer der größten Filesharing-Websites der Welt: The Pirate Bay. In einer Szene gewährt Peter Sunde, einer der Gründer der Seite, der Kamera Einblick in einen kleinen geheimen Raum. Dort präsentiert er etwas, das wie eine viereckige Schachtel aussieht, die er mit beiden Händen halten könnte. Diese kleine schwarze Kiste ist der größte Tracker der Welt und koordiniert 50% des BitTorrent-Traffics auf unserem Planeten. Die Datenmenge und die Art der Informationen, die dieses kleine Plastikgerät bewältigt, sind kaum vorstellbar. Führt man den Gedanken fort und wandelt diesen Satz in eine Frage um, so lautet sie: Ist es vernünftig und sicher, jede kleinste Information auf einem digitalen und fragilen Stück Hardware abzulegen?
Michael Staniaks Kunstschaffen ist vom Surfen im Internet geprägt und bringt außergewöhnliche Gemälde hervor, deren Inspiration die digitalen Medien sind. Die drei Arbeiten in *The Future of Memory* gehören zur *DATA-Serie* (2014), in der es um Themen rund um die Veränderlichkeit und die Unbeständigkeit von Geräten geht, die unsere Daten enthalten. Parallel zu dieser Problematik hinterfragt die Serie die Daten-Sicherheit und die Folgen möglicher Ausfälle dieser Geräte – sollten sie denn passieren. Werden diese Apparate fortbestehen? Wenn ja, wie lange? Das permanente Optimieren und Verarbeiten allen elektronischen Materials scheint darauf hinzudeuten, dass das, was wir in Händen haben, noch nicht sicher genug ist. Die „Cloud" und das Internet scheinen zurzeit die einzig sicheren Orte zur Aufbewahrung von Informationen zu sein, denn was ins Netz geht, bleibt dort für immer. Diese Aussage verkompliziert unseren Zugang zu diesem Problem merklich.
Während sich Staniaks Arbeiten ganz klar mit digitaler Ästhetik auseinandersetzen, werden in ihnen auch Merkmale analoger und digitaler Prozesse nahtlos miteinander verknüpft. Das Ergebnis sind glatte Kunstwerke, die stark an flache Digitaldrucke erinnern. Bei jeder Arbeit benutzt der Künstler eine Farbe, die er selbst aus verschiedenen Arten digitaler Speichermedien gewinnt. Diese Speichermedien sind vorher zu kleinem Granulat pulverisiert worden. DVDs, M-Discs und Silicon Wafers, alle mit einer Haltbarkeit zwischen fünf und eintausend Jahren, werden zu Fluessigem transformiert. Sobald Abbildungen der Gemälde ins Netz hochgeladen werden, beginnen sie, in diversen Suchmaschinen in Umlauf zu sein und im unendlichen Bildermeer auf Google zu treiben. Ähnlich wie in einem Kreislauf der Informationsbewahrung wandelt sich die digitale Hardware zu einem einfachen Bild – und zu einem wesentlichen Bestandteil des dauerhaften Universums, das sie einmal speichern sollte. (EL)

Michael Staniak
DATA_901 (VLSR), 2015
Acrylic and resin on canvas and steel
frame / Acryl Harz auf Leinwand mit Stahlrahmen
180x135cm

<-   *DATA_760 (1081GB)*, 2015
Acrylic and resin on canvas and steel
frame / Acryl Harz auf Leinwand mit Stahlrahmen
180x135cm

Courtesy the artist / der Künstler; Steve Turner
Contemporary, Los Angeles

Philipp Timischl

The Blair Bitch Project

Philipp Timischl's installations are based on a close personal connection to the subject at hand. His artistic approach relates to medium-specific criteria; for instance, in one exhibition he presents only banners that feature both an unfinished video with him as main performer as well as press texts and discussions with friends, thus thematising the format of the solo exhibition itself.

Timischl makes inventive use of found or selected materials, motifs and video clips in various formats. In this way he produces sculptural objects that reference media-related or historically-influenced modalities of representation. Within his own oeuvre, too, Timischl connects new and existing works in a self-referential cosmos that initially seems not to demonstrate any clear external points of reference. In his works, an important role is fulfilled by the re-use of older forms of representation in formats that appear unfinished. This creates the impression of a permanent grappling with processes of image creation and the incompleteness of the artistic act. One work that is characteristic of this basic approach is *The Blair Bitch Project*, which creates formal and intertextual links between multimedia content and contemporary youth culture. A flatscreen TV and a canvas each present collages of graphic wallpaper and images of the performers in the American TV series *Gossip Girl* (2007-2012). Theme music for the series supplies a musical refrain, which is played at regular but unpredictable intervals. The painting depicts a sports car that bears the wording: "You know you love me xoxo," a phrase spoken by the anonymous female protagonist — the "gossip girl" — during the opening credits of the TV series.

The show Gossip Girl is about a group of wealthy young people from New York who attend an elite high school. Gossip Girl, a mysterious character who remains unknown during the show, has a website that is linked to the characters' smartphones and disseminates gossip about the teenagers. The gossip relays incidents that repeatedly defy moral boundaries and reveals the insincerity typical of their social circles. In the series, social interaction mostly takes place through smartphones and is driven by the eponymous off-screen character. Besides narrative intrigues, love stories and a hedonistic lifestyle, the show's most riveting aspect is clearly the way it showcases how sensitive, personal information gets disseminated through digital media in everyday life. The title of Timischl's work is taken from the name of an episode and refers to one of the show's main protagonists, Blair Waldorf, an upper class queen of intrigue and scandal. The installation is composed of seemingly disparate materials that represent the microcosm of the series between the poles of hype and triviality. (ME)

*1989 in Graz. Lives / lebt in Wien.

Philipp Timischls Installationen basieren auf einer engen persönlichen
Bindung zu dem jeweiligen Sujet. Sein künstlerischer Ansatz knüpft an
medienspezifische Anhaltspunkte an, wenn er beispielsweise in einer
Ausstellung ausschließlich Banner präsentiert, auf denen sowohl
Ausschnitte aus einem unfertigen Video mit ihm als Hauptdarsteller als
auch Pressetexte und Gespräche mit Freunden zu sehen sind und so das
Format der Einzelausstellung selbst thematisiert wird.
Gefundene oder ausgewählte Materialien, Motive und Videoclips
unterschiedlicher Formate setzt Timischl in seinen Werken dezidiert ein.
Dabei entstehen skulpturale Objekte, die mediale oder historisch
geprägte Repräsentationsmodalitäten berücksichtigen. Auch innerhalb
der eigenen Praxis vernetzt Timischl neue und bereits existierende Werke
in einem selbstreferentiellen Kosmos, der zunächst keine klaren
Bezugspunkte nach außen aufzuweisen scheint. Die Wiederaufbereitung
älterer Repräsentationsformen und das Zeigen des Unfertigen spielen
dabei eine wichtige Rolle. Sie vermitteln den Eindruck einer permanenten
Auseinandersetzung mit Bildwerdungsprozessen und der
Unabgeschlossenheit der künstlerischen Handlung. Kennzeichnend für
diese Grundhaltung ist die Arbeit *The Blair Bitch Project*, die formell und
intertextuell Verknüpfungen multimedialer Inhalte und zeitgenössischer
Jugendkultur demonstriert. Die amerikanische TV-Serie Gossip Girl liefert
den Jingle, der in regelmäßigen, aber unvorhersehbaren Abständen auf
einem Flachbildschirm abgespielt wird. Über dem Screen ist das
Gemälde eines Sportwagens zu sehen. Auf dem Fahrzeug verläuft der
Schriftzug: „You know you love me xoxo", ein Satz, den die anonyme
Protagonistin im Intro der TV-Serie sagt. Bildschirm und Leinwand
wiederum überlagern eine Fototapete mit Abbildungen der
Seriendarsteller.
Die Fernsehserie *Gossip Girl* (2007-2012) handelt von einer Gruppe
Jugendlicher aus der gehobenen Gesellschaft New Yorks, die eine
Elite-Schule besuchen. Gossip Girl ist auch eine Website, die mit den
Smartphones der Charaktere verlinkt ist und Klatschgeschichten über die
Jugendlichen verbreitet. Diese geraten immer wieder an moralische
Grenzen und offenbaren die Durchtriebenheit wohlhabender
Gesellschaftskreise. Soziale Interaktion findet in der Serie weitestgehend
über Smartphones statt und wird von dem immateriellen Gossip Girl
gesteuert. Neben den Intrigen, Liebesgeschichten und dem
hedonistischen Lebensstil faszinieren die Brisanz des Umgangs mit
persönlichen Informationen und deren Verbreitung durch digitale Medien
im Alltag. Der Titel von Timischls Arbeit ist dem Namen einer Episode
entlehnt und verweist auf die Hauptfigur Blair Waldorf, die als
Klatschbase und Königin der Intrigen fungiert. Die Installation ist aus
scheinbar disparaten Materialien zusammengesetzt, die den
Mikrokosmos der Serie im Spannungsfeld von Hype und Belanglosigkeit
repräsentieren. (ME)

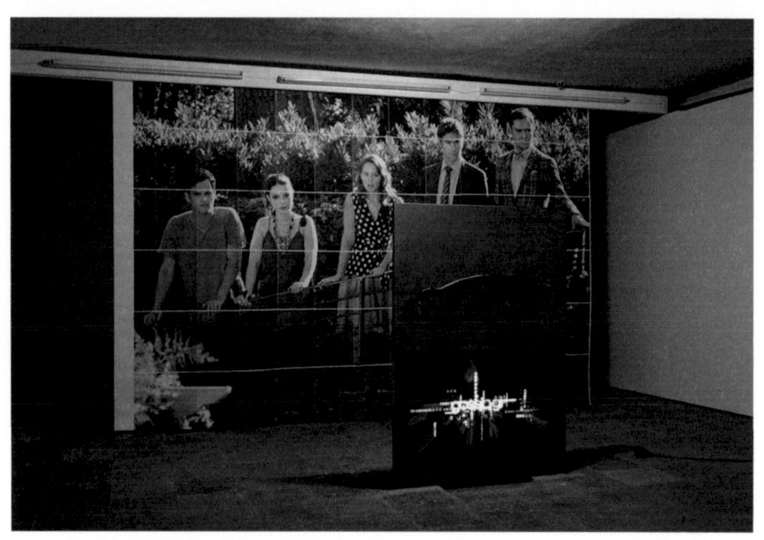
gossip girl

Amalia Ulman

Excellences & Perfections, 2014

Intertwined with her own image, Amalia Ulman's practice is informed by an analysis of class differences, power, and the social anxiety that may result from these things. Gender issues in contemporary culture also inform Ulman's work, especially in *Excellences & Perfections*, an online performance conducted through Instagram and Facebook. For four months, the artist underwent a semi-fictional makeover and staged it in carefully composed pictures, which gained Ulman the peculiar status of *Internet famous*. This virtual performance displays a privileged and self-branded lifestyle, presented through visually pleasing and seemingly inconspicuous images, all fabricated by the artist or taken from other online sources. From expensive items and luxurious settings to pictures of nudity and plastic surgeries (*the artist faked breast implants but underwent a real nose job for the piece*) the work is not only concerned to highlight the manipulation of fiction and facts on social media, it also questions compliance to female appointed stereotypes and the idea that femininity can be purchased. As the performance unfolds, the body becomes the central element of the work, morphing into an online commodity. Ulman explains: *"Excellences and Perfections is a project about our flesh as object, your body as an investment. How do we market this flesh, how do we price this meat and how long will it stay fresh for?"* Entirely constructing her narrative beforehand, the artist meticulously researched and scripted a storyline that follows the clichéd yet recurrent fantasy amongst young women of *the provincial girl turned model in the big city.* The script narrates the rise and fall of this woman through three distinct sequences Ulman named *innocence*, *sin* and *redemption*. To build the different images of the character as she passes these phases, Ulman identified stereotypes of women celebrated on social media (*The cute girl, the gangsta girl*, and *the girl next door*) and made use of their associated codes and aesthetics. To release the images, the artist then methodically followed the rhythm and the vocabulary of social media, stirring confusion even among her close circles of friends, who grew unable to separate the online and the real persona.
The full performance piece has now been archived on the art website Rhizome to be preserved in its original format, escaping the ephemerality of social media. Alongside the myriad of gender issues casually displayed in the work, it also serves as a record of online image manipulation and suggests the public's easy acceptance of what is being presented as the truth. (EL)

*1989 in Buenos Aires. Lives / lebt in London & Gijón.
www.amaliaulman.eu

Verknüpft mit ihrem eigenen Bildnis, geht es in Amalia Ulmans Schaffen um die Analyse von Klassenunterschieden, um Macht und um die sozialen Ängste, die daraus resultieren können. Geschlechterthemen in der zeitgenössischen Kultur kommen in Ulmans Arbeiten ebenfalls vor, speziell in *Excellences & Perfections*, einer Online-Performance auf Instagram und Facebook. Vier Monate lang unterzog sich die Künstlerin einer Reihe von semi-fiktiven körperlichen Veränderungen und inszenierte diese in sorgfältig komponierten Bildern, wodurch Ulman den eigentümlichen Status einer „Internet-Berühmtheit" erlangte. Die virtuelle Performance stellt einen privilegierten Self-Branding-Lifestyle zur Schau, der auf visuell ansprechenden und scheinbar unauffälligen Bildern basiert; die jedoch alle von der Künstlerin optimiert wurden oder aus anderen Internetquellen stammen. Zu sehen sind teure Gegenstände und luxuriöse Ausstattungen, aber auch Nackt-Bilder und Aufnahmen plastischer Chirurgie (die Künstlerin tat nur so, als ließe sie sich Brustimplantate einsetzen, unterzog sich für die Performance aber einer realen Nasenoperation). Die Arbeit betont nicht nur die mögliche Manipulation von Fiktion und Fakten in den sozialen Medien. Sie hinterfragt auch die Zustimmung zu Stereotypen, die als „weiblich" definiert werden und zur Idee einer Weiblichkeit, die durch materielle Güter erkauft wird. Im Verlauf der Performance wird der Körper zum zentralen Element der Arbeit und verwandelt sich in einen Online-Artikel. Ulman erläutert: *„Excellences & Perfections ist ein Projekt über unseren Leib als Objekt, über unseren Körper als Investition. Wie vermarkten wir unseren Leib, wie setzen wir einen Preis für dieses Fleisch fest und wie lange bleibt es frisch?"*[1]

Die Künstlerin hat ihre Erzählung komplett im Voraus erstellt. Sehr genau hat sie eine Handlung recherchiert und entwickelt, die der klischeehaften, aber unter jungen Frauen immer wiederkehrenden Phantasie vom Mädchen aus der Provinz folgt, das in der großen Stadt als Model entdeckt wird. Das Skript erzählt vom Aufstieg und Fall dieses Mädchens in drei Szenen, die Ulman *Unschuld, Sünde* und *Erlösung* nennt. Um das jeweils unterschiedliche Image der Figur in diesen Szenen zu erschaffen, hat Ulman beliebte Frauenstereotypen in den sozialen Medien ausgemacht (*das hübsche Mädchen, das Gangsta Girl* und *das Mädchen von nebenan*) und sich der ihnen jeweils zugeschriebenen Kodierung und Ästhetik bedient. Die Künstlerin folgt dann bei der Veröffentlichung ihrer Bilder planmäßig dem Rhythmus und der Sprache der sozialen Medien. Dabei stiftet sie Verwirrung sogar in ihrem engeren Freundeskreis, indem sie es unmöglich macht, zwischen der Online-Figur und der realen Person zu unterscheiden.

Die komplette Performance befindet sich nunmehr im Archiv der Kunstwebsite Rhizome. Dort bleibt sie in ihrem Originalformat erhalten und vor der weiteren Entwicklung in den sozialen Medien geschützt. Neben einer Unzahl an Geschlechterthemen, die beiläufig aufscheinen, wird diese Arbeit auch ihr Ausmaß an Bildmanipulationen auf der Online-Ebene in sich bewahren – und die schnelle Zustimmung des Publikums zu dem, was ihm als Wahrheit präsentiert wird. (EL)

[1] Do you Follow? Art in circulation #3, ICA. Video talk

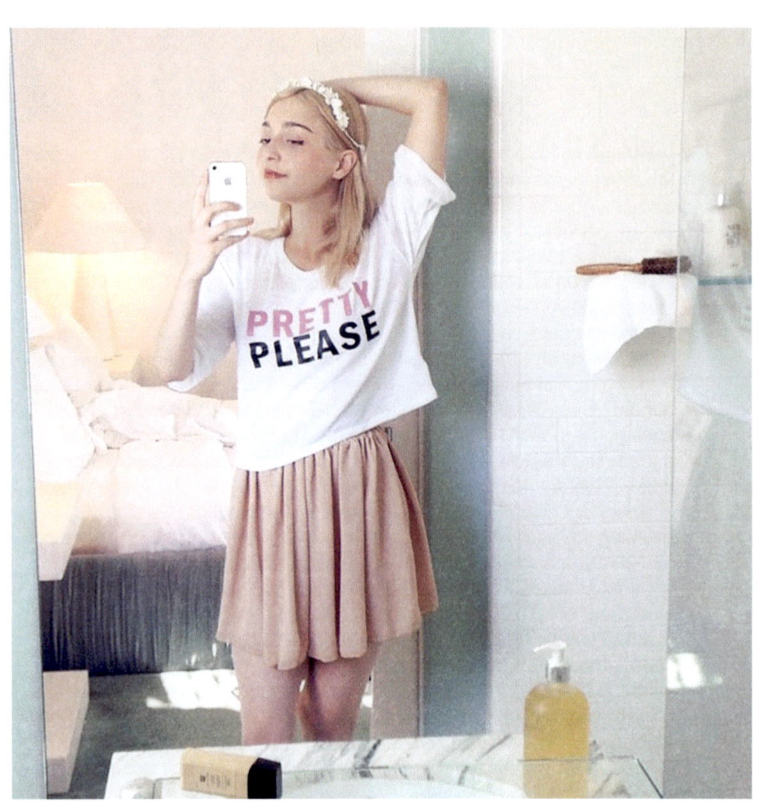
PRETTY
PLEASE

Amalia Ulman
Excellences & Perfections, 2014
Online performance
Courtesy the artist / die Künstlerin

Ignacio Uriarte

60 seconds

The phenomenon we call "time" is composed of time awareness and time measurement, of social and physical time. However, time itself does not fit into the conceptual order of this dualism. Like other phenomena, it refuses classification as objective or subjective, natural or social. Nonetheless our determination of time, which is based on chronological time measurement, follows the primacy of time as a measurable and thus quantifiable unit: one day is equal to twenty-four hours, one hour to sixty minutes, a minute to sixty seconds. Almost imperceptibly, Ignacio Uriarte's installation *60 seconds* destabilizes this method of mechanical time measurement that determines our daily life. The sixty wristwatches that he has linked together and arranged in a circle do indeed reflect the actual time, but each of the watches is one second faster in comparison to its predecessor. This creates a time space of sixty seconds that can be read on the watch dials, progressing at a speed of one revolution per minute. Moreover, at each full hour a beep tone jumps from one watch to the next and signals that another sixty minutes have passed.

Uriarte, who studied economics and who has worked for various large companies, often focuses in his works on standardized systems and forms of administration. In the clear structure of his works and his broad eschewal of subjective artistic gestures he references conceptual movements of the 1960s and 70s which he adapts to the everyday aesthetic of our managed, administered world. In his minimal-laconic works, issues of time, structure, order and monotony are juxtaposed with the creative potential of time that would seem to be spent inefficiently, for instance when one scribbles something apparently meaningless on a notepad during a telephone call. Precisely at the point where maximum efficiency is promoted, it creates a routine that often leads to boredom. In the sense of empty time, boredom in turn can be transformed into a positive energy, generate new ideas, trigger creative processes and new actions. Such potential is contained in the act of rendering time visible in a plastic manner, and thus also revealing the passing of time as a transformation of the present into the past. The wristwatches laid out on the ground have a radius of four metres. Like a magical force field, they draw a line around an empty space that seems to be filled with time as an abstract material. Can this be put to meaningful use? Or is it perhaps exactly this abstraction of the system of time, transforming this system into a dictate, which determines our lives?

In 2014, Uriarte designed a sound installation for the foyer of the Berlinische Galerie, in which one hears the monotonous voice of a man counting for eight hours. His unit of measurement is syllables: he devotes one second to each syllable, and in this way the German-speaking enumerator reaches the number 3599 in the space of eight hours — a period corresponding to a typical working day, but also the daily opening period of the museum. Here, time as an abstract quantity encounters the potential of language to name and to define this, and to translate it into a system that is divergent, phonetic and simultaneously poetic. (VJM)

*1972 in Krefeld. Lives / lebt in Berlin.
www.ignaciouriarte.com

Das, was wir Zeit nennen, setzt sich aus Zeitbewusstsein und
Zeitbestimmung zusammen, aus sozialer und physikalischer Zeit. Die
Zeit selbst passt jedoch nicht in das begriffliche Schema dieses
Dualismus. Wie andere Gegebenheiten entzieht sie sich einer
Klassifizierung als objektiv oder subjektiv, natürlich oder sozial. Unsere
auf der chronometrischen Zeitmessung basierende Zeitbestimmung folgt
dennoch dem Primat der Zeit als messbarer und damit quantifizierbarer
Einheit: Ein Tag entspricht 24 Stunden, eine Stunde 60 Minuten, eine
Minute 60 Sekunden. Ignazio Uriartes Installation *60 seconds* bringt in
diese mechanische, unseren Lebensalltag prägende Zeiterfassung fast
unmerklich Unruhe, denn die sechzig Armbanduhren, die er aneinander
gebunden und zu einem Kreis formiert hat, geben zwar die reale Zeit
wieder, aber jede der Uhren geht im Vergleich zu ihrem Vorgänger jeweils
eine Sekunde vor. So entsteht ein an den Zifferblättern ablesbarer
Zeitraum von 60 Sekunden, der mit einer Geschwindigkeit von einem
Kreis pro Minute fortschreitet. Jede volle Stunde springt zudem ein
Piepston von einer Uhr zur nächsten und signalisiert, das nun bereits 60
Minuten vergangen sind.
Uriarte, der Wirtschaftswissenschaften studiert und für verschiedene
Konzerne gearbeitet hat, bevor er sich der bildenden Kunst zuwandte,
beschäftigt sich in seinen Werken häufig mit standardisierten Systemen
und Formen der Verwaltung. Durch die klare Struktur seiner Arbeiten und
den weitgehenden Verzicht auf einen subjektiven künstlerischen Gestus
zitiert er konzeptuelle Strömungen der 1960er und 70er Jahre, die er der
alltäglichen Ästhetik unserer verwalteten Welt anpasst. Fragen zu Zeit,
Struktur, Ordnung und Monotonie stehen bei seinen minimalisch-
lakonischen Werken dem kreativen Potenzial scheinbar ineffizient
verbrachter Zeit gegenüber, wenn man etwa während eines Telefonats
scheinbar Belangloses auf einen Block kritzelt. Gerade dort, wo
maximale Effizienz gefordert wird, entsteht schließlich eine Routine, die
häufig zu Langeweile führt. Langeweile wiederum als Gefühl leerer Zeit
kann, ins Positive gewendet, zur Ideenfindung, zum Anstoßen kreativer
Prozesse und neuer Handlungsinitiierung führen. Die plastische
Sichtbarmachung der Zeit und damit auch des Vergehens von Zeit als
Verwandlung von Gegenwart in Vergangenheit birgt ein solches
Potenzial. Die auf dem Boden liegenden Uhren haben einen Radius von
vier Metern. Wie ein magischer Bannkreis ziehen sie eine Linie um einen
Leerraum, der angefüllt zu sein scheint mit Zeit als abstrakter Materie.
Kann diese sinnvoll verwendet werden? Oder ist es vielleicht gerade die
Abstraktion des Zeitsystems, die dieses in eine Diktat verwandelt, das
unser Leben bestimmt?
Für die Berlinische Galerie hat Uriarte 2014 eine Klanginstallation im
Eingangsbereich entworfen, bei der die monotone Stimme eines Mannes
zu hören ist, der acht Stunden lang zählt. Seine Maßeinheit sind Silben:
Jeder Silbe widmet er eine Sekunde, wodurch der deutsch sprechende
Zähler innerhalb von acht Stunden – einer Zeitspanne, die einem
typischen Arbeitstag entspricht, aber auch der täglichen Öffnungszeit
des Museums – bis zu der Zahl 3599 gelangt. Zeit als abstrakter Größe
trifft hier auf die Möglichkeit der Sprache, diese zu benennen, zu
definieren und in ein abweichendes phonetisches, gleichermaßen aber
auch poetisches System zu übersetzen. (VJM)

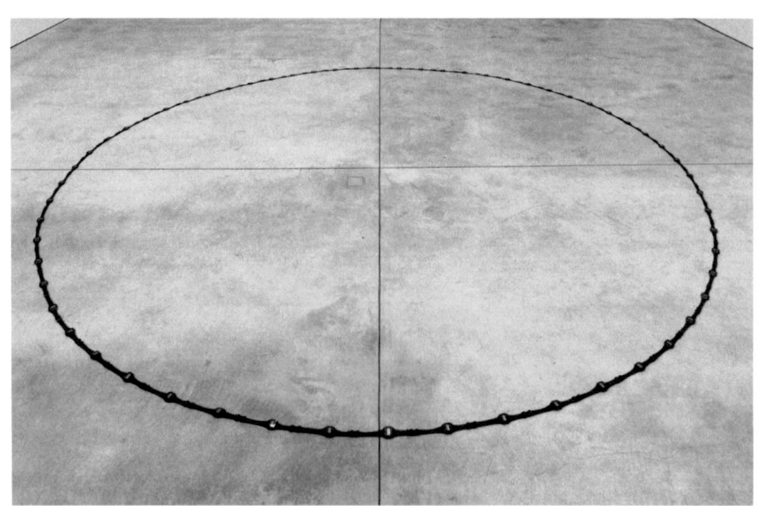

Ignacio Uriarte
60 seconds, 2005
Installation
Wristwatches / Armbanduhren
Diameter / Durchmesser 400 cm
Photo / Bild © VG Bild 2014
Courtesy the artist / der Künstler; Galerie Nogueras Blanchard,
Barcelona / Madrid

Dragana Žarevac

Resist: Disappearing Happiness

Because I'm happy
Clap along if you feel like a room without a roof
Clap along if you feel like happiness is the truth
Clap along if you know what happiness is to you
Clap along if you feel like that's what you want to do

Because I'm happy — this line from the refrain of the pop song Happy by Pharrell Williams was played on radio, TV and internet channels all over the world in 2014. In the song, the American artist sings about feeling good and having a positive attitude to life: "Here come bad news talking this and that / Give me all you got, don't hold it back / I should probably warn you I'll be just fine [...] Because I'm happy."
Nothing can spoil the singer's good mood; in the accompanying music video he moves through urban environments, dancing and smiling, his gaze on the camera. This video clip of the song appeared as a short version lasting around four minutes and as a twenty-four hour version online. The concept of this work, and of the countless private clips that were created and posted after it, generally remains the same: one or more people dance happily in public space. The song, medium, and choreography provided an internationally popular template for creating multiple new versions of the video, which were then uploaded to the online platform YouTube. For her work *Resist: Disappearing Happiness*, the Serbian artist Dragana Žarevac compiled a selection of the videos posted on the Internet, which are played simultaneously and side by side. Included in the selection is an interpretation by a group of Iranian teenagers who, in response to their version of Happy, were arrested and punished because their clip was said to offend public morals. In other videos we see residents of Gaza or Syrian refugees as they dance. In addition to shots of major international cities, footage of demonstrations and civil wars in Africa form part of the mix. Žarevac includes videos that direct attention to global conflict zones and whose makers advocate for what is implied by the title of the work: a resistance to the disappearance of happiness.
Both the song and video collage compel the viewer to decide either for or against an optimistic attitude to life and can be interpreted in contrasting ways. Facing the collection of video clips from areas of conflict, the chorus "Happy" finally relates to the images in a very cynical way. The supposed optimism uniting the "Happy"-fans, is flipped by Žarevac and turned into ignorance, opposing an uncritical attitude towards it.
Considering two recent articles by Nils Minkmar[1] (FAZ) and Fraser Nelson (Telegraph) the piece could be read in a different way. Both argue history has reached a turning point with 2014 as one of its best years, and even better prospects for 2015. Minkmar posits that the general negativity of intellectualized social and media criticism become insignificant when compared to the popularity and afterglow of Pharrell Williams' Happy. But in view of *Resist: Disappearing Happiness* this hypothesis also appear a cynical one. (ME)

*1959 in Belgrad. Lives / lebt in Belgrad.

Because I'm happy
Clap along if you feel like a room without a roof
Clap along if you feel like happiness is the truth
Clap along if you know what happiness is to you
Clap along if you feel like that's what you want to do

Because I'm happy – dieser Refrain des Popsongs „Happy" von Pharrell Williams wurde 2014 weltweit im Radio, Fernsehen und Internet gespielt. In dem Lied werden gute Laune und positive Lebenseinstellung besungen. „Here come bad news talking this and that / Give me all you got, don't hold it back / I should probably warn you I'll be just fine [...] Because I'm happy." Nichts kann das Gemüt des Interpreten trüben. Im zugehörigen Musikvideo tanzt er auf der Straße und lacht in die Kamera. Den Videoclip gibt es als Kurzversion von etwa vier Minuten Dauer und als 24-stündige Fassung. Das Konzept dieses und der von Fans aus der ganzen Welt produzierten Clips bleibt in der Regel gleich: Eine oder mehrere Personen tanzen in der Öffentlichkeit. Die Choreographie des originalen Musikvideos lieferte eine Vorlage zum Nachdrehen eigener Versionen, die auf die Video-Plattform YouTube hochgeladen wurden. Für *Resist: Disappearing Happiness* kompiliert die serbische Künstlerin Dragana Žarevac eine Auswahl dieser Videos, die gleichzeitig nebeneinander gezeigt werden. Teil der Selektion ist die Interpretation von „Happy" durch eine Gruppe iranischer Jugendlicher, die in Reaktion auf ihre Initiative verhaftet und bestraft wurden, da ihr Clip als sittenwidrig eingestuft wurde. In anderen Videos tanzen Bewohner Gazas oder syrische Flüchtlinge. Neben Aufnahmen aus internationalen Großstädten sind Filme von Demonstrationen und Bürgerkriegen in Afrika Teil der Zusammenstellung. Žarevac adaptiert Videos, die Aufmerksamkeit auf globale Krisengebiete lenken und deren Macher proklamieren, was im Titel der Arbeit anklingt: Widerstand gegen das Verschwinden des Glücklich-Seins.
Sowohl der Song als auch die Video-Collage fordern dazu heraus, sich für oder gegen eine optimistische Grundhaltung zu entscheiden oder können auf konträre Weise interpretiert werden. Angesichts der Gegenüberstellung von Clips aus Krisengebieten verhält sich der Refrain „Happy" schließlich zynisch zu den Bildern. Der vermeintliche Optimismus, der die Fans von „Happy" vereint, wird von Žarevac ins Ignorante verkehrt und entlarvt eine unkritische Haltung gegenüber aktuellem Zeitgeschehen. Anders kann die Arbeit vor dem Hintergrund zweier Artikel von Nils Minkmar[1] (FAZ) und Nelson Fraser (Telegraph) gelesen werden. Beide argumentieren, die Geschichte hätte einen Wendepunkt erreicht, da 2014 eines der besten Jahre aller Zeiten gewesen sei – mit noch besseren Aussichten für 2015. Minkmar postuliert, die generelle Negativität intellektueller Sozial- und Medienkritik, halte dem Vergleich zur Popularität und zum Afterglow von Williams „Happy" nicht stand. Mit Blick zurück auf *Resist: Disappearing Happiness* wirkt jedoch auch diese These zynisch. (ME)

---

[1] Nils Minkmar, "Unser Glück", Frankfurter Allgemeine Sonntagszeitung Nr.1/2015, 4.Januar 2015, S.29.

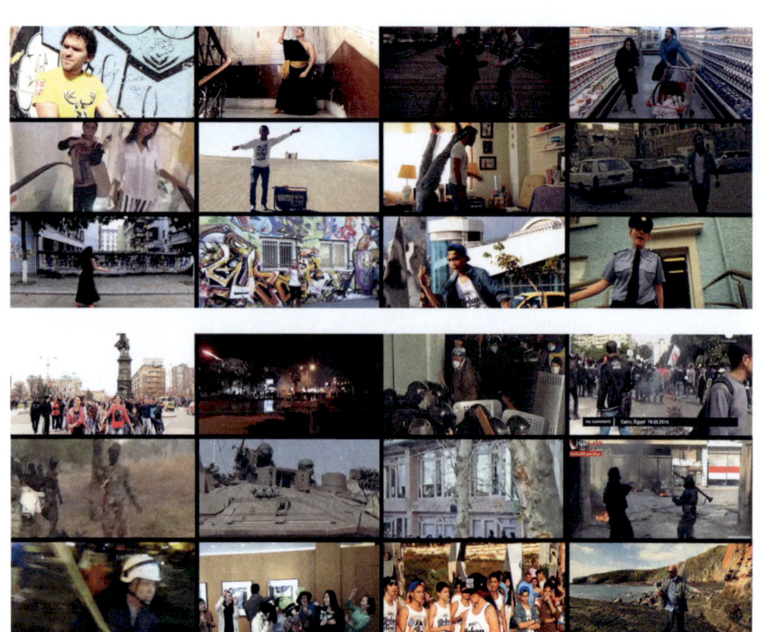

Dragana Žarevac
Resist: Disappearing Happiness, 2014
Video installation, 4 Min.
Courtesy the artist / die Künstlerin

List of works / Werkliste

Julius Von Bismarck
*Unfall am Mittelpunkt Deutschlands
(Accident at the centre of
Germany)*, 2013
Fictive story / Fiktive Geschichte.
Courtesy the artist / der Künstler;
Alexander Levy, Berlin

Igor Bošnjak
Hotel Balkan, 2013
HD Video, 10 Min.
Courtesy the artist / der Künstler

Antoine Catala
Le Petit Antoine, 2014
New Feelings, 2014
Various materials / Verschiedene
Materialien
Courtesy the artist / der Künstler;
47 Canal, New York

Logo to Self-Consciousness, 2014
Various materials / Verschiedene
Materialien
Courtesy the artist / der Künstler;
47 Canal, New York; Greene
Naftali Gallery, New York

Collective Feelings Memory (), 2015
Various materials / Verschiedene
Materialien
Courtesy the artist / der Künstler;
Galerie Christine Mayer,
Munich / München

Julian Charrière
Polygon XII, 2014
B/W Photography / S/W Fotografie
Courtesy the artist / der Künstler

Keren Cytter
Ocean, 2014
Video, 15:40 Min.
Courtesy the artist / die Künstlerin;
Galerie Nagel Draxler, Berlin;
Galerie Pilar Corrias, London

Edith Dekyndt
Carousel, 2010
Dia projection / Diaprojektion
Courtesy the artist / die
Künstlerin; Galerie Greta Meert,
Brussels / Brüssel

Simon Denny
*The Startup Way Snapchat Legal
Evidence*, 2014
You Disruptive Technologies, 2014
*The Process SeedCamp American
Tour*, 2014

Digital prints on billboard
mesh, digital prints on
aluminium / Digitaldruck auf
Netzstoff, Digitaldruck auf
Aluminium

Startup Case Mod: Snapchat, 2014
Various materials / Verschiedene
Materialien
Courtesy the artist / der
Künstler; Galerie Buchholz,
Berlin / Cologne / Köln

*Berlin Startup Case Mod:
Sociomantic*, 2014
Various materials / Verschiedene
Materialien
Courtesy Alastair Cookson

Aleksandra Domanović
Turbo Sculpture, 2010-2013
Video, 19:44 Min.
Courtesy the artist / die Künstlerin;
Tanya Leighton, Berlin

Dani Gal
Wie aus der Ferne (As from Afar),
2013
HD Video, 26 Min.
Courtesy the artist / der Künstler,
Freymond-Guth Fine Arts, Zürich /
Zurich

Florian Hecker
Modulator, 2012
One-channel electro-
acoustic sound, loudspeaker
system / 1-Kanal elektroakustischer
Ton, Lautsprechersystem, 33:48
Min.
Courtesy the artist / der Künstler;
Sadie Coles HQ, London; Galerie
Neu, Berlin

Leon Kahane
19-1-2014, 2014
One-channel / 1-Kanal full HD video,
30 Min.

Xerox, from the series *FRONTEX*,
Warsaw, 2009
Flipchart, from the series *FRONTEX*,
Warsaw, 2009
Situation Room, from the series
FRONTEX, Constanza, 2009
Office left, from the series *FRONTEX*,
Warsaw, 2009
Jacket, from the series *FRONTEX*,
Warsaw, 2009
Flowers, from the series *FRONTEX*,
Warsaw, 2009
Self adhesive print on pressboard / Print
auf Spanplatte
Courtesy the artist / der Künstler

Daniel Keller
*Absolute Vitality Inc. Offshore
Subsidiary (Visit Beauty Atoll LTD,
British Virgin Islands)*, 2013
*Absolute Vitality Inc. Offshore
Subsidiary (Blues Via Totality LTD,
Belize)*, 2013
*Absolute Vitality Inc. Offshore
Subsidiary (Sea But Volatility LLC,
Nevis)*, 2013
*Absolute Vitality Inc. Offshore
Subsidiary (To Value Stability LTD,
Gambia)*, 2013
Courtesy New Galerie, Paris; Kraupa-
Tuskany Zeidler, Berlin.

*Absolute Vitality Inc. Offshore
Subsidiary (Bailouts Yet Vital LTD,
Seychelles)*, 2013
Various materials / Verschiedene
Materialien
Courtesy Private collection /
Privatsammlung

Hanne Lippard
Postisms, 1:06 min
Locus, 4:45 min
Pandoras Cat, 6:20 min
Beige, 6:05 min
Sound installation
Courtesy the artist / die Künstlerin

Deimantas Narkevičius
Books on Shelves and Without Letters,
2013
HD video, 40 Min.
Courtesy the artist / der Künstler;
Galerie Barbara Weiss, Berlin

Katja Novitskova
*Dream Jobs 009 / Special Bonds
011 / Dissemination And Proliferation
012 / Prediction Market 017 / Benefits of
complexity 008*, 2013
Digital prints on Papyrus / Digitaldrucke
auf Papyrus

Dodoli de Luxe Grey, 2014
Elektrische Babywiege,
Polyurethanharz, Datenbankbild von
Eiweißmolekülen, Fischköder, Kabel /
Electronic baby swing, polyurethane
resin, stock image of protein molecule,
fishing baits, cable hose
Courtesy the artist / die Künstlerin;
Kraupa-Tuskany Zeidler, Berlin

Yuri Pattison
RELiable COMmunications (http://
reliablecommunications.net) 2013
webpage (html, css, javascript, php,
jpeg, gif & png)
Commissioned by Legion TV, London;
co-presented with the New Museum,
New York / Auftragswerk für Legion
TV, London; co-präsentiert mit New
Museum, New York

Pale_Blue_Dot, http://www.kxol.com.
au/images/pale_blue_dot.jpg <- sums
it up for me, 2013
Hyperlink & jpeg Image / c-type print,
Hyperlink & jpeg Bild / C-Print, Größe
variabel
Courtesy the artist / der Künstler

Jon Rafman
Mainsqueeze, 2014
Video, 7:23 Min.
Courtesy the artist / der Künstler

Adriana Ramić
*The Return Trip is Never the Same
(After Trajets de Fourmis et Retours
au Nid, M. Victor Cornetz, 1910)*,
2014
E-Book, 82 Pages / Seiten
Courtesy the artist / die Künstlerin

Antoine Renard
1110533_Capture Name (Bob),
2015
SYNTHOS XPS PRIME S 30
Styropor

*2553418_Why do cats sleep on the
newspaper (何故、猫は新聞に乗る
のか?)*, 2015
SYNTHOS XPS PRIME S 30
Styropor
Courtesy the artist / der Künstler

Mandla Reuter
City, 2014
Holz, Stahl, Schlauch, Pumpe,
Evian-Wasser, andere Materialien,
Maße variabel
Wood, steel, PE water pipe, pump,
Evian water, other materials,
dimensions variable
Courtesy the artist / der Künstler;
Galerie Mezzanin, Vienna / Wien

Meggy Rustamova
L'invitation au voyage, 2014
HD Video, 13 Min.
Courtesy the artist / die Künstlerin

Augustas Serapinas
Marie, 2015
Installation / Performance
Courtesy the artist / der Künstler

Michael Staniak
DATA_901 (VLSR), 2015.
Silicon wafers
DATA_012 (1128GB), 2015.
Millennium Discs
DATA_760 (1081GB), 2015.
Digital Versatile Discs
Acrylic and resin on canvas and
steel frame / Acryl und Harz auf
Leinwand mit Stahlrahmen
Courtesy the artist / der Künstler;
Steve Turner Contemporary, Los
Angeles

Philipp Timischl
The Blair Bitch Project, 2013
Poster, flatscreen, painting / Poster,
Flachbildschirm, Gemälde
Courtesy the artist / der
Künstler; Galerie Emanuel Layr,
Vienna / Wien

Amalia Ulman
Excellences and Perfections, 2014
Online performance
Courtesy the artist / die Künstlerin

Ignacio Uriarte
60 seconds, 2005
Installation, Armbanduhren /
Installation, wristwatches
Courtesy the artist / der Künstler;
Galerie Nogueras Blanchard,
Barcelona / Madrid

Dragana Žarevac
Resist: Disappearing Happiness,
2014
2-Channel video
installation / 2-Kanal-
Videoinstallation, 4 Min.
Courtesy the artist / die Künstlerin

Colophon / Impressum

Publication / Publikation
The Future of Memory
Published by Kunsthalle Wien GmbH
ISBN 978-3-852470-57-3

Published on the occasion of the exhibition The Future of Memory
at Kunsthalle Wien, 4 February to 29 March, 2015 / Diese Publikation
erscheint anlässlich der Ausstellung The Future of Memory in der
Kunsthalle Wien, 4. Februar – 29. März 2015.

Editor / Herausgeber: Nicolaus Schafhausen
Assistant Editor / Redaktionsassistenz: Emilie Lauriola

Contributors / Beiträge von: Clint Burnham, Michaël Connor, Marie Egger,
Emilie Lauriola, Vanessa Joan Müller, Nicolaus Schafhausen

Copy editor / Lektorat: Marie Egger, Rosemary Heather,
Vanessa Joan Müller
Translation / Übersetzung: Linke & Schreier

Video: Maximilian Pramaratov
Installation shots / Installationsansichten: Stephan Wyckoff
Design / Gestaltung: eCulture.biz
Printing / Druck: Books on Demand GmbH
Realization / Umsetzung eBook: Felix Werner

This catalogue is available as free eBook via iBooks and
www.kunsthallewien.at. / Dieser Katalog ist als kostenfreies eBook in
iBooks und auf www.kunsthallewien.at erhältlich.

Exhibition / Ausstellung
The Future of Memory
4/2 – 29/3 2015

Curator / Kurator: Nicolaus Schafhausen
Assistant / Assistenz: Marie Egger

Exhibition management / Ausstellungsmanagement: Karin Haas
Construction Management / Bauleitung: Johannes Diboky

Technicians / Technik: Beni Ardolic, Frank Herberg, Mathias Kada,
Othmar Stangl

External Technicians / Externe Technik: Hermann Amon (Video, Audio),
Dietmar Hochhauser, Alfred Lenz, Danilo Pacher

Art Handling / Ausstellungsaufbau: Marc Dumoulin , Chris Fortescue, Johann Groebner, Scott Hayes

Marketing: Dalia Ahmed, David Avazzadeh, Katharina Baumgartner, Bernadette Vogl, Christina Dopplinger (Intern / Praktikantin), Claudia Peintinger (Intern / Praktikantin)

Press and Communication / Presse und Kommunikation: Katharina Murschetz, Stefanie Obermeir, Hannah Kocevar (Intern / Praktikantin)

Education / Vermittlung: Isabella Drozda, Belinda Hak, Anna May Education Team / Kunstvermittler/innen: Wolfgang Brunner, Daniela Fasching, Maximiliano Kostal, Ursula Leitgeb, Alexandra Matzner, Martin Pfitscher, Michael Simku

Finances / Buchhaltung: Mira Gasparevic, Doris Hauke
Visitor Service / Besucherservice: Christina Zowack

The Kunsthalle Wien GmbH is the institution of the City of Vienna devoted to international contemporary art and discourse. / Die Kunsthalle Wien GmbH ist die Institution der Stadt Wien für internationale zeitgenössische Kunst und Diskurs.

Director / Direktor: Nicolaus Schafhausen
CFO / Kaufmännische Geschäftsführung: Ursula Hühnel-Benischek
Assistant CFO / Assistenz der Geschäftsführung: Sigrid Mittersteiner

Kunsthalle Wien GmbH
Museumsplatz 1, 1070 Vienna, Austria
www.kunsthallewien.at
+43 (0) 1 5 21 89-0

Kunsthallewien.at
Blog.kunsthallewien.at
Facebook.com/KunsthalleWien
Instagram.com/KunsthalleWien
Twitter.com/KunsthalleWien
#Future

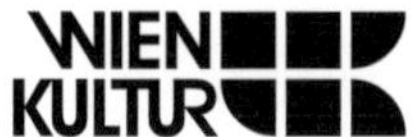

With the kind support of / Mit freundlicher Unterstützung:

KRINZINGER
PROJEKTE